Foreign Fighters and International Peace

Foreign Fighters and International Peace

Joining Global Jihad and Marching Back Home

Cholpon Orozobekova

HAMILTON BOOKS
an imprint of
Rowman & Littlefield
Lanham • Boulder • New York • London

Published by Hamilton Books
An imprint of The Rowman & Littlefield Publishing Group, Inc.
4501 Forbes Boulevard, Suite 200, Lanham, Maryland 20706
www.rowman.com
86-90 Paul Street, London EC2A 4NE, United Kingdom

British Library Cataloguing in Publication Information Available

Library of Congress Cataloging-in-Publication Data Available
ISBN 978-0-7618-7370-9 (pbk. : alk. paper) | ISBN 978-0-7618-7371-6 (ebook)

∞™ The paper used in this publication meets the minimum requirements of American National Standard for Information Sciences—Permanence of Paper for Printed Library Materials, ANSI/NISO Z39.48-1992.

Contents

Foreword

John Heathershaw

The phenomenon of the foreign fighters who left their homeland to join the violent extremists of Iraq and Syria has garnered much international attention over the last ten years. A great deal of this attention has taken the form of stigmatization where radical ideas and claims of the protagonists are taken as prima facie evidence of their wickedness. Much of this work has been policy analysis which has framed these people and their families as a problem to be solved. How may they be 'deradicalized'? How might their examples be used to deter others from following in their stead? How can they be repatriated without creating an internal extremist problem? These are urgent and perhaps necessary questions, but they are almost always approach from an 'external' perspective, by those who have had minimal contact with foreign fighters and their family members or show little or no ability to empathize with their predicament.

Cholpon Orozbekova takes a different approach. First, she is originally from the post-Soviet space of the foreign fighters that she studies. Most work on foreign fighters is written by outsiders. But as a compatriot of her subjects, she demonstrates a willingness to consider them as a 'domestic' matter in that, as she argues in her introduction, "jihadists and terrorists are not adversaries that came from abroad, but products of our societies." Foreign fighters are not an aberration from but a reflection on the Central Asian transition, how its states and societies have evolved in the thirty years since the end of the Soviet Union.

Second, Cholpon writes her book from a first-hand perspective which explores the everyday lives and concerns of the many who have been left in the foreign fighter camps since the violent extremist groups were defeated. Her interviews and observations over the period 2018–2021, particularly with women and children, are revealing for their empathetic perspective and emphasis on the complex pathways that have led from alienation at home to fighting abroad, and then from internment camps abroad to, in some cases, eventual repatriation. At no point are her interviewees demonized or presented as Others to their societies and states. Their significance is not as members of extremist group but as subjects of the traumas of transition.

Third, Orozbekova presents 'radicalization' and repatriation as universal moral challenges. Her perspective is not the security imperative of protecting Us from Them, secular states from Islamists, everyday life from extremists. Orozobekova shows that their lives are ours. They are secular as well as religious. They are ordinary and extremist. She raises the humanitarian question of how we have disintegrated as a society and how those Central Asian women and children stranded in the camps after the fall of ISIS may be reintegrated into their own countries. There remains very little organized extremism in Central Asia; jihadism has shallow roots in the communities of the region. But a surprisingly large number of post-Soviet citizens have responded the vicissitudes of their economies and societies, by embarking on routes to, and searching for meaning in, violent jihad. This is a moral question as well as a political one.

The fact that so many Central Asians have gone to join overseas extremists has shocked many within and beyond Central Asia. It is easy to fall back on simple explanations which stigmatize the fighters and their families. Detailed research and nuanced reportage are the antidotes to this problem. Cholpon Orozbekova's provides just such a treatment in this fascinating and insightful book.

John Heathershaw is Professor of International Relations at Exeter University, UK. He founded the Exeter Central Asian Studies (ExCAS) research network and directed its Central Asian Political Exiles (CAPE) project 2015–2020. He was a member of the board of the Central Eurasian Studies Society and the European Society for Central Asian Studies. He is the author of Post-Conflict Tajikistan: The Politics of Peacebuilding and the Emergence of Legitimate Order *and coauthor of* Dictators without Borders: Power and Money in Central Asia. *Professor Heathershaw is a senior fellow of the British Academy / Leverhulme Trust under the Saki Ruth Dockrill Fellowship in Contemporary History and International History (2021/22).*

Acknowledgments

During the writing period of this book, which took two years, I have encountered many new people. I feel indebted to many of them, including those who were willing to share their stories with me. I am particularly grateful to the Geneva Centre for Security Policy (GCSP), which I have been lucky to call my rich and intellectual home for many years. After obtaining a MA degree from the joint program of the GCSP with University of Geneva in 2014, I have been privileged as an alumna to continue gaining more knowledge and experience, which inspired me to write this book. I thank my professors, colleagues and mentors at the GCSP such as Marc Finaud, Christina Liang, Mohamed Mahmoud Mohamedou, Pal Dunay, Siobhan Martin, and Isabelle Gillet for their endless support. I also thank my colleagues at the Bulan Institute for Peace Innovations, for their support during this research period. I am deeply grateful to my colleagues Sarah Wolfe, Melissa Magalhaes, Saboor Stanikzai, Jennifer Torner, Leslie Kassongo, and Leou Chen for reading and commenting on the chapters. Finally, I have an inexpressible debt to Professor John Heathershaw, from the Exeter University, for his guidance and support to this book. And of course, I am grateful to my family for their unconditional support and encouragement.

Introduction

"We are having good life now, because Allah rewarded us for our jihad. We will depart to Jihad if God calls us," said the twelve-year-old boy in Tajikistan who was repatriated from Iraq. Her mother remains in the Iraqi prison serving her sentence term for joining ISIS. Some children in Kazakhstan called psychologists and social workers kaffir when they returned during the operation Zhusan. Children perceived their home country as a place full of infidels. Such imprints ISIS left on the minds of children who were taken to the Middle East and raised under ISIS. After the fall of ISIS, thousands of ISIS-linked women and children left behind in Syria and Iraq. They have been held in camps in the desert by the Kurdish forces, and several countries repatriated women and children, who were family members of ISIS fighters.

Kyrgyzstan repatriated seventy-nine children from Iraqi prisons. They were held in Iraqi prison for almost four years with their mothers who had been charged with terrorism and sentenced. Children returned to Kyrgyzstan in the winter of 2021 and were very happy to see the snow. Despite the cold day, they were running in snow and did not want to go inside. While in the Iraqi prison, children did not go out, even did not have a window for four years. In the rehabilitation center, children were just looking outside, through the window of their room for hours nonstop. Social workers in Kyrgyzstan told me how bigger children were hugging their small siblings, and they were looking through the window for hours. No words, just silence and the window. Living in the crowded cell with more than fifty people for almost four years is terrible. It is terrifying to imagine how children survived with no access to fresh air and food.

The ISIS ideology left huge imprint on mental and physical health of children. Children were deprived of education but were fully indoctrinated by having planted the radical religious ideology in their minds. Boys were deeply immersed into the radical misinterpreted and mutated concepts such as jihad, tawhid and takfir, while little girls also perceived the world through the gender-related patterns of the radical ideology. Uzbek children who were repatriated from Syria were given toys. Uzbek girls, as other many girls under ISIS, were mainly forced to read Quran at home and had rarely seen real toys in the Middle East were given beautiful dolls. After having settled in the rehabilitation center, at first night the repatriated girls decided to change clothes of dolls. In the morning, all dolls were wrapped into niqabs. Social workers were quite shocked seeing how they show their world perception even in playing with dolls. Both girls and boys under ISIS were taught from their early age to comply with norms of the Salafi-Wahhabi ideology. It was remarkable even after repatriation how older children continued controlling smaller children if they were not stepping away from what they had been taught in Syria and Iraq. If someone forget to read Namaz or dress differently they directly started blaming in apostasy. Social workers told me that in the beginning if children argue each other so only about religious traditions and call each other kaffir or apostate. These kinds of behavior have been addressed by psychologists, social workers and theologians to make children to focus on more important tasks such as preparing to school, gaining new skills, adapting to new life.

ISIS was defeated in March 2019 after the last black flag was lowered in Baghouse, which was its last stronghold. After the fall of ISIS, the Kurdish forces captured about 11,000 male fighters in Northeast Syria. They have been held in the makeshift prisons in the Hasakah region in Northeast Syria. They wear orange jumpsuits in the prisons. ISIS dressed its captives in orange before beheading them so it is symbolic why SDF decided to put on captured fighters into orange. When they first were asked to put orange jumpsuit on them, many ISIS fighters were shocked thinking they were about to be killed. The prisons are overcrowded by holding male fighters of different nationalities and different ages. Thousands of ISIS fighters, who urgently must undergo legal assessment and stand before a judge, have become a global urgent problem that requires more than sixty countries to come together to develop an enduring long-term solution.

Meanwhile, about 70,000 women and children who were family members of ISIS fighters, have been held in Al-Hawl and Roj camps in the desert in northeast Syria. The family jihad created the dilemma of how to manage returning fighters, and mainly their family members. There are small children who were born under ISIS, whereas some children were brought to the Middle East by their parents. The world had never witnessed the mobilization of foreign fighters at this scale. We had never seen small children and women traveling to conflict zones to join terrorist groups. The second complication stems from the fact that more than 70,000 affiliates of terrorist groups are being held in the desert in northeast Syria by a non-state actor, which is unprecedented in modern history. This lack of state authority is a source of ambiguity states refer to when they refuse to repatriate or take other concrete actions. Many states maintain a firm position that former ISIS fighters and their associates should be brought to justice in the territory where they committed their crimes.

ISIS destroyed thousands of families across the globe and brought enormous tragedy to people's souls. Many parents in northeast Syria did not know that their son or daughter reached the Middle East, but rather thought that they were migrants in Turkey or Russia. A father died of a heart attack when the Amir called from Syria to inform him that his son had died as a martyr. The voice on the other side repeated, "You should be grateful to your son, he died for the mercy of the God," but the father could not believe this and fell down from shock. The next day he died in the local hospital in Kyrgyzstan. I interviewed another father who was desperately looking for a way to bring back his two daughters, his wife and his little son held in Roj camp. He was among the initiative group of parents in Kyrgyzstan and was actively advocating for repatriation of women and children. In several months, I was shocked learning that he died from a heart attack at his home in the Chuy region of Kyrgyzstan. Arman's story is in the fourth chapter of the book. There are hundreds of weeping mothers mourning their daughters and sons who joined ISIS, while other thousands of families in grief whose sons and daughters were killed by ISIS.

There are tragic cases of disappearances of whole families which joined ISIS, with sometimes more than ten family members nowhere to be found. They lured each other to the Middle East one by one. Twenty-nine family members, including their eighty-one-year-old grandmother, siblings and their small children, headed to Syria from Kyrgyzstan six years ago.[1] Their houses in the village in Tong district remains empty. Nobody knows where its former occupants are now. These cases should be lessons learned against becoming a hostage of radical ideologies.

The main purpose of the book is to examine the emergence, gradual change and internationalization of jihadism, radicalization processes of people who dreamt of a caliphate and how the world should deal with them now after the defeat of ISIS. Why did they reject their home countries and had chosen to live in a so-called Islamic state? Is there a link between their incentives, grievances and their radicalization? Do states have responsibilities toward foreign fighters and their associates trapped in Syria? Should we demand states to take responsibility for their citizens who joined ISIS and are now trapped in the desert? I address these questions in the eight chapters of the book. I argue that jihadists and terrorists are not adversaries that came from abroad, but products of our societies. Radicalization starts from people`s grievances, which can be socioeconomic, political or related to personal loss or trauma. Grievances produce further developments in conjunction with other cycles of the radicalization process. I propose the radicalization theory- non-enigma cycles of radicalization- that consists of six casual cycles. The Salafi-Wahhabi ideology plays a crucial role as it is a soft power that poisons minds of people.

It is striking to see how ISIS achieved the emergence of the so-called family Jihad. How could a woman take her small children and travel to the conflict zone? This question had been wondering in my head and made me seek answers to understand and analyze their motivations. In 2018, I had a chance to meet my first interviewee, a voluntary returnee in Kyrgyzstan who managed to escape ISIS, reached Turkey and knocked on the door of the Embassy of Kyrgyzstan in Istanbul asking for help. Then I reached out and interviewed thirteen other voluntary returnees in Kyrgyzstan. I continued looking for relatives of fighters and interviewed parents of those who were in Syria. Then, the repatriation operations in four countries in Central Asia provided me a chance to look closer at the profiles of returnees. I had access to both returnees and psychologists, theologians and social workers in these countries who were involved in rehabilitation programs and directly worked with repatriates. Then, the conversations with parents from Kyrgyzstan, Kazakhstan, Russia, Azerbaijan, Uzbekistan and Tajikistan, whose children and relatives were held in camps in Syria and who were advocating for their repatriation, helped me gain more insights on the motivations of fighters and their associates. This network of parents helped me to connect and to interview women who have been living in Roj and Al-hawl camps in northeastern Syria.

During fifteen months, I reached out to those who held in Al-Hawl and Roj camps in Northeast Syria and interviewed more than twenty women about their pre-ISIS and post-ISIS lives through WhatsApp and Telegram. I analyzed the profiles of forty returnees in Kazakhstan and Uzbekistan in open-sources who were repatriated during the operations Zhusan and Mehr. I conducted twenty-five interviews with people who were directly affected, having lost their loved ones in Syria or waiting for their repatriation. The most striking conversations were with women who have been held in Roj and Al-hawl camps in northeast Syria via WhatsApp, Telegram and phone, having found them through their relatives. I also had a chance to read the diary of Sabina, who was living in the Roj camp at the time of the interview (February 2021). She agreed to publish some pages of her diary, so I have added them to Chapter 3.

I am concluding this book with mixed feelings, as profiles of men and women are tremendously different. Russian speaking women held in Al-Hawl camp call themselves in Russian—Рабы Аллаха, which means "slaves of Allah." They post photos with this slogan on the Telegram channel named LagerHol. In the introduction of the channel, you can read that "the channel is about everyday life of women and children detained in Al-Hawl camp in Syria." While observing the social media channels of women in Northeast

Syria on Instagram, Telegram and their WhatsApp status messages, one can be in dismay. They call their sons "lion cubs" and say that "our lions are growing up and will restore our dignity." In 2021, they published several videos where three or four women spoke and called Muslim men to come and save Muslim captives in the camps. But while many women still seem very radicalized and determined to fight for an Islamic state, there are also women who realized they were deceived and are ready to return to their normal lives.

I interviewed dozens of returnees, both repatriated and voluntarily returned, and dozens of other women who are still trapped in northeast Syria. All of them are from former Soviet republics. Interviews with people who had been part of terrorist groups has its own challenges. First, it is hard to reach out and convince them to give an interview. Second, their answers can be limited or selective. Some of them can be very emotional, others can be reserved and discreet. Many of them were afraid to recall their stories because of two reasons: it is emotionally hard to recall them as brings heavy memories and secondly they were afraid to disclose something that would make them to be prosecuted. Thus, returnees were careful and selective in their answers. However, I thank civil society leaders, social workers and psychologists, and theologians who directly worked with returnees for their firsthand information. The interviews with both practitioners and returnees were conducted between July 2019 and June 2021. So, all information given by the respondents refer to that time when the interviews were conducted and their situation may have changed since then. It is also important to highlight that many women trapped in Syria and other voluntary returnees did not want their names to be in the book. All names of fighters and their associates have been changed upon their request. They hope to be repatriated and fear stigmatization. Some of them asked to change their name, some were afraid even to name their countries. I conducted interviews with the state officials of dozens of countries. As the issue of repatriation is very complex and sensitive, many officials from governments preferred to remain anonymous. I had two officials from European governments who gave interviews and then changed their minds and refused that the interviews be published. They changed their minds simply because this issue is a very tough and a sensitive question within their countries. After having spent enormous time on finding and reaching out to respondents, I am happy that the book provides firsthand information with direct interviews with former ISIS fighters and their family members, and the governmental officials.

Researching the issue of returning foreign fighters is important as the world should deal with them now. This is indeed a complex and urgent issue that demands both thorough diplomatic efforts and political will as it will have long-term effects on international peace as well as source countries. States should learn how to deal with such situations through the experience of repatriation, prosecution, rehabilitation and reintegration. The most urgent actions needed is for the destinies of children who were heavily affected by it all, and who are innocent. Children did not make the decision to go the Middle East, but were taken by their parents. Moreover, about 20,000 children were born under ISIS in Syria and Iraq. States are under a legal obligation to resolve this situation in the best interests of children. Thus, children should be repatriated urgently and deserve to stand at the first row of the repatriation queue. However, there are many challenges to identify these children, conduct DNA tests and restore their documents.

I hope that this book will contribute to the international debate and will give useful insights to all stakeholders and decision makers. Most importantly, states and other international actors will hear the voices and personal stories of women and children but, at the same time, we must also be mindful of the concerns of states about national security. This book aims to show the complexity of the current situation with former fighters and also how crucial it is to make the right decisions by shared responsibility. States are the main players of the game, who should prevent further radicalization and networking. Thus, the UN member states have obligations under international law and need to find a law-compliant and efficient solutions to manage the given situation. Regarding women who have been stranded in the camps, they are losing their hopes that states will repatriate. Russian speaking women living in Al-Hawl camp frequently publish their plea to Muslim men in the world, urging them to free them by paying buyout to the Kurdish forces. Parents from Russia, Azerbaijan and Kyrgyzstan, whose daughters are held in Al-Hawl, told me that women in the camps are tired of waiting and have lost any hope that their countries will repatriate them. So they decided to reach out to the Muslim communities to ask help. "Quran says that Muslims should free those who are in custody. So my daughter is hoping that Ummah will save them" told me one of the parents. This precedent is dangerous for international peace, and the situation should be solved only by the United Nations and member states. ISIS fighters and their associates should not be released by ransom, but have to be under jurisdiction of states, repatriated, prosecuted and reintegrated.

This book consists of eight chapters. The first chapter analyzes the global jihad, its roots, emergence and gradual change. The chapter traces genealogies of jihadism and analyses historical grievances of jihadis groups` motivations to consider the West as an adversary. It sheds light on how jihadists misinterpreted and used distorted concepts of Islam to justify their violence. The chapter also analyzes the nature of the Salafi-Wahhabi ideology and how Islamic fundamentalism emerged from the colonial era. The second chapter is devoted to the radicalization process of jihadists. It proposes the non-enigma cycles radicalization theory that consists of six casual cycles. Each cycle is crucial in the radicalization process and they have a strong causal relationship by complementing each other.

The third chapter analyzes the fall of ISIS, its war and genocide crimes and international efforts to bring ISIS fighters to justice. The United Nations established three international bodies: the UNITAD investigative team, the Independent International Commission of Inquiry on Syria, and the International, Impartial and Independent Mechanism. However, there is still a main question of how and where to try fighters. The fourth chapter is devoted to the post-ISIS lives of fighters and their family members, and the current situation and living conditions of women and children living in Roj and Al-Hawl camps. The chapter contains voices of women who gave interviews to the author from these camps. There is an excerpt of Sabina's diary, who shared it with the author and her feelings and thoughts give some understanding on how the women live and what they dream about. The book has separate chapters on women and gender analysis, and also on children, as ninety percent of the habitants of Al-Hawl and Roj camps are women and children. The attention of the international community has been focused on them. A family jihad is a phenomenon that was successfully deployed by ISIS, thus exploiting gender-biased assumptions as a tactical weapon.

The seventh chapter analyzes state policies towards ISIS fighters and the dilemma of bringing them to justice. The options to deal with former ISIS fighters and their family members includes the establishment of an ad hoc tribunal, stripping citizenship, transferring them to Iraqi prions, repatriation and rehabilitation and sentencing in absentia. The final chapter is about repatriation operations carried out by several countries such as Kosovo, Tajikistan, Uzbekistan and Kazakhstan. Since I have observed and researched this closely, the chapter gives a more detailed and interesting insight into repatriation, rehabilitation and reintegration programs of Kazakhstan, Kyrgyzstan and Uzbekistan.

NOTE

1. Ulanbek Egizbaev, twenty-nine residents of Tong went to Syria, RFE/RL Kyrgyz Service/Azattyk, available at https://www.youtube.com/watch?v=xXO9X8esYpM

Chapter 1

Global Jihadism

Emergence, Gradual Change and Search for Enemies

The world has been witnessing the transformation of political violence and the emergence of transnational armed non-state actors as a new threat to international peace. The rise of jihadism has its history and serious implications for international peace. Jihadism is not about military confrontation, but about a black-white mindset that perceives the secular state system as nefarious, and it targets non-Muslims as infidels and regards westernization and Western countries as adversaries. If jihadism constituted only military confrontation between states, it would present a more familiar challenge to the contemporary world. Rather, jihadism is about "soft power." It is a powerful and dangerous ideology that cannot be defeated by military might. Bombing, invading, even armed drones are not effective to defeat jihadism; to the contrary, they strengthen and embolden jihadists, equipping them with new narratives. It is apparent that international efforts to combat jihadism have been a "colossal failure."[1] Although ISIS was defeated and lost its territory, the jihadist ideology of terrorist groups is not dead today. It has become a powerful soft power that will continue winning the minds of people.

The confrontation between jihadist terrorist groups, who see the West as the cause of their tribulations of the past centuries, and the West, which is overly concerned with Islamist groups and perceives them as a threat, is a deeply troubling problem for the modern world. A salient feature of this confrontation is its lack of borders. When the conflict touches boundaries of faith and religion, it is indeed dangerous and difficult to manage. As Dominique Moïsi put it, we are witnessing a "clash of emotions" when "the Western world displays a culture of fear, the Arab and Muslim worlds are trapped in a culture of humiliation, and much of Asia displays a culture of hope."[2] The incentives of Islamic terrorist groups have been spurred by feelings of humiliation, while Western countries build their foreign and counterterrorism policies on a "culture of fear." Scholars observe that after the 9/11 attack, a culture of fear has become more characteristic for Western societies.[3] In the past two decades, jihadism has reached its peak and tensions between the West and the Islamic radical groups reached a new height. Though the confrontation between jihadism and Western values may seem straightforward, but it is a complex phenomenon that emerged from a cumulation of historical and political factors, as well as from contemporary grievances that drive individuals to take radical paths. The core powerful component is jihadist ideology, which proposes an alternative utopian society based on jihadi values.

An analysis of genealogies of jihadism demands a careful and thorough study of the history of Islam and the Middle East. It further demands deep analysis of the foreign policies of Western countries, such as the United States, France and the United Kingdom. A complex twine of historical and political factors contributed to the rise of jihadism and the eventual confrontation between the West and global jihadism. There is an erroneous association of Islam with violence, as current jihadist movements cannot be considered followers of true Islam. Islam is an old and peaceful religion with over 1,400 years of history. It is one of the main world religions with rich traditions, holy books, and sets of legal texts that are open to new interpretations, as are those of any other religion. However, misinterpretations of certain Islamic concepts and their mutations made by radical groups cannot be considered as Islam itself. As Francis Fukuyama says, it is doubtful that there is something inherent in Islam as a religion that makes it hostile to Western modernity.[4] Islam is not hostile to the West by its nature, but Islamic fundamentalism has become hostile due to several factors. First factor is historical context and grievances that came from the colonial era.

ROOTS OF JIHADISM AND THE BIRTH OF THE RADICAL IDEOLOGY

Political Islam and fundamentalism emerged due to the hard and humiliating experience that Muslim societies had to overcome during the colonial era. As Francis Fukuyama stated, Islamic radicalization stems from poverty, economic stagnation and authoritarian politics in the Middle East. The U.S. and other Western countries always offered economic aids through the World Bank or bilateral dealings, but Arab countries did not open up their countries to the global economy having delayed the foundation for sustainable development. As Fukuyama said, Middle Eastern countries preferred to create a "society of corrupt rentiers, who over time have become more and more fanatically Islamist."[5] However, this isolationism should also be considered as a product of imperial and colonial relations. As Neuman stated, when Muslim countries were colonized by the West, they felt that their social and cultural norms were threatened.[6] Both the debasing experience of colonial violence and the feeling of cultural effacement led to the emergence of Islamic movements that sought to protect their religion and values from Western influences and preach for the return to a pure and uncorrupt Islam. Consequently, "both movements, the Deobandis and the Salafists, emerged from contact with the West and its colonialism."[7]

As Fred Halliday argues, this contemporary image of Islam as a threat has three sources. The first is the history of conflict with the West and Christianity that stretches back over a millennium. The second source derives from the end of the Cold War with the revival of this ancient conflict. The third source is that "the Islamist movements reject Western values of secularism, democracy, the rule of civil law, equality between men and women, and between Muslims and non-Muslims."[8] However, the first waves of jihadism never pursued global political goals, nor did they target far enemies. Further, jihad in Islam does not suggest war and violence. The Arabic word jihad does not mean a war; its literal translation is "striving." Jihad appears in the Quran about forty times in two ways: the main jihad in Islam refers to making efforts for the sake of God in order to improve one's attitude and habits. One should strive to improve oneself for righteous conduct and utter dedication. The second jihad is about the protection of the house and land from an external aggressor, but it does not encourage the killing of innocent people or offensives against other countries. The main problem is that jihadists want to impose the radical ideology in every sphere of people's lives. Jihadists interpret the world through the prism of the radical ideology and envision solutions applying mutated Islamic concepts. They misinterpret religious texts and holy books according to their political agendas of fighting infidels and creating a caliphate.

The roots of jihadism trace back to the Medieval Age when religious scholar Ibn Taymuyya (1262–1328) presented his personal interpretation of jihad in response to the Mongol threat to the Muslim community. The declaration of apostate and infidels started from Tamaya's teachings and laid the foundations of Salafism. He believed that solely the first three generations of Muslims followed the correct path of Islam, thus establishing the takfir concept denouncing fellow Muslims of apostasy. Tamaya's ideas about jihad against apostates, or kaffurs, are echoed in the works of Al-Wahhabi, whose ideology conceived the Wahhabi doctrine. Wahhabi started his teaching 400 years later in response to European expansion in Arab countries. He emphasized the necessity of one ruler for all Muslims, basing his ideology on the "three main pillars: one ruler, one authority, one mosque."[9] Wahhabism and Salafism are the main ideologies that stand behind jihadism. Both are radical, rejectionist and backward. As Neumann states, Salafi-Wahhabi jihadism is a "combination of Qutb's violent theory of revolution and Wahhabist religious doctrine."[10]

The first waves of jihadism, in a more subdued state than that of today, started taking shape in the Muslim world in the 1920s. It emerged as a political mobilization for Islamic awakening. As Vijay Prashad states, political Islam "emerged in the 1920s as a part of a global movement to draw Islamic resources toward the anticolonial struggle."[11] However, things started changing when the Muslim Brotherhood of Egypt was established in 1928, a faction that laid the foundation for the Salafi-jihadist movement and jihadism in general. Sayyid Qutb, a member of the Muslim Brotherhood, became a principal ideologue of the narrative portraying Muslims "as victims of a corrupt, materialistic, secular society created by the West." Qutb saw the existence and the foreign policy of the United States as the root cause of the difficulties of the Muslim world, demanding jihadi aggression. However, Qutb's teachings called to target near enemies before addressing far enemies. As the Muslim Brotherhood battled against certain Arab state rulers whom they considered apostates, special services of Western countries supported the Muslim Brotherhood. Later members of the Muslim Brotherhood were forced to go underground, and many of them later joined jihadist groups. Qutb's teachings continue to inspire thousands of jihadists who believed that Muslims should act against those they perceived to be infidels.

THE SALAFI-WAHHABI IDEOLOGY: REJECTIONIST AND MUTATED

To challenge jihadism, one must understand its ideology. Salafism is one such ideology that drives jihadist groups and justifies the global jihadi movement. As Michael R. Kelvington suggests, the Salafi-jihadist ideology is "the intangible 'soft power' of the adversary."[12] It rejects the international state system and secularism. It rejects democracy and human-made laws and conventions. What is wrong with the Salafi-jihadist ideology is that it justifies actions and violence of the jihadi groups through selective citation of Islamic texts, which are misinterpreted to serve a malicious agenda. It is a rejectionist and totalitarian mindset which "utilizes medieval violence to forcibly manifest their vision into reality, and they do so with the backing of scripture."[13] Salafi-jihadist ideology pursues political goals based on theological concepts. Thus, they exploit several religious concepts. Shiraz Maher identifies five such elements: tawhid, takfir, hakimiayya, al-wala wa-l-bara and jihad.[14] My analysis and interviews with ISIS fighters and associates showed that the main religious concepts that jihadi groups exploit to attract followers are a bit different. I identified seven religious concepts which exist in norms and traditions of Islam, but as Maher observed they have "undergone significant ideational mutation in Salafi-Jihadi understanding."[15] These are the seven essential religious elements of jihadi ideology: takfir, umma, Al-Wala`wal Bara, tawhid, jihad, hijrah and jannah. The main element is takfir, which is an Arabic word used to describe the practice of accusing another Muslim of apostasy. In this view, the world is divided into two camps: Dar-al-Islam (House of Islam), which means Muslim countries, and Dar-al-Harb (House of War) referring to non-Islamic countries. The next concepts of tawhid, umma and Al-Wala`wal Bara are interrelated. Tawhid is the concept of monotheism in Islam which holds God as one and unique. Umma in its turn refers to the worldwide Muslim community, and the caliphate is a state governed by sharia law. Further, the jihad concept is misinterpreted as a holy war against infidels, while the hijra concept is about the emigration of Muslims to escape persecutions. To sum up, these religious concepts have been distorted and mutated to justify violence and reproduce the religious basis to conceptualize their radical movements.

Internationalization: Victimization and Confrontation with the West

Jihadism has changed gradually over the last several decades. The emergence of internationalized violent jihadism started evolving in the 1980s. Its most salient feature is that it targets the West, considering it as a direct enemy, and strives for its eradication. Jihadism is a product of a rejectionist mindset dividing the world into believers and nonbelievers, along with a complex combination of historical grievances, religious idealist worldview, lack of trust in man-made laws and conventions, self-victimization and creation of far and near enemies, and monopolization of violence to assert the supremacy of sharia law. Why do such ideologues target the West? The source of this rivalry is twofold: first, jihadist ideologues reject the secular state system and assent only to the establishment of God's sharia law. Second, jihadists accuse the U.S. and other Western countries of humiliation and aggression against Muslim countries. At the same time, the United States and European countries fear Islamic radicals and perceive them as a threat to security and democracy. In many European countries, there is public fear about this growing threat and debate about why Muslim immigrants appear resistant to integration and tend to be subject to radicalization and marginalization. Many Europeans believe that the source of radicalization is a supposed Muslim "anti-integration attitude and innate hostility to democratic and civilized ideals that breed Muslims' anti-state orientations—not socioeconomic marginality, political exclusion, repressive tactics of the police, and lack of opportunity."[16] However, more significant than contemporary grievances in jihadists' narrative to justify violence are historical grievances, such as military intervention and occupation of Muslim countries in premodern and modern history.

The direct confrontation between the West and radical jihadist groups started in the 1990s, even earlier than the 9/11 attacks. In 1996, Usama bin Laden, leader of Al-Qaeda, issued the fatwa "Declaration of War Against the Americans Occupying the Land of the Two Holy Places." He published a second fatwa in 1998 calling all Muslims to fight against Americans. Bin Laden urged to kill Americans stating that "they want to occupy our countries, steal our resources, impose on us agents to rule us, and then want us to agree to all this." Regarding Western foreign policies, there are serious grievances that Muslim countries can put on the table. Western countries historically pursued their national interests and "sought to harness the power of radical Islam to serve the interests of their own foreign policy."[17] Scholars argue that the foreign policies of the USA, UK and France, which supported and armed various armed groups for short-term military, political and diplomatic advantages, directly contributed to the rise of Islamic terrorist groups. As Atwan argues, "betrayal, manipulation, and self-interest were, and remain, the name of the game when it comes to Western meddling in the Middle East."[18] Take the United States alone; since 1980, Washington intervened in the affairs of dozens of Muslim countries: Iran, Libya, Lebanon, Kuwait, Iraq, Somalia, Bosnia, Saudi Arabia, Afghanistan, Sudan, Kosovo, Yemen, Pakistan, and Syria. Some were invaded by the military and bombed. If we look back on the colonial era, the UK and France played a significant role in the Middle East, changing its history and redrawing its borders. Both countries negatively impacted prospects in this region, not only colonizing their controlled territories but enforcing false borders and involuntarily contrived states. The jihadist movement uses this narrative as its first weapon to justify violence and denounce false borders in the Middle East. For this reason, ISIS leader Abu Bakir al-Baghdadi declared the caliphate and announced the end of Sykes-Picot, the agreement secretly signed between France and UK in 1916.

Jihadist groups cite the Sykes-Picot agreement as the main source of nearly 100 years of endless conflicts in the Middle East. After the collapse of the Ottoman Empire, France and Britain sought to impede the re-emergence of the powerful Islamic state, thus dividing the Arab territories of the former Ottoman Empire into spheres of influence. Two diplomats, Mark Sykes and Francois Picot, took pencils to a map, and drew the new borders that would create modern-day Palestine, Israel, Jordan, Lebanon, and Syria. The consequences of their disregard for local ethnic and religious groups have shaken the region for a century. Many Middle Easterners cite the closed-door Sykes-Picot agreement as the source of the pervasive violence in the Middle East. Thus, historical grievances are at the core of jihadist narratives; Al-Qaeda and other jihadist groups "compel Muslim audiences to view contemporary conflicts through the prism of a wider historical global attack on Islam and Muslims by a belligerent 'Zionist-Crusader Alliance.'"[19] Usama bin Laden consistently repeated in his fatwas that Muslims have suffered from aggression, inequity, and injustice by the Zionist-Crusader alliance, that the Muslim's blood became the cheapest, and that their wealth was looted in the hands of the enemies.

Indeed, jihadist terrorist groups exploit the victimization narrative by highlighting a deep trauma and resentment. Prior to the 1980s, the main narratives were of Kashmir and Palestine. The Palestine issue is "the most commonly recognized and longest-running grievance of Muslims worldwide."[20] Britain took control of the Palestinian territory after the defeat of the Ottoman Empire in World War I. Palestine was previously inhabited by a Jewish minority and an Arab majority. Britain issued a declaration in 1917 recognizing Palestine as a homeland for the Jewish diaspora, despite the fact that Arabs constituted the majority ethnic group. Subsequently, in 1948, Britain left the territory and Jews created a state- Israel. The problem of Palestinian Arabs being rendered stateless is a significant grievance among Muslim communities that has been weaponized by jihadi groups. As Khosrokhavar notes, in regard to the respective Palestinian, Afghan, and Iraqi questions, the disregard for their dignity by the West, particularly by the United States, is a "deep wound that induces a movement of absolute violence and the praise of death as the only solution to the dilemma of this denial."[21] Jihadism indeed is also about recognition; the demand for recognition of one's political and economic rights constitutes a significant motivational factor in jihad enlistment. Offended dignity, humiliation and victimization are integral parts of the doctrine of jihadism. Jihadist ideologues skillfully use these narratives to attract thousands of followers. These grievances are to serve for justifications that may be availed of over the course of many years in light of the absence of economic equality, peace, and a feeling of justice in the region.

The internationalization of jihadist movements started at the end of the 1970s. Its origins stem from the Afghan-Soviet war with the Soviet invasion of Afghanistan in December 1979. Palestinian Islamic scholar Abdullah Azzam was a godfather of the global jihad, mobilizing fighters and organizing the transfer of thousands of fighters to Afghanistan, by establishing a Services Office in Pakistan. His rhetoric on defending Islamic territory from infidel occupants inspired Usama Bin Laden, who was a wealthy son of a Saudi construction tycoon. Bin Laden found a mentor for his jihadist journey, and in exchange, Azzam received financial support for the Service Office, which played a crucial role in the fight against the Soviet Army. Usama bin Laden established a training camp in Peshawar and his troops later became legendary for their victory over Soviet troops in battle. Azzam and Bin Laden became key figures in mobilizing fighters by developing, nurturing, and disseminating jihadist ideas. After the defeat of the Soviet Army and its withdrawal from Afghanistan, thousands more Arab fighters were galvanized, for whom the victory was not the end of the fight, but the beginning. The vision of Muslim victory and their fight against occupation by infidels had begun its journey. Azzam and Bin Laden understood that their war just started, while Azzam envisioned an army of Muslim fighters at the ready to protect Islamic lands from "infidel" occupation worldwide and started realizing his dream.

The Arab fighters, armed and trained to defeat the Red Army of the USSR, laid the foundations of modern terrorist groups. Arab fighters, mobilized in Afghanistan to fight against the Soviet Union, were supported and armed by the United States, Pakistan, and Saudi Arabia. As Nelly Lahoud states, it is ironic that jihadists' big victory over the Soviet Red Army was facilitated and ultimately empowered by none other than the "unbelieving despots and imperialists the jihadists sought to eliminate in the first instance, namely the United States and Arab regimes."[22] These thousands of Arab Afghans who fought in the Afghan-Soviet War were "a U.S.-Saudi creation that later turned against its patrons"[23] and were abandoned without further policies and action. Abandonment of fighters without demobilization, disarmament and reintegration led to their further networking, radicalization, and mobility, resulting in the emergence of Al-Qaeda and ISIS. Their nomadic structure allowed them to "move to new conflict zones, principally Bosnia, but also Algeria and Egypt."[24] At that time, jihadism was not yet global, but the internationalization process was just emerging. During the Bosnian war (1992–1995), Usama bin Laden was offered refuge in Sudan, where he lived while building networks and brainstorming a new strategy while presenting himself as an engineer and businessman. Azzam's legacy, who was killed in a bomb attack in 1989, was powerful in attracting fighters to Bosnia. His speeches had been circulated widely throughout the Middle East and Central Asia since his death and inspired thousands of fighters. While Afghan Arab fighters were looking for a new war to join, the conflict in Bosnia provided them with a new jihad to join. Subsequently, about 5,000 foreign fighters went to Bosnia to fight. According to scholars, "the Arab commanders from Afghanistan entered the country between 1992 and 1993."[25] These foreign fighters fought in the special unit called "El Mudžahid," which was a separate battalion within the Bosnian Armed Forces.

As Hegghammer explains, since 1980 between 10,000 and 30,000 fighters have inserted themselves into conflicts from Bosnia in the West to the Philippines in the East.[26] According to Hafez, some Arab volunteers returned to their home countries or established a haven in Peshawar, Pakistan. After the end of the Soviet-Afghan War and the complete withdrawal of the Red Army, there was a large influx of people in Afghanistan and Pakistan who sought to take advantage of a safe haven and to get trained in the camps of the Mujahiddin, who had fought against the Soviets. The training camps established during the Afghan-Soviet War, which were set up by Pakistani intelligence services and run by Mujiahiddin, were further expanded and played a crucial role in terrorism. Thousands of fighters were trained and "became the trainers of future jihadists in Afghanistan, Bosnia, Tajikistan and Chechnya."[27] The Arab Afghan fighters, who fought against the Soviets, had become main networkers for future jihadist networks throughout the world. Those who returned to their home countries likewise maintained ties that endured for decades and helped recruit trainees.

In 1996–1999, during the Chechen war, foreign fighters trained in Pakistan and Afghanistan established camps and started training not only Chechens, but other Muslims from the Caucasus, Central Asia, and Russia. The contribution of Arab fighters thus "changed the dynamics of the Russo-Chechen wars."[28] Thus, it is important to draw lessons from how the fighters of the Soviet-Afghan War were trained and how they were treated after the conflict. They developed skills and networks that allowed them to disseminate radical ideology and tactical know-how acquired in training camps. Their skills empowered terrorists, subsequently led to the creation of Al-Qaeda, and heavily impacted global security. Al-Qaeda was established in the 1980s to wage a war against the U.S., whom Usama bin Laden and his associates blamed for troubles in the Middle East. In 1998, Al-Qaeda organized terrorist attacks on the US embassies in Kenya and Tanzania and emerged fully towards the 9/11 events, "leading to a militarization of the world amid IS would be born."[29] As Mohammad-Mahmoud Mohamedou, author of the historiography of ISIS, Al-Qaeda is an ancestor of ISIS as "the group holds the key DNA of IS."[30]

The Emergence of ISIS and a New Global Shape

The next stage of global jihadism, a period marked by the triumph of Al-Qaeda and ISIS, starts from the 9/11 attack. Indeed, during the last two decades, jihadism took a new shape and became global. Al-Qaeda and ISIS are the product of a sequence of conflicts in the world, notably the Soviet-Afghan War, the Gulf War, the Iraq War, the War on Terror, and the Syrian War. Each of these conflicts contributed to the rise of the deadliest jihadist groups. Scholars have published invaluable works on the rise of ISIS and Al-Qaeda, with most of them analyzing the genealogy of jihadism (Mohamedou, Hegghamer, Cooper, Sangeman, Rashid, Hafez, Harling, Robinson). Mahomedou sees the Afghan-Soviet War as a principal cause, saying "Moscow's ill-fated crossing into Afghanistan" was regarded by Islamists as a "casus belli" which served as a ground for jihad (religious struggle).[31] Some scholars conduct cross-case analyses of foreign fighters in different conflicts of the last thirty years (Hegghamer, 2011), or trace the origins of jihadism until Wahabism and Qutbism (Sageman, 2011), and others still distinguish between waves of jihadism throughout history (Robinson, Jaffe, Hafez).

The emergence of Al-Qaeda and ISIS should be analyzed in parallel with the War on Terror, the Iraq War, and the Syrian War. Each contributed to the new wave of jihadism. Robinson (2017) identifies four waves of jihadism: (1) from 1979–1990, Arab fighters fought in the Afghan-Soviet War, (2) from 1996–2011, the second wave undertook an "America First" approach to global jihad given the failures of local jihads in Egypt, Algeria, and elsewhere, (3) from 2003–2017, the destruction of the Iraqi state and, later, the civil war in Syria gave rise to the third wave of global jihad, and (4) the most recent wave of global jihad emerged from the destruction of the Afghan "emirate" under the Taliban and the essential defeat of Al-Qaeda and focuses on worldwide Islamic "resistance" (muqawama) in the form of an endless series of decentralized and small scale "personal jihads" (jihad fardi) around the globe.[32] While all waves identified by Robinson are important, the Afghan-Soviet War was detrimental, as it produced the initial key figures who conceptualized and set the foundation for Al-Qaeda and ISIS. Each wave of jihadism has been directly linked to different wars in the Middle East.

Tensions mounted after the declaration of the War on Terror by the United States in 2001, which was almost framed as a new Cold War. As Buzan posits, the USA took a securitization approach by declaring that the West should protect itself from terrorists who wish to destroy western civilization. He argues that after the end of the Cold War, the United States sought an enemy that could replace the USSR "to reassert and legitimize its leadership of global security."[33] The experience of a threat deficit was present throughout the 1990s. Thus, as Busan states, the Al-Qaeda attacks on the United States in 2001 solved this deficit by introducing a new enemy to the stage which was successfully constructed and embedded as the great new struggle.[34] The US President at the time, George W. Bush, Defense Minister Donald Rumsfeld and other US officials mainstreamed the discourse around a common enemy against whom the world should fight. For example, Donald Rumsfeld said in one of his speeches that terrorists are determined to force the U.S. and American values to withdraw from the world. "We have a choice—either to change the way we live, which is unacceptable; or to change the way that they live, and we chose the latter," said Rumsfeld.[35]

The US foreign policy shifted towards military intervention after 9/11 with the US invasion of Afghanistan, Iraq, and others. Washington also conducted drone attacks in Pakistan, Afghanistan, and Iraq that targeted terrorist suspects, but also killed hundreds of civilians. The invasion of Iraq, the Arab Spring, and the Syria War became critical factors that enabled global and transnational jihadism to grow. According to Hegghamer, the invasion of Iraq gave the global jihadists a strategic and emotional focal point at a time "when movement was strategically disoriented, having lost its territorial base in Afghanistan."[36] Of course, the invasion of the Islamic territory and its subsequent occupation have increased level of frustration in the Islamic world regarding American foreign policy; thus, jihadist groups easily mobilized and channelled radical forces to Iraq. Furthermore, Iraq became a haven, replacing Afghanistan as a "training ground where a new generation of Islamist militants can acquire military expertise and build personal relationships through the experience of combat and training camps."[37]

For jihadi ideologues, it was important to have new symbols of Muslim suffering and create narratives accordingly. When examples of Muslim suffering are salient and explicit, jihadist ideologues have more success in attracting followers. As Farhad Khosrokhavar says, "victimization brings Muslims together within an imaginary community where suffering is the paramount feature: Bosnia, Iraq, Afghanistan, Palestine, Chechnya, etc."[38] The Iraq War became a strategic battle; jihadi ideologues considered it to be a just and politically legitimate war, urging other Muslims to participate. As Hegghamer highlights, the Iraq War and the occupation created "new and powerful symbols of Muslim suffering."[39] The suffering of Muslims in Iraq served as a trauma that jihadists exploited for the mobilization of fighters.

The key figure in the Iraq War was Abu Musab al-Zarqawi who arrived in Iraq in September 2002 and founded Al-Qaeda in the country. As Shiraz Maher states, the Iraq War was instrumental in giving shape to Salafi-jihadist ideology as a tool to drive followers. "Salafi-jihadist ideology first began to emerge during the Algerian civil war, but it was really during the Second Gulf War that something more concrete, coherent, and discernable appeared."[40] Indeed, the period of the Iraq War became an ideologically significant period when Al-Qaeda in Iraq produced numerous pieces of literature that justified and explained their violence. For every act of violence, they found justification referring to false interpretations of scripture. This is what Hegghammer calls a "new strategic studies genre of the jihadist groups that emerged during the Iraq war." Ideological actors, including religious scholars, strategic thinkers, and social media writers emerged and started writing and disseminating books and fatwas about their ideology and explaining how to fight common enemies.

The United States and its allies did not expect that the Iraq War would have such a long-lasting spillover of terrorism. Nobody predicted that veterans of the Afghan War would join jihadi groups and turn against the West. The Iraq War played a crucial role in awakening Afghan War veterans striving to share their guerrilla skills. The main endurable strength of jihadist groups comes from human capital. Hundreds of veterans who fought in the Afghan War returned to battle to share their guerrilla skills with younger generations. The Iraq War also brought strategic changes to jihadist groups, adding greater numbers of European countries to their enemy list.

However, the Syrian War brought an astonishing impact on the globalization of jihadism. It certainly has become the most transformative period among jihadist groups, particularly for ISIS. The Syrian War presented the opportunity for jihadists to emerge as a global political project, occupy territories of two countries, create a caliphate, evolve ideologically and technically, mobilize unprecedented numbers of followers worldwide, and introduce new leaders and ideologues. As Hamming argues, jihadists have managed "to take their political project further than ever before with the establishment of a tangible political entity in the form of the Islamic State's caliphate."[41] The Syrian War produced unprecedented numbers of foreign fighters and the rise of "family jihad." Thousands of women and children travelled to the Middle East to live under the Islamic State.

The establishment of the caliphate is the main story in Syria. After the death of Zarqawi, his umbrella group was rebranded and renamed the Islamic State of Iraq. In 2010, Abu Bakr al-Baghdadi was elected to command the group. The crisis in Syria offered him an opportunity to establish a jihadist group in the territory of Syria as well. Baghdadi sent Abu Mohammed al-Jolani, his senior fighter, to establish a jihadist fighting group in Syria. Subsequently, Jahbat al-Nusra, a new jihadist group in Syria, was announced in late January 2012. In one year, al-Nusra became a powerful militant group largely composed of Syrian fighters and also functioned as a municipal and judicial authority in towns and villages under its control. In 2014, Baghdadi announced the establishment of ISIS with the merge of the Islamic State in Iraq and al-Nusra. ISIS became the most dangerous and powerful global jihadist group. It grabbed world headlines by its beheadings and executions. Thousands of fighters, including women and children, started travelling to Iraq and Syria to join the group. ISIS secured an image as the most terrifying jihadist group. As Atwan states, even Iraqi soldiers were afraid to fight them. "In early June 2014, when a brigade of 500 ISIS fighters entered Iraq's second city, Mosul, 30,000 regular Iraqi army soldiers surrendered instantly, throwing down their weapons and stripping off their uniforms."[42]

The world witnessed the creation of a brutal and dangerous terrorist organization that managed to establish a caliphate. Now with the defeat of ISIS and the detention of its affiliates in the desert of northeast Syria, what should concern us is their experience. They have learned how to wage a war and how to create a caliphate. They have applied experience and they have networking skills. As Tore Hamming states, "the experiences gained during the 2012–2018 period have generally made the jihadi movement more dangerous, popular, and arguably more mainstream."[43] Creating a caliphate is no longer a utopic dream; they have witnessed a near conception. They have rich lessons and experiences that will be shared widely. This raises concerns about imminent jihadist movements that will be more mature and still better networked. These gains were made in just one decade during the Iraq and Syrian War. In general, conditions for jihadist movements in the 21st century are more favorable than in the 1980s. They have the capacity to master a digital caliphate and know how to use new technologies. The digital mobilization of fighters was successful; thus, ISIS is not dead.

Jihadism is about both the clash of civilizations and the Western dominance and colonization of Muslim states. It is also about a sense of recognition and feeling of humiliation. But most importantly, it is about the failure of governance. As Fukuyama rightly underscored, Arab states failed to build good governance and instead created corrupt societies that disregard human rights and modernity. Many Muslim societies are not open to development and Western liberal ideas. They reject the secular state system and liberal values. Islamic fundamentalism sees a political solution only in Islamic dogmas. Yet, religion cannot be a solution for all political and economic problems. Jihadi groups see no separation between the radical ideology and governance, perceiving instead mutated and misinterpreted Islamic concepts as the solution. They perceive the radical religious concepts as ready recipes how to live. Instead of thinking and looking for solutions, they prefer to consider them as the set of rules and values to follow. Jihadists believe that issuing a fatwa is sufficient to wage war, but neglect the legitimacy problem. In the international system, only entities recognized as a state can be full members of the international community. Non-state actors cannot act as a state and their declarations do not have legal power.

Samuel Huntington's clash of civilizations sparked spirited debates. Some of his arguments concerning Islam, which is incompatible with other civilizations, might be weak. However, he is correct in asserting that, uniquely, the West has had a major and at times devastating impact on every other civilization. It is misguiding to believe that Western values are universally valid and that non-Western nations should commit to them. Why should Muslims westernize? Any country or culture will seek to sustain its traditions and values. As Huntington says, "what is universalism to the West is imperialism to the rest."[44] While non-Westerners are not happy with the hypocrisy and double standards that the West displays in its actions, non-Western countries should accept a universal secular legal system. It is because some of the Islamic legal norms do not cover full human rights values, especially with regard to women. However, Huntington erroneously indicates Islam itself as the underlying problem, not Islamic fundamentalism. We need to distinguish Islamic fundamentalism from Islam itself. Islam is a rich civilization with long history. However, Islamic fundamentalism is a different strand that emerged from colonial resentment and a feeling of humiliation. Civilizations are not antagonistic by nature, but historical and political circumstances may create collisions and different factions between them.

The next chapter of the book analyzes the root causes and motivations of individuals who join jihadist groups. Based on the findings of my analysis and personal interviews with the ISIS fighters and their associates, I conclude that there is a complex interaction between jihadi narratives, personal grievances that offer fertile ground, and religious concepts that lure individuals by proposing a utopian alternative. Those who travelled to live under a caliphate are products of this intersection between personal grievances, resonant narratives created by jihadi groups, and religious concepts distorted and mutated to lure recruits. The intersection of all the six cycles of the radicalization process are necessary to drive enlistment in jihadist groups. If one is absent, radicalization does not fully materialize. However, grievances and resentment of people are significant, while the radical ideology is a powerful soft power that poisons minds of people.

NOTES

1. Brinjar Lia, "Jihadism in the Arab World after 2011: Explaining its Expansion," *Middle East Policy* 23, no.2 (2016).

2. Dominique Moisi, "The Clash of Emotions: Fear, Humiliation, Hope, and the New World Order," *Foreign Affairs* 86, no. 1 (2007): 8–12.

3. See Barry Glassner, The Culture of Fear: Why Americans Are Afraid of the Wrong Things, Paperback, 2018, ISBN-13: 9780465004430.

4. Francis Fukuyama, Has History Started Again?, The Center for Independent Studies, Feature Article, Winter 2002.

5. Francis Fukuyama, "History and September 11," quoted in Ken Booth and Tim Dunne, *Worlds in Collision, Terror and the Future of Global Order*, (Palgrave Macmillan, 2002), 33.

6. Peter R. Neumann, Radicalized New Jihadists and the Threat to the West, (London-New York, I.B. Tuaris, 2016), 36.

7. Peter R. Neumann, *Radicalized New Jihadists and the Threat to the West*, (London-New York, I.B. Tuaris, 2016), 36.

8. Fred Halliday, *Islam and the Myth of Confrontation, Religion and Politics in the Middle East*, (London-New York, I.B. Tauris Publishers, 1995), 110.

9. Abdel Bari Atwan, *Islamic State: The Digital Caliphate*, (Oakland, California, University of California Press, 2015), 203.

10. Neumann, *Radicalized New Jihadists and the Threat to the West*, 38.

11. Vijay Prashad, *The Death of the Nation and the Future of the Arab Revolution*, (University of California Press, 2016), 27.

12. Michael R. Kelvington, "Global Salafi-Jihadism Ideology: The 'Soft Power' of the Enemy," *International Institute for Counter-Terrorism*, 25 March, 2019.

13. Kelvington, "Global Salafi-Jihadism Ideology: The 'Soft Power' of the Enemy."

14. Shiraz Maher, Salafi-Jihadism. *The History of an Idea* (New York, Oxford University Press, 2016).

15. Shiraz Maher, *Salafi-Jihadism: The History of an Idea*, (New York, Oxford University Press, 2016), 14.

16. Anouar Boukhars, Islam, Jihadism, and Depoliticization in France and Germany, *International Political Science Review* 30, No.3(2009): 297–317.

17. Abdel Bari Atwan, *Islamic State, The Digital Caliphate*, (University of California Press, 2015), 190.

18. Atwan, *Islamic State, The Digital Caliphate*, 192.

19. Akil N.Awan, "*The Impact of Evolving Jihadist Narratives on Radicalization in the West,*" quoted in Simon Staffel, Akil N. Awan, *Jihadism Transformed,* Al-Qaeda *and Islamic State`s Global Battle of Ideas*, (London, Hurst &Company, 2016), 183–199.

20. Tamara Sonn, "Is Islam an Enemy of the West," *Polity Press*, 2016, 66.

21. Farhad Khosrokhavar, *Inside Jihadism, Understanding Jihadi Movements Worldwide*, (London, Paradigm Publishers, 2009), 302.

22. Nelly Lahoud, *The Jihadis' Path to Self-Destruction*, (London, Hurst&Company Publishers, 2010), 255.

23. Thomas Hegghammer, "The Rise of Muslim Foreign Fighters: Islam and the Globalization of Jihad," *International Security* 35, no. 3 (WINTER 2010/11), 53–94.

24. Muhammed M. Hafez, Jihad After Iraq: Lessons from the Arab Afghans, *Studies in Conflict and Terrorism* 32, no. 2 (2009): 73–94.

25. Jeanine de Roy van Zuijdewijn and Edwin Bakker, Returning Western foreign fighters: The case of Afghanistan, Bosnia and Somalia, ICCT Background Note, June 2014, p. 5.

26. Hegghammer, "The Rise of Muslim Foreign Fighters," 53–94.

27. Hafez, "Jihad After Iraq," 73–94.

28. Paul Tumelty, "The Rise and Fall of Foreign Fighters in Chechnya," *Jamestown Foundation: Terrorism Monitor* 4, no.2 (2006), 8–10.

29. Muhammad-Mahmoud Ould Mohamedou, *A Theory of ISIS: Political Violence and the Transformation of the Global Order*, (London, Pluto Press, 2018), 28.

30. Mohamedou, *A Theory of ISIS,* 28.

31. Mohamedou, *A Theory of ISIS*, 28.

32. Glen E. Robinson, "The Four Waves of Global Jihad, 1979–2017," *Middle East Policy* XXIV, no. 3 (2017).

33. Barry Buzan, "Will the 'Global War on Terrorism' Be the New Cold War?" *International affairs* (London) 82, no. 6 (2006): 1101–1118.

34. Buzan, "Will the 'Global War on Terrorism' Be the New Cold War?," 1101–1118.

35. Donald Rumsfeld, "Pentagon Briefing on Military Response to Terrorist Attacks, Donald Rumsfeld's speech on 18 September 2001," *The Washington Post*, 18 September 2001.

36. Thomas Hegghamer, "Global Jihadism after the Iraq War," *Middle East Journal* 60, no.1 (2006), 11–32.

37. Heggmaher, "Global Jihadism after the Iraq war," 11–32.

38. Farhad Khosrokhavar, *Inside Jihadism, Understanding Jihadi Movements Worldwide*, (London, Paradigm Publishers, 2009), 191.

39. Heggmaher, Global Jihadism after the Iraq war, 11–32.

40. Shiraz Maher, *Salafi-Jihadism: The History of an Idea*, (Oxford University Press, 2016), 17.

41. Tore Refslund Hamming, "Global Jihadism after the Syria War," *Perspectives on Terrorism* 13, no.3 (2019), 1–16.

42. Atwan, *Islamic State, The Digital Caliphate*, 126.

43. Hamming, "Global Jihadism after the Syria War," 1–16.

44. Samuel P. Huntington, The Clash of Civilizations and The Remaking of World Order, The Free Press, London 2002, p. 116.

Chapter 2

Why Join ISIS

Conceptualizing Radicalization Process of Jihadists

Scholars have advanced various theories to explain radicalization and terrorism, while each has its limitations and strengths in understanding why people get radicalized. There is no universal algorithm to explain their path and it's impossible to generalize. Each foreign fighter, including their family members, have their own story. Behind those stories, more profound problems of the contemporary world are hidden. Profiles of those who joined ISIS sent the world one important message: they rejected the political system where they lived and fled their countries to find another system to live in. They wanted to erase their previous lives and start from a blind page. They rejected society and the entire political state system, even abandoning their parents and loved ones. The conversations with returnees from Syria and Iraq and those living at the time of interviews in the Al-Hawl and Roj camps, have led me to conclude that their radicalization processes are gradual and complex. Radicalization and becoming a jihadist result from the intersection of several interlinked cycles of complex processes and factors.

The most outstanding feature of the situation is that people rejected the political system they lived in and started seeking an alternative system where they hoped to find just society, belonging, and understanding. People saw an alternative in an Islamic state, even though it is a utopian concept based on the radical religious ideology. The failure of secular states to address political and economic grievances of people, to build effective institutions, and eliminate corruption has become the primary source of the quest for a caliphate, significance for their lives, and a new identity. The main message that the world should receive, digest, and take appropriate decisions is that people are aware of the failures of states, have already become disillusioned, and have started seeking alternatives to the existing political system. And the alternative that they found is perilous, even though it might seem utopian. After the victory of the Taliban, the perspective that terrorists can govern is not a utopia already. It is a fact. Thus, it is crucial to understand and analyze the aspirations and grievances of those who joined ISIS. This chapter will discuss why people joined ISIS. The non-enigma cycles radicalization model has been developed based on the interviews and stories of former fighters and their family members.

In the global context, general processes -colonization, globalization, modernization, and migration—all caused a feeling of insecurity and discontent among people. In a rapidly developing and changing world, people, especially those who live in developing countries, feel unprotected and weakened by having a sense of losing control over their destinies. Even though many developing countries were colonized and exposed to cultural and social transformation, the emergence of new globalization and modernization came as a great shock for non-Western countries.[1] Not all countries have benefited from globalization and modernization, subsequently some Muslim countries that failed to take advantage of economic benefits may perceive globalization as a threat. As Neumann posits for these societies, globalization may "seem to fail to deliver on the promise of prosperity, and it is sometimes viewed as a pretext for the imposition of alien values and culture."[2] Muslim countries have not benefited from globalization as other countries have.

Consequently, some Arab countries perceive globalization as the imposition of Western institutions and values, thus preferring to remain uninvolved in many processes. This uncontrolled process of globalization "not only came with the liberal politics and economics of the West, but it also brought with it its likelihood of cultural transformation. The dominant pattern of the global politics and consumer culture was Western, especially American."[3] Muslims feel threatened by this cultural transformation and reject Western values, while their home countries are left behind economically and socially. There is anger and resentment among the population in the Middle East, Central Asia and other regions. They see a widening difference between the opportunities in developed and free countries and the appalling poverty, unemployment, and repression in their home countries. They first blame their rulers and Western countries for "keeping those rulers in power for selfish reasons."[4] Most Muslim communities understand that the outflow of natural resources, especially oil resources, did not serve the national interests of the country, but the Western countries and the local elites.

The next cause of this unease is global migration. The high influx of Muslims into European countries has become the hallmark of the 21st century. In some European countries, the first generations of Muslim communities came from colonized countries. For instance, in the 1930s, France had to receive thousands of Algerians, as it had colonized Algeria for 130 years.

Other European countries, such as Germany, Italy, and Belgium, received hundreds of Muslims in the 1960s as heavy industries needed cheap labor force. However, European countries did not know that they would face non-stop vast waves of Muslim refugees in several decades. Currently, Europe has been dealing with four generations of Muslim immigrants. The first generation aged seventy to eighty are those who came to work between the 1930 and1960s. The second generation are their family members who later joined them. The third generation are their grandchildren born in Europe, and the fourth generation are the grandchildren's children. Today, Europe is challenged by Muslim communities which are not integrated, feel marginalized, and question their dignity and identity. As Claude Moniquet stated in 2008, "Europe is living with this problem and paying for it." "So today, parts of the Second and Third generations make no efforts to integrate into European society and to adopt European humanist values. However, it has to be pointed out that, until very recently (in fact in the nineties), absolutely nothing was done to help them to integrate. This is the European reality and the European shame. We must live with it and are paying for it," noted Moniquet.[5] A decade later, of this note made by Moniquet, Europe is in trouble with the nonstop arrival of millions of Muslims in the context of the severe problem of integration and incapacity of finding appropriate policies to eliminate discrimination. Muslims do not feel at home, but rather feel discriminated against and treated as a potential threat. In such circumstances, Muslims have started questioning their sense of identity and dignity. As Neumann states, global migration "has created hybrid identities, especially among the second-and third-generation descendants of immigrants."[6] Muslim communities in Europe not only get challenged by their identity, but also feel economically marginalized. As scholars posit, marginality can explain the appeal for radicalization. Muslim residents in Europe "live for the most part in ghetto-like segregation, receive second-rate schooling, suffer much higher unemployment than the general population, and those who work are more likely to have low-wage, dead-end jobs."[7] Benjamin states that the Madrid cell members were mainly marginalized Muslims, drug dealers, part-time workers, and drifting students. Many European jihadists are indeed products of failed policies of European societies that will discuss later in the chapter.

High levels of global migration have mounted for the last two decades. Some migrate due to unemployment, others escape war, and conflicts. According to the UN Migration Report of 2020, the number of international migrants is estimated to be almost 272 million globally.[8] Of this number, 164 million are migrant workers, 30 million are refugees, and the number of internally displaced persons is 42 million. Their new home brings on its social context, prejudices, rules, culture, and mentalities. After the 9/11 attack, the perception of being an immigrant has changed. As Coolsaet highlights, "it became standard practice to equate 'immigrant' with 'Muslim.'"[9] Tensions are mounting, and antipathy towards immigrants is sharpening while "Christian Europe continues to shrink and Muslim Europe grows."[10] Indeed, the number of Muslims in Western countries is growing rapidly. There is an urgent need to reconsider integration policies, weigh all pros and cons, and take preventive measures to stop discrimination and marginalization.

NON-ENIGMA CYCLES OF RADICALIZATION: FROM GRIEVANCES TO NETWORKING

There is existing literature that explores sources of terrorism and radicalization (Krueger, 2007; Sageman, 2004; Roy, 2004; Neumann, 2009, Haffez and Mullins, 2015, Wiktorovicz 2005). Each study has its contribution and significance, and several interesting models have been developed. Borum proposes a four-stage conceptual model for the emergence of a "terrorist mindset."[11] His model explains how grievances and vulnerabilities are transformed into hatred of a target group and how that hatred can be transformed into a justification or impetus for violence. Kruglanski, Bélanger, and Gunaratna developed the significance quest theory, which posits that an individual who experiences humiliation will seek to have significance. This process starts with a "feeling of a loss of significance" and follows with one's significance quest. "This search typically entails seeking guidance from a group and its shared values and beliefs. We call this phenomenon a 'collectivistic shift,' representing a transition from one's individual identity to one's social identity as the member of some group."[12] The authors highlight that radicalization has three main pillars: need, narrative, and network.

While many theories address major important factors of radicalization, I argue that two critical cycles, that are crucial for the radicalization, should not be under regarded: the religious and ideological basis that serves as a soft power and the grievances of people that serve as a fertile ground. People's grievances, both individual and collective, are significant. However, grievances alone cannot produce radicalization. One cannot suddenly get radicalized due to own frustrations. It is a long, complex, and gradual process that intersects several important cycles. The second essential factor is a religious radical ideology that poisons people's minds—the Salafi-Wahhabi ideology. The interviews that I conducted with men and women who joined ISIS have proven that their religious beliefs, even though they had limited knowledge about Islam itself, played a crucial role in deciding to travel to the Middle East. They truly believed in the distorted concepts of Islam and their whole mindset was occupied by it. However, when I say religious belief, I am not referring to Islam as a whole religion, but to Islam's distorted and mutated concepts that jihadists use to justify violence. It would be impossible for them to justify their narratives and mobilize fighters and their family members without religious justification. Thus, radicalization has a strong ideological pillar which is very significant.

The model that I propose consists of six puzzling cycles. Each cycle plays an important role, and they form a causal relationship between each other, whereas complement each other. Thus, I call it "non-enigma cycles radicalization." It was developed based on the interviews I conducted with the women and men who joined ISIS and the analysis of open-source profiles of dozens of other fighters. The model consists of six cycles: (1) grievances and resentment, (2) cognitive opening/searching, (3) encountering the narratives, (4) soft power/religious dogmas, (5) search for belonging and identity, and (6) brotherhood networking and channels. I called them non-enigma cycles because, while each person has their own story and destiny, and paths may look puzzling, but if you analyze their motivations and paths, it is not enigmatic as each cycle has a causal relationship with one another. While the model's causal cycles may seem sequent, they intersect and interact; the causal relationship between cycles is very strong.

My empirical evidence proved that the background condition for radicalization is people's grievances and resentment. Everything starts from what was happening in their pre-ISIS lives, where they were unhappy, unemployed, had low-paid jobs, felt discriminated against or mistreated, lived with uncertainty, did not receive education etc. The feeling of injustice was the central element, even though how they presume justice might vary. Grievances and resentment of people are the fertile ground that produces the cognitive opening condition where a person starts questioning their own life, asking themselves why it is happening. This condition is significant as it opens a door for looking around and sinking into an in-search position. It can be a search for justice, revenge, or a search for belonging and significance. This search condition could have remained inactive unless it encountered the jihadis' narratives. Jihadist groups target the vulnerabilities and grievances of people and create narratives to exploit their weaknesses and propose utopian solutions. Subsequently, in-search people in an uphill battle with their endless social and economic problems encounter the narratives conveyed by jihadist groups.

Narratives can speak about the evil state system with corrupt leaders, historical grievances of Muslims, the humiliation of Muslims or apostate regimes, and also about Western military interventions such as the Iraq war, for example. Jihadist groups create victimization narratives and target both near and far enemies. The narrative easily catches those who hate their governments because of poverty and corruption, the "evil secular system" and apostate governments. Narratives help to awaken and mobilize people by exploiting their grievances and vulnerabilities. The next important cycle is rationalization and justification of actions through the Salafi-Wahhabi ideology. Jihadi groups use distorted and mutated concepts of Islam to justify their violence. I identified seven religious concepts that exist in Islam's norms and traditions, but as Shiraz Maher states, these concepts have "undergone significant ideational mutation in Salafi-Jihadi understanding."[13] Shiraz Maher identified mutated concepts, but his list is different from mine. These are seven essential religious elements of jihadi ideology that I identified: tawhid, takfir, umma, al-Wala'wal Bara, Jihad, Hijrah, and Jannah. The next cycle of the radicalization process is networking through different channels and heading to the Caliphate. Networking is done through the internet, but also mainly through friendship, kinship, or other contacts.

FERTILE BACKGROUND: FEELING OF INJUSTICE AND GRIEVANCES

After having interviewed more than thirty former fighters and their wives, and twenty five family members, and having analyzed forty other profiles of returnees in Kazakhstan, Kyrgyzstan, Russia, Azerbaijan, Tajikistan, and Uzbekistan, I have acquired a more bottom-up approach. In understanding one's path of radicalization and joining ISIS, we need to zoom in on their grievances, which serve as a fertile ground for radicalization. There has been a debate among scholars on the role of grievances and on how deep we need to zoom in on them. I agree with Ahmed Ajil that "a grievance-based analysis may help 're-politicize' and 'dehystericize' discussions on PIV."[14] In the context of the 9/11 attacks, research on terrorism and radicalization has been depoliticized, and thorough engagement with people's grievances, such as frustrations and dissatisfactions, has been limited. There has been a tendency in research "since 9/11 is overwhelmingly engaged with the phenomenon on the individual and group level and tends to displace elements related to grievances, especially of a socioeconomic and political nature."[15] Especially government officials of developing countries are reluctant to mention socioeconomic grievances in their home countries, while EU governments have a tendency not to focus on grievances of immigrants, such as discrimination and marginalization. In research, there is also a tendency to underestimate a grievance-based analysis. However, some scholars have taken a grievance-centric approach in their models (Borum 2011, Wiktorowicz 2005 and Hafez and Mullins 2015).

Hafez and Mullins propose a contextualized approach where four factors come together to produce violent radicalization: personal and collective grievances, networks and interpersonal ties, political and religious ideologies, and enabling environments and support structures. Borum's model also centered on the grievances of people who think it is not right and their feeling of injustice which says it is not fair. Wiktorowicz (2015) also proposed a four-stage radicalization process with an initial stage with a "cognitive opening" that occurs following personal or group grievance. My analysis also shows that grievances and resentment are significant because they are the main source to find a target and justify violence.

The interviews with men and women who joined ISIS have proved that the main central line is a feeling of injustice. The majority lived in poverty, struggled with unemployment, or suffered from endless violence at home or from conflict within their own family. The most striking feature for me was that they had a common desire to escape their own life, more accurately their existing problems in their lives. Raya, a thirty-five-year-old woman from Russia, who was living at Roj camp at the time of our interview, told me that she was tired of her life in Russia. She was married to a Dagestani man, and lived together with his parents. "My relationship with his parents was very complicated. They hated me because of my Russian nationality. They did not believe that I converted to Islam and always thought I was just pretending. My husband and I also were tired of police who sees us as an extremist just because we are Muslims," she said. "I wanted to change my life and live freely somewhere else." At the time of the interview, her husband had been held in prison near Hasaka guarded by the Kurdish forces, whereas she lives in Roj camp with her son. The interview was conducted on WhatsApp in February of 2021. During the interview, she recalled a moment when ISIS was fully defeated. "I cried heading to the Kurdish camps, cried because of the feeling of failure. We failed to have our dream to build a Muslim country. I could not believe that our dawla (in Arabic means state) does not exist anymore," she told me. She had a clear goal to live in a caliphate and never return.

Another common line present among interviews that I conducted with both returnees and those still trapped in Northeast Syria, was the feeling of injustice in their home countries. Many of them struggled to live with unemployment, poverty, or discrimination. Many of them claim they sought to fight for justice. What kind of justice? Each of them spoke about their truth, and they wished to seek the justice they presumed for themselves. Political scientist Viktor Mikhaylov, Director of Center to Study Regional Threats in Uzbekistan, researched the motivations of foreign fighters in Central Asia. He informed me during an interview that many foreign fighters understand Jihad as a fight for justice. "They are telling the truth when they talk about justice. They are fighting for justice because they saw injustice according to their views. Some of them refer to unjust decisions of their governments. Some may refer to drone attacks conducted by the USA, which killed civilians in Afghanistan and Pakistan. They say that Muslims are suffering, and we cannot tolerate it any longer," said Mikhaylov.[16] However, most of the time, foreign fighters have grievances about problems in their home countries. "It is mostly about corruption, how government officials are living luxurious lives while ordinary people struggle in poverty. They [the government officials] live in big houses, organize luxury weddings, and drive expensive cars. Their children go to nightclubs to have fun—all these facts are perfect conditions for recruitment," said Mikhaylov.

People rightly perceive they are living with injustice when their human rights are violated. It can be about their right to social guarantees, economic opportunities, access to education, or access to medical services. The UN Secretary-General Antonio Guterres rightly stressed that religious extremism and terrorism "do not arise in a vacuum." "Actual or perceived injustice and promised empowerment become attractive wherever human rights are being violated, good governance is being ignored, and aspirations are being crushed," said Mr. Guterres.[17] Citizens feel the injustice when they don't have access to equal conditions, equal payment, or social welfare due to neglect and discrimination by corrupt governments. As the UN Secretary-General stressed, "terrorism is fundamentally the denial and destruction of human rights." To counter terrorism, certain social conditions should be facilitated by the states where the human rights of every citizen are respected. When we protect human rights, we are tackling the root causes of terrorism. Scholars stress that high levels of state-sanctioned human rights violations and political authoritarianism have been the core features of the politics of some regions, and "until these social conditions are changed, there is no reasonable expectation that the ISIS crisis can be ameliorated."[18]

Justice is directly connected to human rights and the dignity of people: human rights are upheld, if only governments build institutions that function effectively and abuse of power is minimized. In such a just society people are less likely to take extremist actions. From a psychological perspective, extremism starts from protesting against something aggressively. Lola Shakimova, a psychologist who worked with extremists and former foreign fighters in Kazakhstan, explained that extremism is an extreme norm of behavior either in politics or religion. "The basis of extremist behavior always includes aggression. Aggression comes from resentment of the social environment. When a person is unhappy with something in their social environment, is not happy with themselves or the environment, that is what their aggression can manifest," said Lola Shakimova.[19]

In many developing countries, people are frustrated with socioeconomic problems and lack of opportunities. State leaders have been incapable of resolving massive socioeconomic problems in the Middle East, North Africa, Central Asia, and South Asia. As Benjamin and Simon maintain, the delegitimation of regimes and the emergence of religious violence are unquestionably linked to the failure of leaders to cope with these problems.[20] Within

Muslim countries, including Arab countries, radicals have occupied people's minds by constant religious discourses and narratives about unjust societies and humiliation of Muslims. Indeed, the radicals may have not yet won the war against the state, "but they have won the theological debate"[21] by nonstop propaganda and discourses that dominate societies.

In Central Asia, most foreign fighters who traveled to Syria wanted to overcome economic difficulties. Most of them were brainwashed and recruited in Russia, where they were labor migrants. Many foreign fighters harbored resentment toward the political and economic system at home. They expected fair conditions, adequate resources, and sufficient social welfare. Some were disillusioned with the state in which they lived and believed that their frustrations and grievances would never be addressed in their home countries. The majority of Central Asian fighters were recruited from Russia, where they faced discrimination and loneliness. They went to Russia to avoid poverty and unemployment in their home countries. However, a hostile environment in a host country turns them to seek justice in religion. I interviewed Komal, who returned voluntarily to Kyrgyzstan. He went to Russia to earn money to help rebuild his parents' house, which was burnt during the ethnic conflict in Osh in 2011. However, his life in Moscow turned out to be even more frustrating. "I could not find a job and left without money. Nobody wanted to help me. I am an ethnic Uzbek, and they treated me as someone dangerous. Nobody wanted to hire me. I felt alone. I could not return to Kyrgyzstan as my old parents hoped that I would earn money. I did not want to disappoint them. My friend invited me to come to the mosque in Moscow. I found support and compassion there. Several men talked to me, even gave me some money. I did not know that they were recruiters. One day, I was proposed to travel to Syria and help Muslim brothers," said Komal. At that moment, he was happy to travel to a Muslim country and truly believed that Muslims working there would treat him equitably and with compassion. Many labor migrants from Central Asian countries who travelled to Russia to earn money were sent to the conflict zone.

Grievances can not only be individual, but also collective. My empirical evidence from the interviews with returnees has proved that people eventually switched from their personal grievances to group grievances. Most of them believed that Muslims, in general, are being humiliated and mistreated in the world. They believed that there is a general tendency in most countries to make Muslims suffer, and blamed the Western countries for such unfair treatment. Dozens of fighters, whom I interviewed, referred to the Iraq war, the Palestinian crisis, and the Afghan war, saying that Islam and Muslims have been in danger due to the colonial behavior of Western countries. Some fighters believed that infidels were killing Muslims in Syria; thus, they had a duty to protect them from infidels. Another line of discourse was about the evil secular state system. One Kyrgyz man I interviewed told me that he considers the secular system a blind, corrupt and evil system whose eventual goal is to make Muslims suffer. "Corruption is everywhere, and its main source is man-made law. I still believe that only Sharia will save Muslims from corruption, repression, and poverty; we will come to it one day," he told me. He truly believed that Muslims in Kyrgyzstan are victims of the Western-imposed secular system working against Muslims and their values in the country. He was not talking about his grievances, such as unemployment and uncertainty but preferred to hold a collective account of the problems in his life.

Extensive research is conducted on how groups' grievances may lead to violent extremism. For instance, some scholarly works study group identity explaining the significance of horizontal inequalities for conflicts (Ostby, 2008; Cederman et al., 2010; Brown, 2010). Horizontal inequalities mean that groups of people, who share a similar religion, identity or culture, or other similarities, suffer from economic, political, and social inequalities within their country. This includes inequalities in income levels and employment opportunities and inequalities in power distribution, political participation, and access to health, education, and social services. There is vast research on the link between political exclusion, minority discrimination, and terrorism. When people face oppression and discrimination based on their ethnicity or religion, they are more likely to turn violent to protect their group's status and interests. James Piazza conducted a statistical analysis of 172 countries between 1970 and 2006. He found a strong link between economic discrimination of minority groups and higher rates of domestic terrorism. "Countries that feature economic discrimination against minority groups experience around six more incidents of domestic terrorism per year," concludes Piazza, adding that "discrimination matters."[22] Other significant research works found evidence on how groups' wealth low levels compared to the country average may lead to conflicts or civil wars (Cederman et al., 2010; Brown, 2010).

Group grievances are significant catalysts for civil wars and radicalization to join terrorist groups. That group can be a minority group or just a social group that unites people with the same social status. They can be unemployed, underpaid, or living in poor villages. They will be united by the feeling of living in an unjust society and lacking equal economic opportunities. Individuals feel comfortable being in a group which shares their frustrations instead of being alone with their problems. There is another significant component of the group grievances, which is a group identity. Jihadist ideologues build narratives to construct a group identity and attract people by exploiting historical events. In the case of Al-Qaeda and ISIS, they recall the Afghan war, the Palestinian issue, drone attacks, the Iraq war, etc. As France Stewart observed, political leaders adopt a strategy of "a reworking of historical memories" to engender group identity and find group cohesion.[23] According to

Stewart, any society where "some differences in individuals' circumstances—including cultural, geographic, economic—which provide the construction of group identity as a source of political mobilization."[24] Stewart observed rightly saying that "leaders often seize on, change and exaggerate cultural or religious differences—or symbolic systems—as a mechanism of group mobilization." In the case of jihadi groups, they exaggerate Islamic concepts to mobilize people and justify violence.

Group identity is also about Fukuyama's politics of resentment. When people switch from individual grievances to group grievances, it is not about material self-interest. They do not pursue finding a good job, buying a house, or having a car, but it is more about dignity and recognition and the group's identity. This is a very strong motivation that is much harder to weaken. As Fukuyama observed, "a humiliated group seeking restitution of its dignity carriers far more emotional weight than people simply pursuing their economic advantage."[25] Because they become more fanatic, more dangerous, and more committed in the group. Because the group provides them with the common political goal and feeling of belonging and safety. Individual grievances may remain inactive without further steps, but united actions will follow once individuals switch to group grievances. Group grievances are a very strong basis for cohesion and mobilization.

COGNITIVE OPENING AND ITS ENCOUNTER WITH NARRATIVES

After living with long-lasting individual and group grievances, people start to undermine their current lives and values. This is the moment that Wiktorowicz called a "cognitive opening," which I also use to describe this moment. Some scholars call this condition unfreezing mechanism. Unfreezing means searching for a new connection because of feeling alone or losing someone very close. As McCauley and Moskalenko observed, "unfreezing is radicalization to escape fear and pain."[26] My empirical evidence also proves that people wanted to escape that unfreezing moment, which has its main features such as grief, loneliness, uncertainty, fear and pain. An individual who faces poverty, socioeconomic crisis, family conflict, painful divorce, discrimination, and political repression starts questioning his life and realizes that he cannot continue living in the same way. He devaluates what he has and becomes vulnerable and receptive to the narratives conveyed by radical groups. Narratives are very important as they bring essential messages that awaken, guide, and mobilize people. As Akil Awan observed, while narratives are important pull factors, but they have to find fertile ground as "the individual's context and their personal circumstances are central to whether or not this narrative resonates on an individual level."[27] The narratives about injustice and corruption among secular evil governments, the humiliation of Muslims worldwide, and the secular system, which is considered to be evil and corrupt, make those in-search conditions switch to the awakened condition. This kind of awakening brings them to searching for new ideas, new meaning, or belonging. They see Jihadist groups as an ideal community that promises an ideal society where all Muslims live in harmony.

The interviews conducted with female returnees in Kazakhstan, Azerbaijan, Kyrgyzstan, and Uzbekistan showed uncertainty, pain, humiliation, and different conflicts in their previous lives in their home countries. They had an endless struggle with socioeconomic problems. They wanted to avoid this self-uncertainty, and thus narratives of the Jihadist group gave them hope. By joining the Muslim community, they pursued group identification that was supposed to reduce or eliminate the uncertainty and pain. The Azerbaijani woman I interviewed told me that she had a feeling of emptiness and full uncertainty about her future and the future of her two children. She lived with her husband under constant financial constraints. "I was at home with my children. My husband was a driver. His salary was not enough to cover our expenses. I thought our future was dark, and we failed to build our children's future too. One day, my husband showed me videos on YouTube about the Caliphate. We watched videos at night when children were sleeping. In several months, we found people who helped us to connect with those who were in Syria," she told me. She truly believed that only the Caliphate could resolve her socioeconomic problems. However, most importantly, she believed that the association with the Umma and Muslim community would save her from uncertainty and emptiness in her soul. Another Kazakh woman, repatriated from Syria, told me she also had emptiness and uncertainty. "I lived like a robot which has no soul. My heart was empty. Feeling that emptiness was painful for me. The idea about a Muslim country gave me hope that I can start everything from zero," she told me.

The narratives spread by the jihadist group brainwashed their minds by several significant lines. First, black-white thinking that identifies the secular state system as evil, and the Sharia law system is to be human and effective. People in constant troubles facing discrimination, unequal economic opportunities, and poverty were disillusioned by their own lives. They were very receptive to this kind of mindset. They witnessed corruption, repression, human rights violations and were morally prepared to accept this kind of white and black mindset. The subsequent narrative was about an ideal society within a caliphate under Sharia Law. YouTube propaganda videos showed how those who had reached Iraq and Syria were living in comfortable houses, how they smiled at each other, and how they were receiving medical and social benefits. People blindly believed that the Caliphate was an ideal state in which people felt accepted, respected, and whose dignity was restored.

Another narrative was about the far enemy-Western countries, which colonized and threatened Islam and the whole Muslim community worldwide. Jihadist groups' main argument has been that Islam is under siege and Muslims have been humiliated. So they present people's lives in their home countries as meaningless and useless; only Islam can guarantee security, order, and acceptance. As I discussed before, each foreign fighter or woman who joined ISIS sought to live in a just society. Each of them has its presumed justice. It can be imagined justice, but it was their justice. Thus, the feeling of injustice is at the center of the radicalization process. Scholars also observe that a feeling of injustice is very important in the radicalization of people as they are angry due to the absence of justice in their lives. As Bruce Hoffman notes in *Inside Terrorism*, they have a "burning sense of injustice and dispossession." My empirical evidence also suggests that each of them lived with this burning sense of injustice. Several returnees in Central Asia told me that their countries have been ruled by apostate and corrupt leaders, thus they had never seen justice in their lives. "My father worked his whole life as a teacher with a small salary. My mother was unemployed. I was also unemployed. I could not marry because we all lived in a small house in the village. While we make ends to meet, look how rich the corrupt politicians are. Compare their lives to ours. When we will have at least 10 percent of what they have? I wanted to reject such a miserable life, but later understood that I chose a wrong way," said one of the voluntary returnees in Kyrgyzstan. Everyone speaks about own justice. Their presumed justice can be about different things and what they perceive as justice can be contested. Knowing this context, the narratives of jihadi groups presented Islam as a guarantor of justice or a valid reaction to injustice. These narratives were powerful in gaining new followers, brainwash and mobilize them.

"SOFT POWER": RATIONALIZATION AND SANCTIONING

The Salafi-Jihadist ideology constitutes the ideological pillar of the radicalization process of people who joined jihadist groups. Religious dogmas are essential mechanisms as they not only give justification and rationalization for violence, but also for their rejectionist mindset and behavioral change. As Michael Kelvington states, the Salafi-Jihadist ideology is "the intangible soft power"[28] of jihadi groups that contests the international system and the existence of modern nation-states. The religious pillar of radicalization is powerful by its two features. First, it is a soft power that rationalizes, sanctions and resonates with the appeals of terrorist groups. Second, its powerful contribution is that it gives each person personalized benefits and rewards. People believe that God sees their efforts in Jihad and rewards them. As Juergensmeyer notes, religion personalizes the conflict. "It provides personal rewards-religious merit, redemption, the promise of heavenly luxuries."[29] Jihadists attract people by promising personal rewards that come directly from God as if there were a direct deal between God and a person. They use selective citation of Islamic texts and misinterpret, exaggerate, and manipulate them. I have identified seven Islamic concepts which the Salafi-Jihadist ideologues have misinterpreted. These concepts have been mutated to serve their radical political ideology. The main concepts that Jihadist groups use to brainwash people are: takfir, tawhid, Al-Wala' wal Bara,' hijra, Jihad, Umma, and Jannah.

The central concept is tawhid which rejects the secular state system and liberal values. In Islam, tawhid means oneness. It refers to the oneness of God and also the oneness of humankind. The latter means that humans may look different because of their nationality, gender, or race, but as humankind, we are all the same. Tawhid has a profound philosophy of unity and equality of mankind in Islam. However, the Salafi-Wahhabi ideology interprets it differently, giving it a rejectionist mindset. Jihadist groups present tawhid as total exclusionist by asserting that God only has sovereignty and nothing else man-made can decide both state government and individual destinies. They assert that only Sharia-based law and the only government that applies tenets of Islamic law can exist on the earth. God has sovereignty, and subsequently, human beings cannot make laws. Jihadist groups believe that "democracy, liberalism, human rights, personal freedom, international law, and international institutions are illegal, illegitimate and sinful."[30] Thus, they call to build a caliphate and urge all Muslims to live under the Caliphate.

The next mutated concept is Takfir. In Islam, the pronouncement of Takfir is possible. If someone's acts constitute disbelief in Islam, another person can declare him an apostate. Nevertheless, there is a very strict rule that by declaring someone an apostate, that person should provide clear evidence. If he fails, it is considered a big sin in Islam. Jihadists use the takfir concept to blame and target secular states and Muslims who do not join the Jihadist groups. ISIS published several documents explaining the Takfir publicly. In the *Aqidah Wa Manhaj Al-Dawlah Al-Islamiyah Fi Al-Takfir* (IS' Creed and Methodology of *Takfir*), they published a list of infidels: all parties based on communism, secularism, nationalism, and liberalism, proponents of democracy, and those who participate in its process and all governments that do not rule by the *Shari`ah* law were considered as infidels and apostates. They call the rest of the world infidel or kaffir, both Muslims and non-Muslims who do not support their radical ideology. However, the main problem is that fellow

Muslims can easily become Kaffir. As Lahoud observed, "whenever jihadist disagree among themselves over doctrinal issues, they believe they must resort to Jihad against the internal enemy to eliminate their differences and purify the group from any perceived signs of unbelief."[31] ISIS indoctrinated small children from an early age with the rejectionist mindset. Children who were repatriated from Iraq and Syria, upon their return, regarded other people as kaffirs. Children, who were repatriated in Kazakhstan, called social workers and psychologists kaffir simply because some were Russian or because women did not wear a hijab. The boy told the social worker: "You are kaffir because you were not with us. We are true Muslims because we built a caliphate." Gulnaz Razdykova, a psychologist who worked with returnees in Kazakhstan, came across a boy in the morning when she was going to her office. The boy was repatriated during the operation Zhusan from Syria. "Good morning! How are you?" she greeted him. She hoped that the boy remembers her, as she worked in the rehabilitation center in Aktau. "Do you remember me? Who am I?" she asked. The boy was direct: "You are kaffir!" This happened several months after their return and the boy was still living with this mindset. However, two years have passed since their repatriation, and now most children have changed their world views. In general, rehabilitation of returnee children have had some positive dimensions but many challenges as well.

Jihadist groups also use the doctrine of Al-Wala' wal Bara' (Loyalty and Disavowal), which is central to the ideology of modern Salafism that identifies the relationship of Muslims with the non-Muslim world. This doctrine is also a logical continuation of tawhid and takfir. Al-Wala' wal Bara' urges Muslims to reserve their love and loyalty for fellow Muslims and to reject and declare war on the rest of humanity. This doctrine has several dimensions, including a political one. It urges to be loyal to rulers who rule according to Sharia law, but "a Muslim leader who does not rule by the shariah in its entirety is an infidel who should be overthrown, by violent means if necessary. The political dimension of Al-Wala' wal Bara' can lead to the Jihadi dimension."[32] Jihad, in its turn, is a central concept that has been associated with war and violence. Jihad never meant offensive war in Islam. The notion of Jihad is very broad, ranging from personal development, gaining knowledge, imparting knowledge, writing a book, earning a living, supporting a family, and so on. The word itself in Arabic means "making efforts." Jihad simply means that every Muslim should do their best to improve themselves. Great Jihad is about personal ego, a believer's internal struggle to live according to the various tenets of the Muslim faith as wholly and authentically as possible. Through this struggle, a believer must improve their attitude, character, habits, and skills.

The second form of Jihad is a lesser Jihad that focuses on building a good society and defending that society when necessary. For this cause, there are several types of Jihad. The first type is Jihad of the Pen, which is about telling the truth to hakims or governors. "If you disagree with injustice, you should tell it to the rulers. If you cannot tell them directly, you must at least condemn it in your heart. Jihad of the Pen also refers to writing articles and books to improve society and to encourage others to do good or to deter them from wrongful actions," said Kadyr Malikov, a well-known theologian and religious leader in Kyrgyzstan.[33] A hadith says, "The best Jihad is the word of Justice in the face of the oppressive sultan," which was applied by some scholars to protests in the Arab world.[34] If one analyzes its pure goal, Jihad of the Pen is a democratic concept that encourages freedom of speech and standing out against oppressive regimes. Jihad of the Pen never implies bloodshed, fighting, or violence; it presumes only speaking and writing. Thus, it suggests peaceful actions and aims only to struggle for a good.

The next type of Jihad is the Jihad of Sadaka, which means sharing what you have earned with others and helping the poor. This is why mosques collect alms from Muslims, particularly during the holy month of Ramadan. It is also not compulsory; alms should be given from the bottom of one's heart and cannot be forced. The next type is a military Jihad or Jihad of the Sword. Terrorist radical ideas have referred to this type of Jihad, although in Islam, it means only to protect the land from outside aggression. ISIS and other terrorist groups have interpreted and promoted Jihad as a holy war against infidels, but this idea is far removed from the fundamental tenets of Islam. Military Jihad has less importance in Islam because priority is given to the greater Jihad, the internal struggle of the person fighting their bad attitudes and habits and seeking to improve themselves internally. Military Jihad is a lesser Jihad meant for acts of self-defense only when outside enemies attack the land.

Western scholars also stress that the misconception of Jihad led to assumptions that Jihad is synonymous with war, particularly in the wake of 9/11.[35] "If an aggressor attacks the land, Jihad can be authorized only by a caliph. The important rule is that a person can participate in Jihad only with the permission of their parents," said Kadyr Malikov. He reminds us that self-defense is a legal norm entrenched in the constitutions of all countries, and the same is considered in military Jihad. However, there are strict rules that should be followed concurrently. Jihad prohibits unnecessary harm and violence: women, children, and innocent people should not be killed; enemies must be treated with justice; wounded enemy soldiers must be treated; the property must not be damaged; poisoning is forbidden; war must cease as soon as the enemy offers peace, etc. "All these rules must be followed. Thus there was no Jihad in Syria due to the absence of any grounds for self-defense and the widespread violence carried out, including the killing of innocent women and children, the beheading of hostages, and the destruction of properties and heritages. They committed war crimes during the civil war that involved religious terrorist groups," said Kadyr Malikov.[36]

In 2014, 126 Islamic scholars worldwide published an open letter which can be considered a fatwa condemning ISIS and other terrorist groups for misinterpreting Sharia laws. The Islamic scholars described how ISIS had misinterpreted and distorted Islam "into a religion of harshness, brutality, torture and murder" that constituted a "great wrong and an offense to Islam, Muslims, and the entire world." They explained that the word 'jihad' is "an Islamic term that cannot be applied to armed conflict against any other Muslim; this much is a firmly established principle." Furthermore, all the scholars agreed that Jihad is conditional upon the consent of one's parents. The justification for this is a well-known hadith about a man who approached the Prophet asking him to permit him to perform Jihad, upon which the Prophet asked "Are your parents alive?" to which he replied: "Yes." And the Prophet told him: "Then perform jihad (struggle) through [serving] them."[37] This Hadith demonstrates that even when it is necessary to protect a homeland from an aggressor, the main condition is to receive permission from one's parents, particularly if they are old and need care.

The next Islamic concept that ISIS exploited was Hijrah. Seven women and two men whom I interviewed informed me that it was essential to undertake Hijrah for them. "Our Prophet Muhammad also had to flee when he was persecuted. So, by relocating, he saved his faith and allowed Islam to prosper. I did not feel comfortable in my country, I could not wear the Niqab in Moscow, so the only solution for me was to relocate and undertake Hijrah," said a twenty-two-year-old woman in Al-Hawl camp. She was living in Moscow with her migrant parents and was originally from one of the Central Asian countries. What is striking is that women and men perceived Hijrah as a duty of every Muslim to relocate to join a Muslim community in order to be able to safeguard their faith. The assumption of Hijrah as a duty for Muslims is inaccurate. According to Kadyr Malikov, a prominent theologian and religious leader in Kyrgyzstan, the Prophet Muhammad did relocate to Medina during the seventh century to escape persecution and live in peace with his community. However, Islam does not recognize any other Hijrah except for that of the Prophet. "In the history of Islam, there is only one Hijrah which is made by the Prophet Muhammad. There is the Hadith of Buhari and Muslims, two legitimate sources for Islam. The Hadith says that there is no Hijrah after the Prophet's, that it is forbidden to repeat the Hijrah of the Prophet, and any attempts to do so will be seen as illegitimate in the eyes of Islam. Islam does not demand its followers to relocate, and any such migration cannot be called Hijrah," said Kadyr Malikov.[38] He stressed how such misinterpretation of Hijrah had led to the recruitment and mobilization of thousands of ISIS fighters and condemned the terrorist group's approach that played on people's religious beliefs.

Erkebulan Karakulov, a theologian and imam from Kazakhstan, worked with repatriated foreign fighters in Kazakhstan as a part of the deradicalization process in Kazakhstan. He graduated from Al-Azhar University in Egypt and worked as a religious scholar at Kazakh National University. He is also the imam at the mosque of Al-Bilal in Chymkent, Kazakhstan. Erkebulan agrees that terrorist groups misused concepts of Islam to attract foreign fighters. "The terrorist groups aimed to attract as many people as possible, so they used misinterpretations of some concepts to convince them to travel to Syria. In Islam, Hijrah should only be announced by the Prophet or highly important religious leaders who have such authority. Nobody can decide on their own to implement Hijrah. None of the foreign fighters had such authority or sufficient education to decide to make Hijrah," said Erkebulan. He stressed that how ISIS misinterpreted concepts of Islam revealed the true evil and insidious nature of the terrorist groups. "ISIS wanted blood and violence, so they needed fighters to fight and achieved its goal through playing on the religious sentiments of people," said Erkebulan.[39]

ISIS's next lure to attract foreign fighters was Paradise or Jannah. ISIS repeatedly presented suicide bombing and being killed as akin to becoming a martyr and an honorable duty for Muslims in its propaganda materials. ISIS indoctrinated children to become suicide bombers and cynically instructed them, saying, "Push the button, and you will immediately go to Paradise." Some were even offered sedatives to calm them ahead of their missions.[40] Not only adult men and children, but also women were forced to wear suicide jackets and were sent to detonate them at the front line. The lure of Jannat, meaning paradise or heaven, was "the deadliest weapon of the terrorist groups."[41] ISIS convinced fighters that dying as a martyr in battle or a suicide bombing would result in an immediate ascent to heaven and the beginning of life in paradise. ISIS built its propaganda on the false idea that death in Jihad is not the end of life, but a start to eternal life in paradise, a real place devoid of problems and full of joy. "Convincing fighters that Paradise is real, that it is a certainty because they die as martyrs to jihad, is what made Islamic State's military forces so fearsome; its suicide bombers so ecstatic."[42] ISIS fighters deeply believed that if they died in Syria, they would head directly to paradise. One of the repatriated foreign fighters in Kazakhstan said in a video interview with local journalists that his main goal was to reach paradise. "If a Muslim person dies for the sake of Allah, their death will be honored, and they will end up in paradise. It is a dream of every Muslim in the world, and of course, I also dreamt of this," he said.[43] He is currently serving his prison sentence in Kazakhstan. Another woman I interviewed via Telegram informed me that many people who joined ISIS believe in Jannah. "We all had and still have this general understanding that Jannah exists. People who have sin, the door of Jannah is closed for them. If you ask why you came to Syria, many will answer that they wanted to get reward of Allah and reach Jannah. Even my husband had this eventual goal to be in Paradise. When we traveled to Syria, he told me that if we both die in that war, we will be reunited in paradise and will be also united with our parents and grandparents there. Now he is in the custody of Kurds, I am here in the camp. And I don't know what to think. But I know that Allah will not let us down" she said. She is currently detained in the Al-Hawl camp with her two children and hopes that her country, Kyrgyzstan, will repatriate them.

ISIS misled people in telling them that dying in Syria was honorable and would earn them the mercy of Allah. In one issue of Dabiq, ISIS described how, when they were burying their martyrs, there was a very strong smell of musk, the most beloved and purest perfume of the Prophet, suggesting that the Prophet Muhammad was with them at that moment. "By giving this (false) example, Dabiq ideologues sought to sanctify the martyrs through the (idea of the) presence of the Prophet."[44] In Islam, the concept of martyrdom does exist, known in Arabic as shahada or shahid. The literal meaning is witness, which refers to Judgement Day upon which a person should testify how he fought and died while defending his land, his parents, his children, or even his property from aggressors. Shahada in Islam should not be associated with committing suicide. The concept is connected to Jihad of the Sword, which is the act of self-defense against an aggressor. Islamic scholars highlight that Islam condemns and rejects the act of suicide. Theologian Kadyr Malikov said that two ayahs in the Quran strongly prohibit it. "When a person wears explosives and commits suicide, it is self-murder, which is prohibited in Islam. Ayahs of the Quran say, 'Do not throw yourself by own hands to death.' Suicide terrorist attacks are, in the first place, self-murder. The Quran states that if you kill yourself, upon the Judgement Day, you will be murdered by the same method through which you committed suicide," said Kadyr Malikov.[45]

Distorted religious concepts played a powerful role as a soft power and gave people the sense of direct relationship with God and as if God guaranteed rewards for them. It could not be impossible to attract thousands of people without rationalization and justification of their violence through religious dogmas. Thus, scholars and policy-makers must take into consideration the religious pillar of the radicalization process, and they should be studied carefully. The majority of those who travelled to the Middle East had no previous knowledge of Islam. They were directly familiarized with the Salafi-Wahabi concepts and believed that it is true Islam. In Kazakhstan, those who joined ISIS had no previous knowledge on Islam. They started learning the Salafi ideology through preaches on YouTube and Internet just before traveling to

Syria. They truly believed that people only need to live by radical ideology. Alina, a Kazakh woman, denied her radicalization, but insisted that she traveled because she wanted to work in Turkey. But she constantly was repeating tawhid and takfir notions. "I am continuing wearing hijab and to live with Sharia law. Because Allah created us and we need follow God's law. I want my children to live only by Allah's instructions," she told me. Another man, who returned to Kyrgyzstan, told me that he wanted to fight against infidels. "Those who hurt Muslims, should be defeated. I wanted to help Muslims and get Merci of Allah. I was told that kaffirs are killing Muslims and I decided to do jihad to save them," he told me. The common words that returnees were repeating are: jihad, kaffir, Merci of Allah, Jannah, infidels and ummah. They use them frequently and refer them. They embraced all mutated concept of the radical ideology, and see and judge the world only through them. Most of the time, they are skeptic about the modern nation-state system. My empirical evidence has shown that the religious ideology is a soft power that is powerful and has tremendous impact on people's minds.

People who joined ISIS, both women and men, tend to deny their radicalization. They consider themselves as religious but not indoctrinated by radical ideologies. At the same time, they deeply immersed in the abovementioned distorted concepts. Their minds are poisoned and judge everyone around them through these radical ideas. They directly deny that they were radicalized and put victimization narratives forward. They don't have a clear understanding or distinction between true Islam and the Salafi-Wahabi ideology. The Azerbaijani woman, whom I interviewed, explains the reason why she joined ISIS, as her intention was to be together with Umma. "I came here for Umma to be with it. But now I am very sad that Ummah is not saving us. Shame on you, all men of Umma. Fifty thousand women of Umma are suffering here in the desert, but Umma has no reaction," she said. Women in Al-Hawl operate several Telegram channels. Several times, they published video statements where several women in black niqabs called Muslim men to save them and free them from custody. They frequently use terms common to the radical jihadist groups such as kaffir, infidel, umma and caliphate. They blame other Muslims for their unwillingness to help them. "Even Kaffirs are helping us by bringing humanitarian aid to the camps. Kaffirs are building hospitals in Al-Hawl and Roj and trying to improve conditions here in the camps. But where Muslims? Where Umma?" wrote a woman in the Telegram channel. The next day there was a post in the same Telegram channel: "We need medical assistance as many women and children are sick. Perhaps you think that we are guilty. But don`t forget that we are part of Ummah, so you cannot ignore us. These children are children of Umma. These sisters are essential part of Ummah. If you ignore us, Allah will replace you with true Muslims." I had observed several Telegram channels in Russian for several months, and in their posts women asked for help from Ummah, but not from their home countries.

AWKWARD IDENTITIES AND SEARCH FOR BELONGING AND MEANING

While Umma, which means spiritual unity and fraternity, is one of the central concepts in Islam, Jihadist groups made it almost synonymous with a caliphate. Through the concept of tawhid, jihadi groups urge Muslims worldwide to unite under one community—Umma—and live in a caliphate. They want to give them a feeling of family unification by saying that they are all children or grandchildren of the umma and conveying "the sense of despair at disunity, they are 'orphans of umma.'"[46] This kind of appeal works efficiently as many people see the umma through the prism of belonging and identity.

Many Muslims who joined ISIS and other jihadist groups had a burning sense of injustice and the feeling of dignity lost. The sense of loss of dignity leads to seeking recognition. As Fukuyama stated, recognizing one's basic dignity has been at the core of democratic movements since the French revolution. When governments fail to guarantee the equal dignity of their citizens, the inner sense of dignity seeks recognition. As Fukuyama observes, "economic distress is often perceived by individuals not as a resource of deprivation, but as a loss of dignity." Loss of dignity and economic position will be translated into a loss of identity and status. People who live in poverty and injustice claim to have lost their dignity and identity. They lose the connection to that country and do not consider themselves part of it even though it is their home country. As Fukuyama said, "national identity begins with a shared belief in the legitimacy of the country's political system, whether that system is democratic or not."[47] Those are the important tenets of the radicalization process directly connected with restoring dignity and seeking a new identity.

Muslims in Western countries feel marginalized, discriminated and lonely. Their feeling of discrimination and social exclusion inevitably leads to a further reactive search for a new identity antagonistic to the host society. As scholars observed, young Muslims in Europe are becoming angrier, more radical, and more active. "Excluded by racist societies, denied equal opportunity, and denigrated by their own Westernized elites, they have developed an exclusivist mindset," stated Benjamin and Simon.[48] Most of them failed to integrate and live with an awkward identity. Newman calls this "hybrid identities." Indeed, global migration has created hybrid identities, especially among the second-and third-generation descendants of immigrants. Young European Muslims who joined Jihadist groups are "computer addicts in search of their parents' roots, looking for heroism and thrill, sick of the permanence of social prejudice and old colonial clichés against the Muslims."[49] They feel left in-between: not fully integrated into European society, but at the same time detached from their original culture. Cherif Kouachi, one of the attackers on Charles Hebdo in Paris, was described by his lawyer as "a confused chameleon" who smoked marijuana, listened to rap music, and described himself as an "occasional Muslim."[50]

Young Muslims in Europe are in a deep identity crisis and seek an answer to the question "Who am I?" It is about a feeling of uprootedness and a lack of feeling of belonging, which some scholars call a "cultural schizophrenia." Double alienation from both a host society and their original society makes them angry- mostly because European societies are not helping them integrate, but instead look at them as potential terrorists. Some scholars call them the "lost generation" or "generation in transition." "They identify neither with the hosting society nor with their families' country of origin."[51] Usually the older generations, their parents, had always been too busy to integrate into the new society and expected their children to naturally become full members of the society. However, most of the time, their children do not naturally become Europeans. They are caught between the host society's culture and their parents' culture. Young immigrants stay close to each other and start seeking their roots and religion as a source of support and identity.

Some scholars argue that the real reason people are drawn to join terrorist groups is not religious or economic, but their "innate need for camaraderie, identity, and a sense of belonging—the pursuit of social satisfaction, not the expression of political or economic frustration, much less the fulfillment of a religious imperative."[52] I interviewed dozens of foreign fighters who, even after returning to their home countries, continue to refer to one another as "sister" and "brother." They receive satisfaction from treating each other as a sister or brother and being a member of that community. After meeting two Kazakh female returnees in February 2020, who were repatriated from Syria and brought to speak at an OSCE conference on foreign fighters in Vienna, I was struck by their manner of speaking to one another. Two returnee women from Kazakhstan and Uzbekistan continue to call each other "sister," suggesting a sense of comfort in being bound to one another through their shared identity and shared experiences of difficult days in Syria. I noticed that all female returnees in Kazakhstan, who spent years together in Syria and Iraq, are still very attached to each other and call each other "sister."

Many people who wanted to go to Syria and live in a caliphate were driven by a sense of belonging. They wanted to see themselves as an integral part of the community and to be identified as members of that community. ISIS targeted young men and women mostly between the ages of seventeen and thirty-two. "Youth populations are the most vulnerable to succumbing to violent ideologies since adolescence is an extremely formative period for identity."[53] Scholars who analyzed profiles of seventy-one individuals associated with ISIS concluded, "A search for belonging, meaning, or identity appears to be a crucial motivator for many Americans (and other Westerners) who embrace ISIS's ideology."[54] Some American fighters acknowledged that they had everything in the US, including fancy amusement parks, entertainment, restaurants, good food, and pricey cars. However, they claimed to be unhappy.

A crisis of identity among young people is not only widespread in Western countries, but also in other developing countries. A study conducted by researchers in Kazakhstan concluded that many men and women had an identity crisis before going to Syria. Erlan Karin, State Secretary of Kazakhstan and Conflicts Analyst, headed a research group that analyzed the profiles of 200 individuals who joined terrorist groups or participated in terrorist acts in Kazakhstan. Researchers concluded that many young people struggled with a crisis of identity. They link this identity crisis with the collapse of the Soviet Union and ongoing economic and political transitions in the country that began after Kazakhstan's independence and continues to this day. "These people could not adapt properly to ongoing economic and political changes. They felt lost, having no feeling of belonging to the country and our society. All of them had doubts about their future and who they were. While in uncertainty and looking for answers, they came across people who spread radical ideologies. So our citizens had an ideological purpose of joining a caliphate and establishing a state naively believing that they would be living in a new state with its norms. Therefore, many Central Asians, including Kazakh citizens, upon their arrival in Syria, burned their national passports demonstrating in front of a video camera," said Karin.[55]

People abandoned their country as they wanted to belong to the Caliphate, where they sought to find belonging and identity. They lost their connection to their home countries, but religion became a source of identity. As Newman observes, religion offers a sense of direction and guidance for those who believe they have lost control over their destiny. The idea of the Caliphate gave them hope, clarity, purpose, and identity. For most young men who joined jihadist groups, the duty of Jihad lifted them from their previous insignificant and boring life to a meaningful life full of purpose and thrill. They were losers, but eventually, they became heroes defending Muslim lands and participating in state-building. As Akil Awan observed, "jihadism serves as an emphatic rejection of the banality and monotonous inanity of daily life, providing, perhaps for the first time, a sense of being part of an elite group that compensates for the shortcomings of one's trivial existence."[56] There was a thrill and a feeling of heroism among male fighters. First, they acquired meaning, and they found belonging by joining a community. They finally escaped what Khosrokhavar calls—"the feeling of malaise from being in-between"—where they have a very fragile sense of being European and their Muslim roots that were constantly being emphasized in the host country. They eventually sought identity and belonging in the religious ideology and believed that the Caliphate would give them camaraderie, support, and a meaningful life. Second, especially male fighters were driven by a sense of heroism. They felt that they became the superior ones who could change the world and run the show. Marthe Crenshaw is right when she says that certain people enjoy stress. "Being in danger and at the center of events is thrilling. Moreover, the publicity that terrorism generates is gratifying. Attention is a reward, especially for people who have felt ignored and neglected by society."[57] Indeed, young, unemployed, and neglected men started enjoying thrill and stress. They felt that they restored their dignity and identity. Most male fighters were not driven by financial and economic purposes, but they were more political and ideological purposes driven. Jihadism is not only about economic and social grievances but also about the feeling of people and their dignity. When states fail to recognize their citizens' dignities and human rights, radical ideologies may propose alternatives.

FINAL STAGE: BROTHERHOOD NETWORKING AND CHANNELS OF RECRUITMENT

The last stage of the radicalization process is exposure to recruitment through networking and family ties. Networking happens mainly through the Internet or personal and family ties. The prevalence of preexisting ties indicates that the radicalization process has a significant component of personal ties through family members, friends, lovers, or co-villagers. The main recruitment channel is a familial connection through relatives who were already in Syria or Iraq, through marriage, or other links of family members. I call this brotherhood networking. In general, jihadists call each other brother and sister, not only because of solidarity and sense of a shared identity, but also because they literally have siblings or whole families involved in the group. Take Tsarnaev brothers (2013 Boston Marathon) or Koachi brothers (Charli Hebdo attack), or those who travelled to Syria with their family members. There are many examples where family members recruit, plan terrorist attacks, or travel together to the Middle East. Sixty percent of my respondents travelled to Syria with their family members. For women, their husbands or male siblings were the main recruiters. Some families lost five or six people at once, as all of them left for Syria to join ISIS. In Kyrgyzstan, twenty-nine people from one family left for Syria. The main person who influenced others was the 81 years old grandmother. She managed to convince her two daughters with their husbands, their children, and her son with his wife and children. So, twenty-nine people travelled from the Tong district of Kyrgyzstan to the Middle East, and nobody knows where they are now and if they are alive or not. In many countries, local mosques served as recruitment platforms. Local mullahs spread the narratives about the humiliation of Muslims and how infidels are killing innocent Muslim children and women. Mosques became a place where recruiters targeted vulnerable young men. The next channel is ISIS's recruitment agents, who worked through the internet. They used different methods to lure people. They targeted mainly young men and women by either calling them to live in a caliphate or deceiving them with a well-paid job in Turkey. It is important to highlight that a group of people were indeed proposed to work in Turkey and had no idea about Syria and Iraq. Especially majority of women and girls were captured by the promise of marriage or well-paid jobs in Turkey.

CONCLUSIONS

The radicalization process of people, who joined jihadist groups, is very complex and gradual. I proposed the model that consists of six puzzling cycles, which I call "non-enigma cycles of radicalization." The model might have its limitations as it does not distinguish how far people were radicalized. The level of radicalization varies, and I identified several groups of people. In a different cycle of the non-enigma cycles, people can drop out or have different motivations. One of the important factors is their vulnerabilities on which the level of radicalization may depend. The main crucial vulnerabilities were the lack of education and the lack of critical thinking. If we imagine a pyramid to give a sense of visualization of their radicalization process, there are several groups. At the bottom of the pyramid is the first group: hardliners or very radicals. They believed in the idea of a caliphate. They fully rejected the secular state system, had a full white and black mindset, and never planned to return to their home countries. They fully embraced the idea of tawhid and takfir, thus saw the world as divided into Muslims and infidels. The second group is identity seekers. This group not necessarily was not frustrated by economic problems had an identity crisis or simply the crisis and emptiness in their soul after a loss, ongoing conflicts in their lives. Loss can be related to love, family conflict, divorce, or after experiencing discrimination or humiliation. So, they wanted to find belonging, meaning and support. Being associated with the Muslim community was expected to provide camaraderie, identity, and association. The next group is economic benefit seekers. These people only wanted to live in a prosperous society where all their economic and social problems would be resolved. They naively believed that the

Caliphate could provide them with economic opportunities. The next group is followers. I would mostly add women, who followed their husbands or other family members to this group. They had no idea about a caliphate and had no choice but to follow other members. The last group is free riders or thrill-seekers. These are mainly young men who could not alienate their friends or villagers; thus, they agreed to join them. They wanted to see adventures and have some heroic experiences. There is one group, which consists mainly of women. They were deceived through the internet and intended to marry someone or find a job in Turkey. They were told or invited to Turkey, but once arrived in Turkey, they were sent to Syria.

Dividing the people into groups by their levels of radicalization is important for understanding how they differ and how each story can have its peculiarities. However, the radicalization process itself and its motivations should be brought under the spotlight since deeper and more profound problems of the contemporary world are hidden behind such people's decisions. Thus, governments should address individual and group grievances as they serve as fertile ground. However, grievances cannot produce radicalization without other factors and vulnerabilities. We cannot ignore people's vulnerabilities, and one salient feature is the lack of education and critical thinking. Especially, young men and women became vulnerable due to the lack of critical thinking. In the next chapters, I discuss how women in Central Asia were weak as they married very early and did not have a chance to study and get a diploma.

My empirical evidence proved that the feeling of injustice was the central essential element, even though it may vary how they presume justice. Grievances and resentment of people create a fertile ground that produces the cognitive opening condition where a person starts questioning their own life asking themselves why it is happening. This condition is significant as it opens a door for looking around and sinking into an in-search position. Individual and group grievances of people are significant and cannot be ignored. We have to talk about failures of governments: corruption, poverty, and repression in developing countries and discrimination, and also about Islamophobia, and marginalization in European countries. As Newmann stated, when secular governance had failed, "religion was the one culturally authentic alternative." This kind of thesis was also developed by Mark Juergensmeyer. He called it a new Cold War which is explained as a confrontation between secular states and religious nationalists.[58] The cycle of bad governance and corruption is the main source of grievances where people are disappointed by the secular political system. I have interviewed both voluntary returnees and repatriated returnees in Central Asia. All five Central Asian states have a high rate of corruption and nepotism. Uzbekistan, Kazakhstan, Turkmenistan, and Tajikistan have lived under authoritarian regimes for more than two decades. Those who left from Central Asia to Syria believed in the narrative that state-building based on Islamic Sharia could prevent corruption and could allow building a just society. They called secular states "evil," where corruption flourishes and serves only a small circle of elites. They all lost hope that it was possible to get a prosperous life in their secular states.

The burning sense of injustice was at the core of all profiles that I interviewed or when reading their stories. People rightly perceive that they are living with injustice when their human rights are violated. Thus, it can be argued that human rights violations are the leading root cause of terrorism. I want to cite again Antonio Guterres, the UN Secretary-General, who stressed, "terrorism is fundamentally the denial and destruction of human rights. To defeat terrorism, states should build a just society where the human rights of every citizen are not denied. When we protect human rights, we are tackling the root causes of terrorism. For the power of human rights to bond is stronger than the power of terrorism to divide."[59] The main problem is that state-sanctioned human rights violations and state-sanctioned repression and corruption are widespread. People see how governments themselves are directly being involved or sanctioning them.

Finally, the essential mechanism of the radicalization process is the radical ideology that serves a soft power. The religious pillar of radicalization is powerful by its two features. First, it is a soft power that rationalizes, sanctions and resonates with appeals of terrorist groups. Second, its powerful contribution is that it gives each jihadist personalized benefits and rewards. People believe that God sees their efforts in Jihad and rewards them. As Juergensmeyer notes, religion personalizes the conflict. "It provides personal rewards-religious merit, redemption, the promise of heavenly luxuries."[60] Jihadists attract people by promising personal rewards that come directly from God as if there were a direct deal between God and a person. The Salafi -Jihadist ideology is a soft power of jihadists which is mighty as it sanctions and justifies everything. It changes how people think and how they see the world. It is hard to contest something when it is about mindset. The radical ideology is changing minds of people and it is impossible to defeat by arms. It is about education, culture, building counternarratives and talking to people. Muslim states and communities should build new policies to raise awareness about Islam as a peaceful religion in order to win discourses of jihadists.

NOTES

1. Simon W. Murden, *Islam, The Middle East, and the New Global Hegemony*, (London, Lynne Rienner Publishers, 2002), 9.

2. Peter R. Neumann, *Old and New Terrorism: Late Modernity, Globalization and the Transformation of Political Violence*, (Polity Press, 2009), 93.

3.Murden, Islam, *The Middle East, and the New Global Hegemony*, 9.

4. Bernard Lewis, *The Crisis of Islam, Holy War and Unholy Terror*, (Modern Library Edition, 2003), 119.

5. Moniquet, C. (2008). The Threat . . . Will Remain at a Very High Level for the Foreseeable Future. In: Perry, M., Negrin, H.E. (eds) *The Theory and Practice of Islamic Terrorism*. Palgrave Macmillan, New York. https://doi.org/10.1057/9780230616509_20

6. Neumann, *Old and New Terrorism*, 93.

7. Daniel Benjamin, "Europe Has Become a Central "Field of Jihad," in *The Theory and Practice of Islamic Terrorism, an Anthology*, (Palgrave Macmillan, 2008), 168.

8.UN , "World Migration Report 2020, International Organization for Migration," 2019, https://www.un.org/sites/un2.un.org/files/wmr_2020.pdf.

9. Rik Coolsaet, "Facing the Fourth Foreign Fighters Wave: What Drives Europeans to Syria, and to Islamic State? Insights from the Belgian Case," Egmont Institute, 01 March 2016.

10. Benjamin, "Europe Has Become a Central Field of Jihad," 168.

11. Randy Borum, "Understanding the Terrorist Mindset," *FBI Law Enforcement Bulletin* 72, no.7 (2003): 7–10.

12. Kruglanski, Arie W., Michele J. Gelfand, Jocelyn J. Belanger, Malkanthi Hetiarachchi and Rohan Gunaratna. 2015. "Significance Quest Theory as the Driver of Radicalization towards Terrorism." In *Resilience and Resolve: Communities Against Terrorism*, eds. Jolene Jerard and Salim Mohamed Nasir. London: Imperial College Press, 17–30.

13. Maher, Shiraz. *Salafi-Jihadism: The History of an Idea*. Penguin Books Ltd, 2016, 14.

14. Ahmed Ajil, Politico-ideological Violence: Zooming in on Grievances, European Journal of Criminology, 00(0) 2020, 1–18.

15. Ahmed Ajil, Politico-ideological Violence: Zooming in on Grievances, ibid.

16.Viktor Michaylov, interview by the author on March 15, 2020.

17. "Terrorism 'spreading and Destabilizing' Entire Regions, Guterres Warns States, at Key Kenya Conference." Ventures Africa. Abuja: SyndiGate Media Inc, 2019.

18. Nader Hashemi, "The ISIS Crisis and the Broken Politics of the Middle East," *Institute on Culture, Religion, and World Affairs,* University of Denver, (November 2016), http://www.bu.edu/cura/files/2016/12/hashemi-paper1.pdf.

19. Lola Shakimova, interview by the author on 05 April 2020.

20. Daniel Benjamin, Steven Simon, *The Age of Sacred Terror*, (Random House Trade Paperback, 2003), 172.

21. Benjamin & Simon, *The Age of Sacred Terror*, 172.

22. James A Piazza, "Poverty, Minority Economic Discrimination, and Domestic Terrorism," *Journal of Peace Research* 48, no. 3 (2011): 349–350.

23. Frances Stewart, "Crisis Prevention: Tackling Horizontal Inequalities," *Oxford Development Studies* 28, no.3 (2000): 247.

24. Stewart, "Crisis Prevention: Tackling Horizontal Inequalities," 247.

25. Francis Fukuyama, *Identity, The demand for Dignity and The Politics of Resentment*, (New York, Farrar, Straus and Giroux, 2018), 164.

26. Clark McCauley, Sophia Moskalenko, *Friction, How Radicalization Happens to Them and Us*, (Oxford University Press, 2011), 220.

27. Akil N.Awan, *The Impact of Evolving Jihadist Narratives on Radicalization in the West*, quoted in Simon Staffel, Akil N. Awan, *Jihadism Transformed, Al Qaeda and Islamic State's Global Battle of Ideas*, (London, Hurst &Company, 2016), 189.

28. Michael R. Kelvington, Global Salafi-Jihadist Ideology: The Soft Power of the Enemy, International Institute for Counter-Terrorism, March 2019.

29. Mark Juergensmeyer, *Does Religion Cause Terrorism? in The Cambridge Companion to Religion and Terrorism*, (Cambridge University Press, 2017), 20.

30. Mary R. Habeck, *Knowing the Enemy, Jihadist Ideology and the War on Terror, in in The Theory and Practice of Islamic Terrorism, an Anthology*, (Palgrave Macmillan, 2008), 66–68.

31. Nelly Lahoud, *The Jihadis's Path to Self-Destruction*, (London, Hurst & Company Publishers, 2010), 8.

32. Mohamed Bin Ali, "Forging Muslim and Non-Muslim Relationship: Contesting the Doctrine of Al-Wala' wal Bara'," Nanyang Technological University, *RSIS Commentary*, (2015).

33. The interview with Kadyr Malikov was conducted by the author, ibid.

34. Mohammad Hashim Kamali, *Shari'ah Law: An Introduction*. (Oneworld Publications, 2008), 204. ISBN 978–1851685653.

35. Amanda Kretsch, "Misconception of Jihad in America," (2016). *Undergraduate Library Research Awards*. 3. http://digitalcommons.lmu.edu/ulra/awards/2016/3.

36. Interview with Kadyr Malikov, ibid.

37. "Open Letter from 126 Prominent Islamic Scholars to Al-Baghdadi and to the Fighters and Followers of the Self-Declared 'Islamic State,'" (2014), http://www.lettertobaghdadi.com/14/english-v14.pdf.

38. Kadyr Malikov, interview by the author on 10 March 2020.

39. Erkebulan Karagulov, interview by the author on 03 April 2020.

40. Anne Speckhard, "Inside the ISIS Machine Turning Children to 'Monsters'," *International Center for the Study of Violent Extremism*, August 25, 2017, https://www.icsve.org/inside-the-isis-machine-turning-children-to-monsters/.

41. Ronald Tiersky, "ISIS's Deadliest Weapon is the Idea of 'Heaven,'" *Huffington Post,* September 19, 2016, https://www.huffpost.com/entry/isiss-deadliest-weapon-is_b_12087084.

42. Ronald Tiersky, Ibid.

43. Official video produced by Committee of National Security of Kazakhstan.

44. Erkan Toguslu, "Caliphate, Hijrah and Martyrdom as Performative Narrative in ISIS Dabiq Magazine," *Politics, Religion & Ideology* 20, no. 1 (2018): 94–120, doi: 10.1080/21567689.2018.1554480.

45. Interview with Kadyr Malikov was conducted by the author, ibid.

46. James Piscatori, Amin Saikal, *Islam Beyond Borders, The Umma in World Politics*, (Cambridge University Press, 2019), 7.

47. Francis Fukuyama. *Identity: The Demand for Dignity and the Politics of Resentment*, ibid.

48. Benjamin & Simon, *The Age of Sacred Terror*, 175.

49. Khosrokhavar, Farhad. Inside Jihadism: Understanding Jihadi Movements Worldwide. Paradigm Publishers, 2009.

50. Andrew Higgins and Maïa de la Baume, Two Brothers Suspected in Killings Were Known to French Intelligence Services, *New York Times*, 08 January 2015.

51. Antunez, Juan & Moreno, "Daesh European Foreign Fighters: Ideology, Motivation and Profiling" (2016) GESI.

52. Charles Mink, "It's About the Group, Not God: Social Causes and Cures for Terrorism," *Journal for Deradicalization* 16, no. 5, ISSN: 2363–9849.

53. Moreno, "Refugees and Terrorism," Ibid.

54. Lorenzo Vidino, Seamus Hughes, "ISIS in America, From Retweets to Raqqa," *The George Washington University, Program on Extremism*, (2015), https://extremism.gwu.edu/sites/g/files/zaxdzs2191/f/downloads/ISIS%20in%20America%20-%20Full%20Report.pdf.

55. Erlan Karin, interview by the author on 20 April 2020.

56. Akil N.Awan, "Jihadism Transformed," 183–199.

57. Marthe Crenshaw, *How Terrorists Think: What Psychology Can Contribute to Understanding Terrorism, in Terrorism: Roots, Impact, Responses*, (Praeger Publishers, 1992), 71–93.

58. Mark Juergensmeyer, *The New Cold War?: Religious Nationalism Confronts the Secular State*. (Berkeley: Univ. of California Press), 1994.

59. Antonio Guterres, "Uniting the World Against Terrorism," June 26, 2018, https://www.un.org/sg/en/content/sg/articles/2018-06-26/uniting-world-against-terrorism.

60. Mark Juergensmeyer, *Does Religion Cause Terrorism? in The Cambridge Companion to Religion and Terrorism*, (Cambridge University Press, 2017), 20.

Chapter 3

Fall of ISIS

Dilemma of Justice and Consequences of a Family Jihad

Since 2012, around 40,000 people travelled to Syria and Iraq and joined jihadist groups, mainly ISIS. They represent more than sixty countries across the globe, about 5,000 of which came from European countries. This is the most extensive scale of jihadist mobilization in modern history. The Afghan-Soviet war mobilized about 10,000 fighters, but only male fighters from Arab countries. The main feature of this current jihadi mobilization is that ISIS also managed to bring women and children to live in a caliphate. Thus, the new phenomenon of a family jihad is having many implications for international peace and their national countries.

After the fall of ISIS, the world has faced the family jihad and its consequences. Since ISIS had a global appeal that aimed to challenge the existing political order, it needed to create an image of a real Islamic state. Women and children were necessary for its state-building project. First, it was a political appeal to the rest of the world that meant that the Islamic State was real and it started taking a real shape by having inhabitants, including women and children. Second, the fact that entire families were arriving and joining, was a demonstration of ISIS's power. However, women and children were not only a demonstration of that power, but were also important actors playing a significant role within the caliphate. ISIS managed to create a realistic picture of state-building by having women and children, building families, bringing more children into the world, and giving an impression of having a normal society. Women played diverse and large-scale supporting roles to maintain an Islamic State, recruiting other women with their children, and disseminating radical ideology. Children had been indoctrinated as a future generation of ISIS fighters and called "lion cubs" of the caliphate. Boys were trained from the age of nine and most of them possessed combatant skills.

They hold up their index fingers and shout "bāqiyya" [remaining] which is ISIS's slogan meaning "remaining and expanding." While fighters were encouraged to train their children to become the next generation of jihadists, women were required to indoctrinate their children from the age of five or six, even four. Many women stayed at home and their main task was to bring up children with the jihadist mindset that divides the world into infidels and true Muslims.

ISIS was defeated in March 2019, after the last black flag was lowered in its last stronghold, Baghouse. ISIS was defeated in a physical sense, as its territories were reclaimed and its fighters were captured. What happened with 40,000 people who had joined ISIS? Thousands of fighters were killed on the battlefield, while other six to seven thousand returned to their home countries. In total, more than twenty thousand male fighters were captured and sentenced in both Iraq and Northeast Syria. Iraq captured 9,000 fighters and charged them with terrorism offenses. Many of them were sentenced to death for atrocities committed by ISIS in Iraqi territories, and the majority has been held in the Nasiriyah Central Prison in southeast Iraq. There are hundreds of ISIS women from third countries in Iraqi prisons, who are held in cells alongside their children. Home countries are allowed to only repatriate children, whereas their mothers should remain in the prison and serve their sentences. However, Iraq tried children too. According to Human Rights Watch (HRW), at least 185 children of foreign nationals were convicted and sentenced to prison terms under antiterrorism laws by midyear 2019. Their prosecution varied by their age: children between the ages of nine were prosecuted for illegal entry, some of them for membership, and others for participating in violent acts.

Currently, about 10,000 male fighters, who surrendered or were captured, are held in prisons in northeast Syria, guarded by the Syrian Democratic Forces. The SDF, which is a Kurdish force supported by the US-led international coalition, played a crucial role in defeating ISIS. While male fighters should be brought to justice for their crimes and atrocities, the main dilemma emerged concerning their family members. An urgent solution is needed for 70,000 women and children who have been held in Al-Hawl and Roj camps in northeast Syria. The majority of them are Iraqis and Syrians, with about 12,000 women and children who represent third countries. The main dilemma is where these people should go. While children can be treated as victims, women's cases should be assessed individually, as some of them may have committed crimes. While the detention camps Al-Hawl and Roj have become prime breeding grounds for radicalization and indoctrination, the international community is failing to find appropriate policies to manage this crisis. Countries are main actors which need to assume that ISIS associates are ticking time bombs for international peace.

BRINGING TO JUSTICE FOR WAR CRIMES AND ATROCITIES

The question of bringing them to justice should be considered separately for male fighters and women. All male fighters who participated in hostilities and committed crimes should be given a chance for a fair trial. ISIS committed the crime of genocide, war crimes and crimes against humanity. Three high-level international bodies were specifically created to investigate and document crimes committed by ISIS, some of which also target other actors who committed crimes alongside ISIS in Syria and Iraq. The United Nations established three international bodies: the UNITAD investigative team, the Independent International Commission of Inquiry on Syria, and the International, Impartial and Independent Mechanism. UN reports and investigations by international NGOs such as HRW, Amnesty International and UN Office of the High Commissioner for Human Rights (OHCHR), and the Independent International Commission of Inquiry have documented evidence for crimes committed by ISIS fighters.[1] The mentioned international bodies have documented crimes committed by the terrorist group in Iraq and Syria.

Firstly, ISIS committed the crime of genocide against the Yazidis, thousands of whom were killed by ISIS fighters. Yazidis is a distinct religious community living in Iraq and Syria whom ISIS regarded as infidels, subsequently subjecting them to unimaginable horrors. The UN OHCHR issued a report about the genocide against Yazidis in 2016, relying on evidence and information collected by the Independent International Commission of Inquiry on Syria.[2] The report analyzed a range of international crimes, with a specific focus on determining whether ISIS committed the crime of genocide. ISIS killed, enslaved, and tortured the Yazidi people; raped their women, sold girls at a market, subjected women and girls to sexual slavery, and took boys away from their parents, forcing them into ISIS training camps. It is evident that ISIS committed genocide, as members of this minority were deliberately and systematically targeted and killed.[3] The investigation by the Commission of Inquiry provides many details based on testimonies of the Yazidi people. The report states the following:

> ISIS has sought to destroy the Yazidis through killings, sexual slavery, enslavement, torture and inhuman and degrading treatment and forcible transfer causing serious bodily and mental harm; the infliction of conditions of life that bring about a slow death; the imposition of measures to prevent Yazidi children from being born, including forced conversion of adults, the separation of Yazidi men and women, and mental trauma; and the transfer of Yazidi children from their own families and placing them with ISIS fighters, thereby cutting them off from beliefs and practices of their religious community, and erasing their identity

as Yazidis. The public statements and conduct of ISIS and its fighters clearly demonstrate that ISIS intended to destroy the Yazidis of Sinjar, composing the majority of the world's Yazidi population, in whole or in part.[4]

The testimonies of hundreds of Yazidi women provided to the Commission are heartbreaking. ISIS fighters exercised powers of ownership over Yazidi women and girls, buying and selling them at will. The report says that many of the Yazidi women and girls interviewed bore physical wounds and scars of the abuse they had suffered. "More apparent, however, was the mental trauma all are enduring. Most spoke of thoughts of suicide, of being unable to sleep due to nightmares about ISIS fighters at their door," said the report. The Commission gathered hundreds of heartbreaking testimonies of women and girls. A seventeen-year-old Yazidi girl told the Commission that she wished she was dead because of what she endured. She also said she could not sleep and that her body felt very heavy.[5]

The report's findings concluded that the actions taken by ISIS to destroy the Yazidi people fall under the Convention of Genocide by meeting all of its norms.[6] ISIS had an intent to destroy the Yazidis as an ethnic group and incremental steps were taken to reach their overall objective against the group.[7] Referring to the obligations of Member States under the Genocide Convention, the Commission and the UN Security Council urged the international community to refer the situation in Syria to the International Criminal Court or to establish an ad hoc tribunal with relevant geographic and temporal jurisdiction.

ISIS also committed crimes against humanity. According to HRW, an international human rights organization that has published several reports on the atrocities of ISIS in Iraq, the terrorist group systematically targeted Iraq's minority communities, not only Yazidis, but also Shia Shabaks, Shia Turkmen, and Christians. ISIS ordered representatives of other religions, such as Christians, to convert to Islam or pay a tax as non-Muslims (*jizya*). If they refused, they would be executed. Since 2011, ISIS has deployed its fighters, including children recruited as soldiers, to undertake hundreds of suicide and car bombing attacks, killing thousands of civilians.[8] According to the Eurojust report, ISIS perpetrated violence against civilians in Syria and Iraq following certain patterns based on the perceived affiliations of their victims to ethnic, religious, or political groups. These groups were subjected to systematic killings, abductions, pillaging and the destruction of their property.[9]

The Independent International Commission of Inquiry on the Syrian Arab Republic issued several reports concluding that ISIS and other affiliated terrorist groups committed crimes against humanity. The Commission explained what constitutes a crime against humanity by referring to the Rome Statute:[10]

> Crimes against humanity occur when certain acts are carried out as a part of a widespread or systematic attack directed against a civilian population and where the perpetrator has knowledge of the attack. For purposes of this report, the relevant crimes constituting crimes against humanity include murder; imprisonment or other severe deprivation of physical liberty in violation of fundamental rules of international law; torture; rape, sexual slavery, or any other form of sexual violence of comparable gravity; persecution; and other inhumane acts of a similar character intentionally causing great suffering, or serious injury to body or mental or physical health.[11]

The Commission issued several reports on crimes committed by ISIS against the civilian population in Syria, which were presented in sessions of the UN Human Rights Council in Geneva.

CRIMES AGAINST WOMEN AND GIRLS

The Commission on Syria published a special investigation on crimes committed by different parties, including ISIS and Hay'at Tahrir al-Sham (led by former Jabhat al-Nusra command), against women and girls. In the report titled "I Lost My Dignity: Sexual and Gender-based Violence in the Syrian Arab Republic," the Commission stated that these terrorist groups caused severe psychological and physical harm to women and girls. The Commission added that ISIS committed crimes that constitute the war crime of murder, and seriously contravened international human rights norms. Those norms include the right to life, liberty and security of a person, the right to freedom from torture and other forms of cruel, inhuman, or degrading treatment, and the right to the highest attainable standard of physical and mental health.[12]

ISIS stoned women and girls on charges of adultery and forced Sunni women and girls to marry ISIS fighters. "ISIL's rule placed women and girls under the control of male relatives, effectively restricting their freedom of movement and removing them from public life. Those found to violate ISIL's strict dress code, most commonly adult women but also girls as young as ten, were punished with lashings," said the report. The Commission stated that these acts constituted the war crime of torture, cruel or inhumane treatment, and offenses against the personal dignity of women. "Executions further constituted the war crime of murder and also amounted to serious breaches of international human rights norms, including denial of the right to life and the right to be free from discrimination," said the Commission.[13] According to the UN report, girls and boys suffered widespread violations, including public executions where children were both victims of executions and forced into the role of executor.[14] In September 2014, a sixteen-year-old girl was beheaded by ISIS fighters in Aleppo because she was accused of membership in the Kurdish People's Protection Unit (YPG).[15]

ISIS committed war crimes against women and girls. Women suffered the most under ISIS as they were killed, raped, and enslaved. The best outcome for these women would be to marry an ISIS fighter. They were forced to remarry once their husbands died; thus, a woman often married three or four times. They lost their dignity and health. Minority women have reportedly suffered the most. Women in minority groups, particularly Christians and Yazidis, have been brutalized under the ISIS banner of jihad al-nikah, roughly translated as "sex in the name of the struggle." ISIS sold young girls on the market and forced them to marry as young as ten to twelve years. Sexual slavery and rape were widespread. Each time the fighters took over new cities or territories, they captured women as slaves or concubines. The terrorist groups used women as human shields during the attacks and trained them to be suicide bombers. Bearing in mind all of the atrocities referred to above, ISIS fighters should be brought to justice for crimes that they committed against women and girls.

The United Nations Security Council has recognized that "rape and other forms of sexual violence can constitute a war crime, a crime against humanity, or a constitutive act with respect to genocide." In UNSC resolution 1820, adopted in 2008, the United Nations urged all states to exclude amnesty provisions for such crimes, to end impunity for perpetrators of sexual violence and to comply with their obligations for prosecuting persons responsible for such acts, ensuring that all victims of sexual violence, particularly women and girls, have equal protection under the law and equal access to justice. Women have been directly targeted by terrorist groups, as gender-based violence was a strategic objective and ideology of some terrorist groups, including ISIS. The UNSC resolution recognized that ISIS used sexual violence deliberately and urged the Member States to investigate, prosecute and punish alleged perpetrators of sexual and gender-based violence. There is a common agreement in the international community that ISIS fighters should be brought to justice for their crimes against women and girls.

Legal experts from the Geneva Academy of International Humanitarian Law and Human Rights conclude that ISIS fighters have been responsible for grave and widespread violations that may amount to war crimes or crimes against humanity. They cite crimes committed by ISIS, such as executions of civilians and other persons no longer participating in hostilities, hostage-taking, ill-treatment and torture of detainees, sexual and gender-based violence, as well as recruitment of children.[16] The Geneva-based experts stress that foreign fighters who fought with the Islamic State may have been involved in such acts and may face prosecution for their involvement, regardless of whether or not they held senior positions within the Islamic State. I argue that, whether they were high ranking or low-ranking fighters, all-male fighters were combatants and therefore should be held accountable.

INTERNATIONAL MECHANISMS ESTABLISHED TO BRING TO JUSTICE

In December 2016, the UN General Assembly adopted a resolution establishing an International, Impartial and Independent Mechanism to assist in the investigation and prosecution of persons responsible for the most serious crimes under International Law committed in the Syrian Arab Republic since March 2011 (commonly referred to as the Mechanism).[17] According to the resolution, the purpose of the Mechanism is "to collect, consolidate, preserve and analyze evidence of violations of international humanitarian law and human rights violations and abuses." In its second report to the General Assembly, the Mechanism informed that it has already collected around four terabytes of evidence consisting of almost 900,000 records, which can be filed and presented in courts or tribunals that have, or may in the future have, jurisdiction over these crimes.[18]

The next international body key to uncovering the crimes committed by ISIS and other terrorist groups in Syria is the United Nations Investigative Team to Promote Accountability for Crimes Committed by Da'eash/ISIS (UNITAD).[19] The important role was played by the government of Iraq, which called upon the international community to assist in ensuring that ISIS members are held accountable for their crimes in Iraq. The UN Security Council responded to this call by adopting Resolution 2379 (2017), in which it requested the UN Secretary-General to establish an investigative team. Pursuant to this resolution, on May 31, 2018, the Secretary-General established UNITAD. The latter's investigative team spent a year in Iraq gathering, storing, indexing and analyzing evidence.

In early 2020, the European Union and UNITAD signed a Contribution Agreement through which the EU committed to allocating 3.5 million Euros to support the digitization and archiving of evidentiary materials regarding crimes of ISIS fighters in Iraq and Syria. The project started in March 2020 and is scheduled to run for 18 months. It aims to collect and document a comprehensive inventory of evidence regarding the crimes of ISIS fighters. Karim Ahmad Khan, Head of UNITAD, thanked the EU for its generous support and underlined that the importance of the project as a contributor to the global efforts to promote peace. "The preservation and organization of evidentiary material about ISIL crimes will serve to deepen the evidential foundations available for ISIL prosecutions. By establishing a comprehensive documentary record of these acts, we also contribute to global efforts in promoting peace and security by ensuring that the ideologically bankrupt nature of ISIL is exposed," said Karim Khan.[20] UNITAD's investigative team is working closely with the Iraqi government continuing to collect, preserve and store evidence in relation to actions by ISIL that may amount to war crimes, crimes against humanity and genocide. UNITAD's Analysis Unit provides impartial, independent and reliable assessments of the evidence collected and the probative value of the evidence, with any information gaps identified. According to Karim Khan, about eighty investigators made up the team that travelled around Iraq to gather evidence and witness testimony. "It's a mountain to climb," Karim Khan told AFP, as the investigative team works to analyze up to 12,000 bodies from more than 200 mass graves, 600,000 videos of IS crimes and 15,000 pages from the group's bureaucracy. "Who could have thought in the 21st century we would see crucifixion or burning a human alive in a cage, slavery, sexual slavery, throwing people off buildings, beheadings," said Karim Khan.[21]

Substantial efforts have been made at the UN level to store, document and analyze the crimes of ISIS and other terrorist groups in Syria. Furthermore, a vast amount of work has been done by international NGOs and research institutes. However, the situation has been complicated in northeast Syria as the territory is under control of the Autonomous Administration of Northeast Syria (ANES) and the SDF, a non-state actor with no legal authority. Subsequently, the international community must decide how to prosecute ISIS fighters held in camps in northeast Syria, currently administered by the Kurdish forces. ISIS fighters who committed crimes, and their associates, against whom there is clear evidence, should be brought to justice. Allowing those individuals impunity will likely abet violence and abandoning the large numbers of people currently held in the camps by not addressing the issue is likely to produce new generations of terrorist networks.

The first response should concern the children and their mothers. The treatment of male foreign fighters is more straightforward: immediate arrest, conviction and sentencing with terrorism charges. Those who committed the gravest crimes should be handed down punishments that reflect the seriousness of their actions. However, the international community is struggling with the following legal questions: where should these suspected terrorists be tried and who specifically should hold court to bring them to justice? Bedran Ciya Kurd, a representative of the SDF, stated in his interview given to the author that their official position being that all foreign fighters should be tried in the Middle East and brought to justice for the murders of thousands of people in the region. At the time of this writing, women living in Al-Hawl and Roj camps expressed their concern that Kurdish forces will try them inside the camps and decide their destinies. Women are afraid of such scenarios and expressed their worries that the Kurdish forces will never guarantee fair trials for them. However, as a non-state actor, the SDF does not have the legal authority to organize court hearings.

CONSEQUENCES OF THE FAMILY JIHAD: WOMEN AND CHILDREN

The most pressing issue is the repatriation of small children, while older children and women should be next in the repatriation queue. In 2019, the United Nations developed a comprehensive set of key principles on the protection, repatriation, prosecution, rehabilitation and reintegration of women and children with links to terrorist groups. If a legal assessment finds evidence of crimes by the women, they should be prosecuted, rehabilitated and reintegrated accordingly. The priority for the international community is to save women and children who are living in deadly conditions in northeastern Syria. As such, states should identify, extract, and assess children and women, while giving priority to small children and avoiding separation from their parents.

The United Nations and its high-level experts have been making significant efforts to convince states to repatriate women and children, particularly through internal negotiations with European states. Indeed, EU states are in the best position to ensure the protection of human rights for children and their guardians in camps in northern Syria, as they are considered to be democratic states that protect human rights. Whilst EU countries remain slow to act, small children continue to face death, starvation, and extreme physical and emotional harm, as do their mothers. Many countries refer to the absence of consulate and the absence of communication by the SDF. However, the Kurdish authorities have made clear their willingness to engage with any country to facilitate repatriation. The SDF has already successfully assisted the repatriation of nationals to several countries, including Uzbekistan, Kazakhstan, and Kosovo.

Since 2019, the international debate has been focused on different policies undertaken by states with leading UN experts subsequently making statements and publishing analyses designed to convince states to repatriate children and women. Four United Nations High-Level Advocates made a joint statement to express their concerns and urge states to implement their legal obligations:

> We call on States to fully implement their legal obligations by accepting those citizens who wish to return to their country of citizenship, granting due process to those who should be prosecuted and reintegrating individuals as appropriate into society. We call on States to treat all survivors of violations, specifically

> boys and girls, humanely and fairly, so to affirm their dignity and rights. We offer our collective support and assistance to all Member States to work towards this end.[22]

Antonio Guterres, Secretary-General of the United Nations, wrote in the tenth report of Secretary-General on ISIS that the Member States hold primary responsibility for the repatriation of their citizens. The Secretary-General also reminded states that they must comply with their international obligations and said the following:

> Concerted efforts remain necessary for the rehabilitation and reintegration of men, women and children who are stranded, especially in conflict zones, including in camps and detention facilities in Iraq and the Syrian Arab Republic. Member States have primary responsibility for the repatriation of their nationals. All measures taken by Member States for the protection, repatriation, prosecution, rehabilitation and reintegration of women and children with links to terrorist groups listed by the United Nations should comply with their obligations under international law, including international human rights law, international humanitarian law and international refugee law, as well as international standards and relevant Security Council resolutions. Relevant General Assembly resolutions should also be taken into consideration.[23]

Many states, including leading Western countries, have adopted administrative measures to prevent their citizens in Syria and Iraq from returning to their home countries. Policies such as the stripping of citizenship, temporary entry bans, or annulation of passports may work to counter the risk of terrorism short term, but they do not work in the long term. A few European countries have decided to repatriate a small number of children; however, this is uncommon. Despite the efforts of the United Nations and other international actors, there is no consensus over the question of how to deal with former fighters of ISIS and their associates trapped in Syria. Repatriation seems the most appropriate solution as it would curb the threat of the creation of new generations of terrorist groups. However, many states do not accept this as a solution. The second widely discussed solution is the creation of an ad hoc tribunal to prosecute the foreign fighters. Both options have their limitations in respect to international law and the current reality. Further in this chapter, I will discuss whether or not states have an obligation to repatriate women and children under international law and the challenges that arise regarding the prosecution of ISIS fighters.

Some EU diplomats told me that for states, the top priority is national security. Some of the state officials question whether states have a direct obligation to repatriate foreign fighters from Syria, but they are confident that administrative measures, such as stripping citizenship, may prevent terrorists from entering their home countries, thereby preventing future terrorist attacks.

However, the situation demands that states find a solution, since the SDF, as a non-state actor, does not have the legal authority and thus has no judicial powers to try those in detention.

According to the UN Special Rapporteurs:

> The urgent return and repatriation of foreign fighters and their families from conflict zones is the only international law-compliant response to the increasingly complex and precarious human rights, humanitarian and security situation faced by those women, men and children who are detained in inhumane conditions in overcrowded camps, prisons, or elsewhere in the northern Syrian Arab Republic and Iraq.[24]

They urged countries to repatriate women and children as a comprehensive response that amounts to a positive implementation of Security Council Resolutions 2178 (2014) and 2396 (2017) and is considerate of a state's long-term security interests.

The legal analyses conducted by two UN Special Rapporteurs as a response to the inquiries of international experts is an important document, which explains why states have obligations to repatriate their citizens from Syria, and how states can exercise extraterritorial jurisdiction. Even though a state's jurisdiction under human rights law is primarily territorial, "it is well established that a State may also have jurisdiction in respect of acts which are performed, or which produce effects, outside its national borders."[25] The UN Special Rapporteurs stress that a state should consider extraterritorial jurisdiction "to avoid allowing a State to perpetrate violations on the territory of another State, which it could not perpetrate on its own." In other words, countries that know foreign fighters have committed crimes, and will continue to do so if necessary actions are not taken, should take appropriate preventative action. Knowing that former foreign fighters may flee prisons and camps in Syria and continue carrying out terrorist acts, states should take necessary measures to repatriate, try, and bring them to justice.

"At the European Court of Human Rights (ECtHR), a State's jurisdiction outside its border is primarily established based on (1) the control that the State exercises over foreign territory (*ratione loci*) or (2) the control that is exercised by the state over a person (*ratione personae*)," stress UN experts.[26] UN experts suggest that states to repatriate their citizens currently held in camps in northeast Syria, are most likely to engage their jurisdiction *ratione personae*. The main idea behind such extraterritorial jurisdiction is to stop violence, stop transnational terrorism and prevent the creation of new generations of terrorist organizations. Despite the death of Abu Bakr al-Baghdadi in October 2019, ISIS remains a threat in Syria with most of its activity "focused on re-establishing networks and extending its influence in rural areas throughout eastern Syria and Iraq."[27]

The main tenet of the repatriation narrative is to save children. They are innocent, considering they were either forcibly moved by their parents or were simply born in the conflict zones. The task given to states is to save children and their guardians, their mothers. All persons have a right to life, a norm entrenched in international law, and the dire conditions in the camps, with no access to clean water, nutrition, or adequate medical assistance, threaten children's lives. The HRW, among other international organizations, raises concern over children dying every day in the two camps from malnutrition and preventable diseases. Subsequently, UN Special Rapporteurs stress that a state's responsibility to protect may thus be invoked extraterritorially in this situation. States should act to protect their citizens' right to life against an immediate or foreseeable threat to life and the condition in the Syrian camps possess risks and foreseeable harm that may lead to death.

The UN experts also refer to the UN Human Rights Committee General Comment 36 on Article 6 of the International Covenant on Civil and Political Rights, on the Right to Life, which affirmed that a State may exercise control over a person's rights by carrying out activities which impact them in a direct and reasonably foreseeable manner.[28] Among international legal experts, there is consensus that states have a shared responsibility in settling the current crisis in the camps in Syria—to repatriate their citizens. The shared responsibility of states is about maintaining international peace by ensuring joint efforts to prevent terrorism and armed conflicts and by complying with the requirements of UN resolutions and other international norms. Every state is a member of the international community; thus, all states have a shared responsibility to resolve the situation in the camps in Northeast Syria. As Deputy Ministry of Kazakhstan, Yerzhan Ashikbaev, said during the side-event at the Vienne conference in 2020, states have to take joint efforts otherwise the world will receive new generations of terrorists. "There is no guarantee that these children will grow up and will return to home countries to carry out terrorist attacks. Today ignoring the problem and turning away means that states are violating their obligations as a state,"[29] said Ashikbaev.

OPTIONS BEING DISCUSSED OTHER THAN REPATRIATION

There are 645 European children and 231 women in Syrian camps have been held by the Kurdish forces. However, EU states had been fully rejected active repatriation of both adults and children. After the pressure coming from the

United Nations and international human rights organizations, some European states softened their position toward children and in the last ten-fifteen months some states have started repatriating small children and a few women. For example, France repatriated already dozens of children in 2021, even though Paris had previously rejected repatriation. The French government even sent a delegation to Northeast Syria to meet with the Kurdish forces in November 2021, which means France is reconsidering its approach. Meanwhile, states have also considered different policies to deal with trapped foreign fighters in Syria. While EU states have practiced different administrative measures to prevent the return of foreign fighters, many have no political will to repatriate them. The following options have been proposed to the international community: (1) Transfer foreign fighters to prisons in Iraq and prosecute them in the host country, (2) Create an ad hoc international tribunal to try all ISIS fighters, (3) Employ existing international institutions such as the International Criminal Court, (4) Sentence foreign fighters in absentia.

The first option is to try foreign fighters in a host country, an option that several European countries have advocated for. I discuss state policies in the chapter 7. For example, France has expressed a firm position on relocating foreign fighters and sentencing them in Iraqi courts. The French government faced widespread criticism for negotiating with Iraq and the SDF over the transfer of French fighters from camps in northeast Syria to Iraq, after having relocated eleven French citizens to Iraqi prisons in 2019.[30] Media reports indicated that those eleven French fighters were sentenced to death by Iraqi courts following their transfer to Iraq.[31] According to the European Council on Foreign Relations, international norms forbid such relocations because the European Convention on Human Rights prohibits any state party from transferring its nationals to a country where they are at risk of capital punishment.[32] The Geneva Academy also concludes that, regardless of their status under international humanitarian law, foreign fighters are protected under human rights law, including its prohibition of refoulement. "Non-refoulement prohibits the transfer of individuals to another authority if there is a clear risk that the recipient state would violate fundamental human rights (freedom from torture and other cruel, inhuman, or degrading treatment; arbitrary deprivation of life)."[33] Geneva Academy lawyers stress that to concerning states that are party to the 1950 European Convention on Human Rights, "the Grand Chamber of the European Court has confirmed that the prohibition of refoulement applies to in-state transfers of individuals detained abroad during an international military operation."[34]

Numerous reports indicate that foreign fighters in Iraq have been sentenced to death, and court hearings lasted for only ten minutes. International lawyers have warned states that it is unacceptable to consider transferring foreign fighters to a country that has not abolished the death penalty. There was discussion about creating a special agreement with Iraq, including the creation of special chambers within the Iraqi justice system to try foreign fighters. The Iraqi government demanded that European countries pay an initial two billion USD to cover the costs of trials and the imprisonment of foreign fighters. However, these discussions were halted due to the concerns in the international community about broader deficiencies in the Iraqi justice system. The UN mandates and international organizations raised concerns about human rights violations, torture, and other issues in the prisons of Iraq.

The next feasible solution is to use the existing international courts to try foreign fighters. There was significant work done to try them in the ICC, and the UN was very close to realizing this option. In 2014, the UN Security Council was unable to adopt a resolution that would have referred the situation in Syria and Iraq to the International Criminal Court, due to vetoes by its permanent members Russia and China. A European Parliament analysis stated that, since EU Member States ratified and implemented the Rome Statute of the International Criminal Court, foreign fighters from these countries could be brought to the ICC to be held accountable for international crimes (war crimes, crimes against humanity, and genocide) committed outside EU borders. However, the international community lost this opportunity in 2014 due to a veto by the two aforementioned countries. Subsequently, no international court hearings have yet begun regarding the crimes of foreign fighters to hold them accountable for war crimes or other international crimes.

Since efforts by the UNSC, to refer crimes committed in Syria to the ICC, continue to be blocked, Sweden proposed the establishment of an international ad hoc tribunal or a similar mechanism. Swedish Home Affairs Minister Mikael Damberg hosted a meeting with eleven European countries in Stockholm in early June of 2019 to discuss the issue. The meeting was attended by the UK, France and Germany, and Switzerland and ended with no decisions taken.[35] No country wishes to take on the burden of such a tribunal. Many diplomats stress that an ad hoc tribunal is costly, as establishing a new court and new prisons requires a common agreement in the first place, as well as an agreement on its location and on who would be responsible for detention and security. Thus, this version of a new tribunal has reached a stalemate.

As UN experts highlight, states have the capacity and de-facto control over the human rights of children and their guardians in the camps, and they should act on their obligations to protect the right to life of their citizens, especially of children and women. At the same time, the international community should seek an adequate solution to try foreign fighters. Taking into account the economic crisis incited by COVID-19, there will be a lack of financial resources to establish new mechanisms. The only appropriate and law-applicable solution would be repatriation and prosecution in home countries, with children as a priority. One of the key principles developed by the United Nations is that children should be treated first "as victims and their treatment must be determined with the best interests of the child as the primary consideration, in line with the Convention on the Rights of the Child."[36]

Children have special rights and protections recognized in international law, applicable in all situations, irrespective of the child's age, sex, or other status, including actual or perceived family or personal affiliation. In 2020, many European countries changed their positions and began to consider the repatriation of small children from Syria. The SDF provided the list of countries and their corresponding number of returned children.[37] However, there are challenges in the repatriation of children. States should consider such repatriation on a case-by-case basis and should not separate them from their mothers. The Kurdish forces refused several European countries' requests for extraction and transport as they sought to repatriate children by separating them from their mothers. During an interview with the SDF representative, he confirmed this information. "It is true that some countries request the return of their children without the mothers, and we do not respond to this request because it is inconsistent with our values, especially since the mothers have not been put on trial yet," the SDF representative informed me. Hundreds of children were born in Iraq and Syria with different fathers, due to the practice of marrying off women to different ISIS fighters. At the Vienna conference, held on February 11–12, 2020, some experts stated that about 20,000 children were born to foreign fighters in Syria throughout the conflict. "This situation is further complicated in practice as many children do not have legal documentation, are orphaned, are accompanied by foreign mothers or fathers whose fates are uncertain, or are separated from their parents or responsible caregivers," UN experts stressed in their key principles for protection.[38] For states, it is not easy to identify children born from their nationals, which is a reason behind Kazakhstan's DNA tests for those children born in Syria, especially orphans.

The United Nations reminds Member States that they have a primary responsibility for their own nationals and, at the same time, international human rights law provides that all persons have the right to return to his or her country of nationality.[39] The very purpose of such principles is to protect the most marginalized. Thus, the UN urges states to seriously consider the following in the prosecution of associates of ISIS fighters: (1) Criminal responsibility is individual. No person should be detained or prosecuted for crimes committed by family members. Many women and children come into contact with United Nations-listed terrorist groups through family links and should be treated by the principle of the presumption of innocence, (2) Children should be treated first and foremost as victims and their treatment must be determined with the best interests of the child as the primary consideration, (3) Member States should accept their nationals and children born to their nationals, grant those children nationality, and take actions to protect them from statelessness, (4) Criminal justice processes must be gender-responsive and female survivors of violence, abuses and other human rights violations must be provided with all possible support.[40]

The priority should be given to children and women. Some women perpetrated crimes, but each case should be assessed individually since it is known women were often exposed to physical and psychological torture and were typically dependent on their husbands. ISIS has systematically violated women's rights, used women as human shields, subjected them to child marriage and rape, and forced them to commit crimes. Many women went to Syria following their husbands, unaware of the real situation there, and many young girls and women were victims of online recruiters who recruited them through false promises in Internet. Some girls believed they would be studying in Turkey or Egypt or would marry a man whom they met on social media. These kinds of circumstances should be taken into account in the legal assessments of women's cases.

CONCLUSIONS

The current situation with family members of foreign fighters, held in the desert in Northeast Syria, is unprecedented. The world has never before witnessed the dilemma of dealing with family members of terrorist groups. Male fighters should be given a chance for fair trial and should be brought to justice. We never thought that the defeat of the terrorist group can leave thousands of children and women behind. Consequences of the family jihad made the world face legal, moral and other challenges. However, countries need to find immediate and effective policies to manage the given situation, as abandonment is not a solution.

To conclude, each United Nations Member State should build its policy according to UN resolutions and comply with the key principles built by the UN and with OSCE guidelines. The principal objective is to maintain international peace and prevent further radicalization and escalation of the conflict. From this point, the situation in the camps and prisons in northeast Syria and Iraq demands urgent and orchestrated action from all actors of the international community. States should build their policies toward foreign fighters with human rights-based approaches and in the framework of international obligations. The aforementioned options to deal with returning foreign fighters such as trying in host countries, building an ad hoc tribunal, or accelerating repatriation to home countries should be discussed further and the international community should come to a final decision. Allowing impunity begets more violence and injustice; male fighters should be brought to justice either in their home countries or by an international tribunal. Evidence documented by the Commission and the Mechanism offers concrete hope for justice, once the international community decides on the process through which foreign fighters can be brought to justice. Even if they are tried in their home countries, states should involve the relevant international bodies, so that all evidence can be presented. Finally, the cases of women and children should be treated strictly in accordance with key UN principles and international norms.

NOTES

1. Amnesty International, "Gruesome Evidence of Ethnic Cleansing in Northern Iraq as Islamic State Moves to Wipe out Minorities," Amnesty International, (2014), https://www.amnesty.org/en/latest/news/2014/09/gruesome-evidence-ethnic-cleansing-northern-iraq-islamic-state-moves-wipe-out-minorities/; "Rule of Fear: ISIS Abuses In Detention In Northern Syria.," (2013), https://www.amnesty.org/en/documents/MDE24/063/2013/en/; OHCHR, "Independent International Commission of Inquiry on the Syrian Arab Republic," (2019), https://www.ohchr.org/en/hrbodies/hrc/iicisyria/pages/independentinternationalcommission.aspx; ReliefWeb, "Report on the Protection of Civilians in Armed Conflict in Iraq: 6 July–10 September 2014," (2014), https://reliefweb.int/report/iraq/report-protection-civilians-armed-conflict-iraq-6-july-10-september-2014-enar.

2. OHCHR, "'They Came to Destroy': ISIS Crimes Against the Yazidis," Human Rights Council 32nd session, (2016), https://www.ohchr.org/Documents/HRBodies/HRCouncil/CoISyria/A_HRC_32_CRP.2_en.pdf.

3. OHCHR, "Convention on Prevention and Punishment of the Crime of Genocide," (2019), https://www.ohchr.org/EN/ProfessionalInterest/Pages/CrimeOfGenocide.aspx.

4. OHCHR, "They Came to Destroy."

5. OHCHR, "They Came to Destroy."

6. "Convention on Prevention and Punishment of the Crime of Genocide." Article II of the 1948 Convention for the Prevention and Punishment of the Crime of Genocide, to which Syria and Iraq are parties, states that the crime of genocide is committed when a person commits a prohibited act with intent to destroy, in whole or in part, a national, ethnical, racial or religious group as such. Prohibited acts are (a) killing members of the group; (b) causing serious bodily or mental harm to members of the group; (c) deliberately inflicting on the group conditions of life calculated to bring about its physical destruction in whole or in part; (d) imposing measures intended to prevent births within the group; (e) forcibly transferring children of the group to another group.

7. The crime of genocide requires that the perpetrator have a special intent to destroy, in whole or in part, a protected group. The genocidal acts must be committed

against a person because of their membership in a particular group and as an incremental step in the overall objective of destroying the group.

8. Human Rights Watch, "Flawed Justice: Accountability for ISIS Crimes in Iraq," (New York, 2017), https://www.hrw.org/sites/default/files/report_pdf/iraq1217web.pdf.

9. Genocide Network Secretariat, "The Prosecution at National Level of Sexual and Gender-Based Violence (SGBV) Committed by the Islamic State in Iraq and the Levant (ISIL)." *Eurojust*, (2017), 5, http://www.eurojust.europa.eu/doclibrary/genocide-network/KnowledgeSharing/The%20prosecution%20at%20national%20level%20of%20sexual%20and%20gender-based%20violence%20committed%20ISIL%20(July%202017)/2017-07_Prosecution-at-national-level-of-sexual-and-gender-based-violence_EN.pdf.

10. International Criminal Court, Rome Statute of the International Criminal Court (The Hague: International Criminal Court, Cop, 2011), 4, https://www.icc-cpi.int/resource-library/documents/rs-eng.pdf.

According to the Rome Statute, an "[a]ttack directed against any civilian population" means a course of conduct involving the multiple commission of acts . . . against any civilian population, pursuant to or in furtherance of a State or organizational policy to commit such attack. See Rome Statute of the International Criminal Court, 17 July 1998 (entered into force 1 July 2002), UN Doc. A/CONF.183/9 [hereinafter 'Rome Statute'], at Art. 7(2)(a).

11. UNHRC, "'I Lost My Dignity': Sexual and Gender-Based Violence in the Syrian Arab Republic" (37th session of UN Human Rights Council, Independent International Commission of Inquiry on the Syrian Arab Republic, March 2018), 23, https://www.ohchr.org/Documents/HRBodies/HRCouncil/CoISyria/A-HRC-37-CRP-3.pdf.

12. UNHRC, "I Lost My Dignity," 1.

13. UNHRC, "I Lost My Dignity," 2.

14. UNHRC, "I Lost My Dignity," 1.

15. UNHRC, "I Lost My Dignity," 7.

16. Sandra Kraehenmann, "*Foreign Fighters under International Law*," vol. 7 (Geneva: Geneva Academy Of International Humanitarian Law And Human Rights, 2014), 55, https://www.geneva-academy.ch/joomlatools-files/docman-.files/Publications/Academy%20Briefings/Foreign%20Fighters_2015_WEB.pdf.

17. International, Impartial and Independent Mechanism , "Terms of reference of the International, Impartial and Independent Mechanism to Assist in the Investigation and Prosecution of Persons Responsible for the Most Serious Crimes under International Law Committed in the Syrian Arab Republic since March 2011" (2020), https://iiim.un.org/terms-of-reference-of-iiim/.

18. Marija Sulce, "The War Report 2018: The Syrian Armed Conflict: Nearing the End?," *The Geneva Academy*, (2019), 8, https://www.geneva-academy.ch/joomlatools-files/docmanfiles/The%20Syrian%20Armed%20Conflict%20Nearing%20The%20End.pdf.

19. UNITAD, "Our Mandate | Investigative Team to Promote Accountability for Crimes Committed by Da'esh/ISIL (UNITAD)," (2020), https://www.unitad.un.org/content/our-mandate.

20. UNITAD, "The European Union and UNITAD Sign Agreement to Support Digitization of Evidence of ISIL Crimes in Iraq | Investigative Team to Promote Accountability for Crimes Committed by Da'esh/ISIL (UNITAD)," (2020), https://www.unitad.un.org/news/european-union-and-unitad-sign-agreement-support-digitization-evidence-isil-crimes-iraq.

21.AFP, "Head of UN Investigators Calls for an IS 'Nuremberg,'" France 24, July 29, 2019, https://www.france24.com/en/20190729-head-un-investigators-calls-nuremberg.

22. Fabienne Vinet, "Joint Statement on Human Rights and Humanitarian Concerns Related to Conflict Affected Women and Children in Syria and Iraq," United Nations Office of the Special Representative of the Secretary-General for Children and Armed Conflict, (2019), https://childrenandarmedconflict.un.org/2019/11/joint-statement-on-human-rights-and-humanitarian-concerns-related-to-conflict-affected-women-and-children-in-syria-and-iraq/.

23. ReliefWeb, "Tenth Report of the Secretary-General on the Threat Posed by ISIL (Da'esh) to International Peace and Security and the Range of United Nations Efforts in Support of Member States in Countering the Threat (S/2020/95)," (2020), 17., https://reliefweb.int/report/iraq/tenth-report-secretary-general-threat-posed-isil-da-esh-international-peace-and-security.

24. Agnes Callamard, "Extra-Territorial Jurisdiction of States over Children and Their Guardians in Camps, Prisons, or Elsewhere in the Northern Syrian Arab Republic: Legal Analysis," (OHCHR, 2018), 1, https://www.ohchr.org/Documents/Issues/Executions/UNSRsPublicJurisdictionAnalysis2020.pdf.

25. Callamard, "Extra-Territorial Jurisdiction."

26. Callamard, "Extra-Territorial Jurisdiction."

27. US Central Command, "Posture Statement of General Kenneth F. McKenzie Jr., Commander, United States Central Command, before the House Armed Services Committee on March 10," (2020), https://www.centcom.mil/ABOUT-US/POSTURE-STATEMENT/.

28. Human Rights Committee, "Human Rights Committee General Comment No. 36 (2018) on Article 6 of the International Covenant on Civil and Political Rights, on the Right to Life," (2018). https://tbinternet.ohchr.org/Treaties/CCPR/Shared%20Documents/1_Global/CCPR_C_GC_36_8785_E.pdf.

29. Yerzhan Ashikbaev`s answer during the side event organized by Kazakhstan on the margines of Vienna conference on 11–12 February 2020.

30. Anthony Dworkin, "Beyond Good and Evil: Why Europe Should Bring ISIS Foreign Fighters Home," *European Council on Foreign Relations*, (2019), https://www.ecfr.eu/publications/summary/beyond_good_and_evil_why_europe_should_bring_isis_foreign_fighters_home.

31.Théo Maneval, "Djihadistes Français Condamnés à Mort En Irak: Vers Une Solution Européenne?," *Europe 1*, June 4, 2019, https://www.europe1.fr/international/djihadistes-condamnes-a-mort-en-irak-vers-une-solution-europeenne-3902646.

32. Dworkin, "Beyond Good and Evil."

33. Sandra Kraehenmann, *Foreign Fighters under International Law*, (Geneva, Geneva Academy of International Humanitarian Law and Human Rights, 2014), 21.

34. Emanuela-Chiara Gillard, "There's No Place like Home: States' Obligations in Relation to Transfers of Persons," *International Review of the Red Cross* 90, no. 871 (September 2008): 703–50, 720, https://international-review.icrc.org/articles/theres-no-place-home-states-obligations-relation-transfers-persons.

35. Julia Crawford, "Do We Need an International Tribunal for Islamic State?," *Justiceinfo*, August 26, 2019, https://www.justiceinfo.net/en/tribunals/mixed-tribunals/42224-do-we-need-an-international-tribunal-for-islamic-state.html. 53 UN, "Key Principles for the Protection, Repatriation, Prosecution, Rehabilitation and Reintegration of Women and Children with Links to United Nations Listed Terrorist Groups," *UNCCT Annual Report*, (2020), 5.

36. According to Bedran Ciya, a press officer of the SDF, European countries have repatriated a small number of children. He provided me with the following list of countries which have repatriated small children by 15 April 2020: the Republic of Trinidad: 2 children, Australia: 8 children, Russia: 43 children, France: 17 children, Denmark: 2 children, Sweden: 7 children, United States of America: 6 children, Uzbekistan: 88 children, Nigeria: 3 children, Sudan: 6 children, Norway: 7 children, Germany: 7 children, Britain: 3 children, Austria: 2 children, Belgium: 6 children, Netherlands: 2 children, Finland: 2 children.

37. UN, "Key Principles for the Protection," 3.

38. UN, "Key Principles for the Protection," 5.

39. UN, "Key Principles for the Protection," 5.

Chapter 4

Post-ISIS-Life

Women and Children in the Desert Nowhere to Go

After the fall of ISIS, thousands of women and children, who were family members of ISIS fighters, had nowhere to go. As ISIS territory shrank and the offense against the terrorist groups intensified, women and children began fleeing the ruins of the cities, left without food and shelter. The influx of people to the camps started in December 2018. Three camps in northeast Syria—Roj, Al-Hawl, and Ain Issa—held women and children who were family members of ISIS fighters. However, the third camp Ain Issa, where 249 women and 700 children were held, was destroyed in October 2019 by a Turkish assault. Kurdish forces stated that some inhabitants were relocated to other camps, but at least 750 people fled the area and dispersed in northeast Syria.[1] According to the International Rescue Committee, the other two camps met a 'breaking point' by March 2019, housing over 65,000 people.[2] The majority of them reached the camps after the last strongholds of ISIS in northeast Syria were defeated. Currently (at the time of finalizing the manuscript in November 2021), more than 70,000 people, 90 percent of them women and children, have been held in the two remaining camps in northeast Syria—Al-Hawl and Roj. Women reached the camps by different means, some of them taken there by the Kurdish forces and others reaching camps with the help of local Syrians, whom they had to pay about 5–7 thousand dollars for the assistance. These women walked through the desert, and about 200 children died on the road to the camps due to starvation and hypothermia. Women were forced to bury their children in the desert before continuing their journey. The largest group of women and children came after the fall of Baghouse. The International Rescue Committee informed that "12,000 women and children have arrived from ISIS-controlled Baghouse in Eastern Syria to Al-Hawl within 48 hours."[3] Baghouse was the last stronghold of ISIS, where women who were very loyal to ISIS stayed until the end. Many women did not reach Baghouse and instead headed to the camps at an earlier stage following the liberation of other cities, after being left in ruins and starving.

It is the first time in the history of the world that thousands of women and children associated with terrorist groups have been left behind after the defeat of such groups and become trapped in the desert. It is also the first time that the camps of former foreign terrorist fighters and their associates have been administered by a non-state actor—the Syrian Democratic Forces. Over two years have passed since the collapse of ISIS. However, the international community has struggled to find a viable strategy to address the issue of trapped former fighters and their associates. The question has become a ticking time bomb for international peace, and the source countries of foreign fighters have been very slow to take concrete actions. There is an ongoing international debate discussing options to deal with them, such as repatriation, host country trials, creation of an ad hoc tribunal, etc.

Who are the Syrian Democratic Forces? The SDF is an alliance that mainly consists of the Kurdish forces. It was founded in 2015 and fought against ISIS. It played an essential role in defeating ISIS. The United States supported the Kurdish forces, which realized at an early stage that they needed to identify and create credible rebel forces that could fight against ISIS in Syria and Iraq. Washington observed how the Kurdish forces fought against an Al-Qaeda franchise and that, without foreign support, they managed to fight Syrian government forces between 2011 and 2013. Therefore, the United States chose the Kurdish forces as a local militia to lead the war against ISIS. The U.S. negotiated conditions and, according to insights from anonymous interviews, the U.S. put two main conditions forward: first, after seizing territories from ISIS, they must not form them into a Kurdish state and must include "other ethnic or religious groups, notably Arabs and Christians, in setting up governance and security."[4] The following critical condition was to avoid attacking the interests of Turkey. This was complicated because the Kurdish forces mainly consisted of militants of the YPG, or People's Protection Unit. Its members, including General Mazloum, were trained by the Kurdistan Workers' Party, or PKK. The PKK was on the U.S. and Turkish lists of terrorist organizations. The group is considered a security threat for previous attacks and waging an insurgency to win autonomy in Turkey.

The United States invested significant financial and human resources to train and equip the Kurdish forces. However, the SDF does not only comprise Kurdish militants. The Kurdish General Mazloum warned Washington that a solely Kurdish militia would be weak and having an Arab wing could mount chances to unite Arab tribal sheikhs against ISIS. So, Americans invested in creating a more significant force, the Syrian Democratic Forces, into which the Kurdish forces merged with new Arab, Turk, and Assyrian militias.

Starting in 2015, the U.S. deployed soldiers to train and advise in the fight against ISIS. Thus, after the fall of ISIS, the SDF inherited a new role to hold captured ISIS fighters in prisons in the Hasakah region and family members in camps in northeastern Syria.

After the fall of ISIS, international humanitarian organizations did not expect such a sizable influx of women and children from liberated cities. None of the parties were prepared for a sudden humanitarian crisis of this scale in light of the fall of the terrorist group and when women began arriving with their small children, some of them were still demonstrating fierce loyalty to ISIS and high radicalization. The representative of the SDF, Mr. Bedran Ciya Kurd, whom I interviewed for this book, stressed how it has been difficult for the Kurdish forces to maintain prisons and camps where ISIS fighters and their families have been held. "We do not have fortified prisons that can accommodate this large number of ISIS fighters. We also lack modern devices and technology that help the security in our work. However, the biggest problem facing the [Autonomous Administration of North and East Syria (AANES)] is that the international community is not cooperative with us to put ISIS fighters on trial so that justice is served to them," said Mr. Bedran Ciya.[5] The SDF has asked the international community to provide the financial resources to build new detention centers to separate male fighters and hold boys above twelve years old. They believe that having separate prisons will facilitate the detention of fighters and their family members.

KURDISH FORCES URGE TO BUILD FORTIFIED PRISONS

Currently, the SDF holds about 11,000 male fighters from over fifty countries in a range of facilities, the largest two near the towns of Hasakah and Dashisha in northeast Syria. The United States is helping the SDF to run and secure its detention facilities to hold male fighters.[6] However prison buildings are not designed to be long-term jails for hardened fighters. They are not solid as were converted into prisons from school buildings or hospitals. The Syrian Democratic forces had expressed its frustration at being left with thousands of fighters in unsecured facilities. They warned during the interview in 2021 about a danger of escaping fighters or being attacked by ISIS. Unfortunately, indeed ISIS attacked one of the prisons in January 2022. The largest prison, with about 5,000 fighters was retaken with the help of US-led coalition. ISIS is regaining strength in Syria and now it has become clear that the situation is alarming. Bedran Ciya Kurd, an SDF representative told me during an interview that the large number of ISIS fighters (in prisons) and their families (in camps) is a significant burden on the Kurdish forces. "We do not have fortified prisons that can accommodate this large number of ISIS fighters. We also lack modern devices and technology that help the security in their work. However, the biggest problem facing the AANES is that the international community is not cooperative with us in putting ISIS fighters on trial so that justice can be served," Bedran Ciya Kurd stated.[7] He also underlined that the camps where ISIS-affiliated families reside, Al-Hawl camp, in particular, pose a substantial risk as they include a large number of radical ISIS women.

The SDF appears to be generally unsatisfied with the support it has been provided by the US-led coalition and aims to seek further assistance. Bedran Ciya Kurd, the SDF representative, expressed his position to me that the international community should assume its responsibility for foreign fighters. "We urge states to assist us in the building of fortified prisons with modern technology, the separation of radical women from the less radical ones. In addition to that, we need help for opening rehabilitation centers for women, schools for children, and recreational facilities until a solution is found for this big problem, which needs to be addressed in coordination with the international community," said the SDF representative. After observing the inaction by many countries, SDF members appear to have envisaged the holding of foreign fighters and their associates as a long-term project. Although they reiterate that they suffer from a scarcity of resources, they may be ready to maintain prisons and camps for the long term, if they were provided greater financial support. Turkey, in turn, has harshly criticized the Kurdish forces and claims that the SDF is allocated an annual income of around 150 million USD. An official from the Turkish MFA declared the following during the interview: "Although the 'SDF' points to insufficient funding for its shortcomings regarding effective control, it has an annual income of around 150 million USD. This amount includes 72 million USD worth of oil trade with the regime, which is a flagrant and direct breach of sanctions imposed by the US and EU."[8] The SDF did not comment on this claim and no clarification followed on the annual budget.

Most male detainees held by the SDF are Syrians and Iraqis, with only about 2,000 foreign fighters originating from more than fifty countries. Kurdish forces previously told researchers that they wanted to create better conditions for them, but they did not have the resources to do so. "These prisoners were our enemies. They raped our women. They killed our brothers and friends. But when they are in our hands, we must treat them properly as prisoners of war," said the guard in one of the main prisons in northeast Syria.[9] Thousands of fighters are clogged in the tiny cells of makeshift prisons. Hundreds of men are crammed in one cell under appalling conditions. But the Kurdish forces guarding them say that, at the very least, they are alive and not subjected to torture or even hanged. "If they were captured in Iraq's territory, they would have already been sentenced to the death penalty there," said a representative of the Kurdish forces who did not wish his name to be publicized.

The SDF maintains a firm position that male fighters and women who committed crimes should be tried in the Middle East. "All men and women who committed crimes should be prosecuted in our region because they committed crimes against the people of this region and caused more than 12,000 deaths and more than 24,000 injured, of which hundreds of them now have permanent disabilities. We have evidence and witnesses that can condemn them here in North-East Syria," Bedran Ciya Kurd said.[10] The Kurdish forces informed me that they carried out internal discussions with a number of European countries to exchange views on the situation of the camps and the trials regarding fighters.[11] They did not disclose the details of these talks but asserted that they will continue the discussion after the current crisis related to the novel coronavirus is tempered.

The SDF stated their intention to create a special court in northeast Syria where they are willing to prosecute the foreign fighters while in detention.[12] However, the SDF has no international recognition, and trials organized by a non-state actor could establish a dangerous precedent. Fionnuala Ní Aoláin, the UN Special Rapporteur for the protection of human rights while countering terrorism, stated that there have been discussions about holding some form of trial managed by the Syrian Democratic Forces. "But to state the obvious, we do not generally have non-state actors running trials, and there is a reason for that, which is that non-state actors have not signed treaties, don't have a judicial system, and may not be in a position to ensure that their trials are fair. So, I do not see that as a solution," she said in an interview.[13] However, it is worth mentioning that none of the states have yet raised or supported the idea of granting rights to the SDF to organize trials over fighters. As the Turkish official noted during the interview, alluding to the fact that a non-state actor could have a role in this would be unacceptable. "This amounts to an attempt to legitimize a terrorist organization by granting it with so-called judicial powers. Indeed, the requirements of a fair trial cannot be ensured in such a pseudo judicial process," stated the official from the Ministry of Foreign Affairs of Turkey.[14] Rather, many states will only seriously consider trials in a host country, meaning Iraq or Syria in this context.

The destiny of individuals held by the SDF demands urgent action as there are several risks. First, they may escape the detention facilities. Second, future control of the Kurdish forces over northern Syria is uncertain. Some sources indicate that they entered into negotiations with the Syrian government, which may eventually lead to a return of government forces to the area.[15] If Syria reclaims control over the territory, the transfer of SDF-held detainees to Syrian prisons is a bleak scenario. The Syrian government has never respected human rights and has already been accused of war crimes.

International human rights law prohibits handing over detainees to countries where they may face torture, cruel treatment, and the death penalty.[16]

HUMANITARIAN CRISIS IN ROJ AND AL-HAWL

The two camps Al-Hawl and Roj, located in Northeast Syria close to the border with Turkey and Iraq, hold about 70,000 women and children with links to ISIS. The majority are Iraqis and Syrians, while 12,000 women and children represent third countries. There is a humanitarian crisis in both camps as infectious illnesses are rampant, and many inhabitants suffer from the long-term effects of starvation, wounds, and injuries caused by the armed conflict in Syria. While walking among tents, one will see "teenagers missing legs and arms, women so sick they could not stand, and children with poorly healed burns across their face and arms."[17] The camps do not have any conditions to resist climate cataclysms, such as heavy rains and high temperatures that turn water floods into pools of garbage, litter, and human waste. Children have no place to play, so they sit and run around such "pools."

The United Nations Office for the Coordination of Humanitarian Affairs (OCHA) published profiles of two camps focusing on Syrian and Iraqi people. The factsheet lacks information about the Annex where foreign women from about fifty countries live. The profile provides an overview of conditions in the Al-Hawl camp: 97 percent of inhabitants live in tents. 47 percent of individuals reported lack of sufficient fuel, 45 percent complained of water leaking into their place of shelter, and 37 percent reported shelter damage. The weather conditions in the desert are indeed harsh, with strong winds and heavy rains. The majority of women whom I interviewed complained about tents. Only a few told me they received their tent for free, but some stressed that new tents are being sold for 100 USD for a piece. "We buy a tent, and it is costly for us. If you buy a used one, it will quickly be torn due to the wind or rains. Sometimes winds destroy our tent, so we try to affix it strongly to the ground," one woman said. Another woman who spent three winters in the camp said the following: "At the beginning, I did not know how to fortify my tent, so my tent would fall over, or we would be in pools of water, only now I eventually learned how to fix my tent to the ground properly."[18]

The Al-Hawl camp has become notorious and most discussed for its large territory and dire conditions. At the outset, the camp did not expect to house such a large number of people. The camp is immense, holding 73,000 people, and according to research institutes, "women and children make up 94 percent of its residents."[19] Al-Hawl camp was initially opened to accommodate the wave of refugees coming from the city of Mosul in Iraq. Then the AANES decided to send internally displaced persons to Al-Hawl as the fighting in Der al-Zour intensified, and Arisha Camp nearby was full. "The [Al-Hawl] camps received family members of ISIS who were in Baghouse and Hajin, the last pockets of ISIS. As a result, the [Al-Hawl] camp was expanded to include nine sections, in which the Syrians, Iraqis, and foreigners are separately distributed, due to the cultural differences among them," told me Bedrun Ciya Kurd, representative of the SDF. The Kurdish forces struggled to resolve conflicts between Syrians and Iraqis until they separated. "Still, problems occur between foreign families; the Camp Administration is now sorting them out according to their nationalities," said Mr. Ciya Kurd.[20]

The conditions in Roj are superior to those in Al-Hawl, so women living there feel very lucky. This is not only due to the electricity and better tents, but also less violence and quite good order inside the camp. However, healthcare in both camps is at the same level. According to a UN OCHA report, while only one hospital exists in Roj, three field hospitals are now operational in camp Al-Hawl.[21] They provide in-patient care, but "none of the hospitals operate at full capacity, mainly due to the absence of a blood bank, recruitment issues, license approvals and delayed medical equipment, impacting the number and type of surgeries."[22] Women living in Roj admit they are indeed lucky to live there. "We have been in contact with other women living in Al-Hawl, and their life is horrible there. They do not even have clean water while we have water and electricity. I am lucky that I am in Roj with my two children. This place is more secure and orderly," a Russian woman told me during the interview conducted via Telegram. However, Roj also has many problems. Although the Roj camp has 110 shower cabins, she never uses them. "We have shower cabins, but they were built near the toilets, and it is filthy. In the beginning, they were normal, but now each time I see overflowing latrines there, and it is disgusting," told me the woman in Roj. She said she takes a shower and washes her two children inside her camp.

The situation regarding health care is very desperate, especially in the Al-Hawl camp. Due to the shortage of medication and medical assistance, there is constant panic and fear among women. "The camp administration does not have enough doctors and medicine to treat us. Children are dying here. Many children are exhausted and weak. Children frequently fall with high fever, and it is not easy to convince the camp administration to take a sick child to the hospital," a Russian woman living in the Roj camp informed me during the interview. Several women told me that there was a spread of contagious viruses in the camp, including COVID-19. One of the women told me the water tracks are the primary source of dangerous infections. "There are big water cauldrons from which we all drink water. Water in these tanks is dirty with worms. People throw in diapers, garbage, and syringes. Children are sick because of this dirty water. We hear all time that some women have AIDS, but we do not know if it is true or not," one woman in Al-Hawl told me. It appears that the lack of clean water has been a source of various illnesses. Children have diarrhea and swollen bellies. "We cannot find clean water even for sick children. There is no medication to treat children. Our children are very weak from malnutrition and the bad living conditions, so they are sick almost every day. We are slowly dying here," a Kyrgyz woman in Al-Hawl told me.

The death of children in two camps in Syria is widespread. In particular, the situation in the Al-Hawl camp is dire, where children are dying from infections, acute diarrhea, and malnutrition. Human Rights Watch visited Al-Hawl camp three times and reported "overflowing latrines, sewage trickling into tattered tents, and residents drinking wash water from tanks containing worms in the Al-Hawl camp."[23] HRW testified that small children were sick with skin rashes, emaciated limbs, and swollen bellies. Their bodies were dusted with dirt, flies, and copious sinking garbage around tents. There is always a putrid stench emitting from garbage, the pool of water, and toilets.

At the beginning of April 2020, the woman living in Roj camp with her two children, whom I interviewed, suddenly disappeared for several days. She did not access her WhatsApp and Telegram accounts and did not see my further questions. Three days later, she connected via Telegram. It appeared she was in the hospital with an orphan girl. "I spent three days with her in the hospital. But she died. She had a high fever for several days then was brought to the hospital. Doctors suspected that she had meningitis, but they could not save her. It was too late. I am so exhausted, did not sleep for three days," she told me. "There are rumors in the camp that this meningitis is contagious, and we are in panic," she said. I tried to comfort her by sharing informational resources about meningitis in Russian to read about the condition.

The next day they buried her. When someone dies in the camp Roj, there is a location outside the camp to bury the deceased. "It is just near the fences of the camp; we never go out from the territory. We washed her body, prepared her for the funeral then Iraqi people came to take her to bury her. We approached the place to watch through the fence," she told me. A nine-year-old girl lived with her grandmother and died from an unidentified infection. She said that her grandmother of almost seventy years of age, is shocked by her loss. The girl's both parents died in Syria. Dozens of children die in two camps every week and the main issue is lack of adequate medical assistance.

The Al-Hawl camp has three sections: the respective Iraqi and Syrian sections hold about 60,000 people, most of them women and children. The third section is the Annex, called the 'foreigners' section,' where nearly 12,000 women and children reside from over sixty countries worldwide. This Annex suffers the worst conditions as it "receives less aid from donors and Annex inhabitants must wait for armed escorts to bring them to the camp market, hospitals, and food distribution center, which Syrian and Iraqi women and children can reach freely, aid workers said."[24] Referring to the situation in this section of the camp, Human Rights Watch describes, "foreign women and children have indefinitely locked in a dustbowl inferno in northeast Syria while their home countries look the other way."[25]

Women in both camps, Roj and Al-Hawl, stressed that they do not have access to international humanitarian organizations. They want to receive international aid as other camps of refugees usually receive. Many women I interviewed expressed their concern because they do not have access to international aid. But in reality, UNICEF, Red Cross and International Relief and other organizations are working hard to help them. "Kurds treat us as criminals. We hear a lot that ICRC, HRW come to see us. However, they do not allow us to meet with them. The last time I saw the car and delegates from Red Cross walking in the camp, I wanted to approach them. The guards pushed me back and said, 'Get away from here.' If we say something, Kurds shout at us, 'You are Daesh,' 'You are traitors.' But I did not want to join ISIS; I was deceived," a woman in Roj told me. They want to talk to journalists and want to be heard. "Sometimes we have English-speaking journalists from Europe; whenever they are in the camp, Kurds become very kind to us," a woman living in Al-Hawl who wanted to stay anonymous, told me.[26]

I interviewed twenty-five people from the inner circle of ISIS associates whose children or siblings are currently in Syria. Many have been active parents constantly searching for ways to bring back their children. Parents in Azerbaijan, Russia, Kyrgyzstan, and Tajikistan remain in touch and exchange information. They have WhatsApp groups and Instagram accounts where they post the latest news about efforts to push their governments to bring their children home. Some of them cry continuously over the phone. The unexpected factor was the COVID pandemic, which hindered any positive movement on the issue. Parents informed me that they sometimes send money to women in Al-Hawl and Roj, which is a risky process as money disappears midjourney. They did not disclose all details, but I understood that their contact persons in Turkey could transfer the money to the camps. However, it is difficult for them to send money. "We exhausted all our resources since last year, and now we do not have more money to send. We are exhausted and desperate," Salima told me. She's living in Moscow, whose daughter is in the Al-Hawl camp. Nevertheless, the International Crisis Group reported that camp administrators allow Syrian and Iraqi women in the main camp areas to make purchases through the *Hawala* alternative money transfer system, but those foreigners cannot do so.[27]

Women living in the Annex for foreigners are upset they receive less support than Syrians and Iraqis and have more violence in their territory. There is a threat of sexual violence for girls and little boys inside the camps. Older boys from Syria and Iraq chase younger boys and women, fearing this and trying to watch their sons. There were cases of older boys who lured and raped younger ones. A European woman told researchers that she had been warned of rapes of young boys and girls in the camp and "was horrified when she found that older boys had come to her tent when she was briefly absent and tried to lure her young boy out of the tent to go away with them."[28] Several incidents occurred when boys captured little boys on their way to the distribution center to receive a bread unit and raped them. Two women I interviewed confirmed these cases and told me that they are afraid for their children's security and always keep their children nearby, not allowing them to walk alone.

AMBIGUITY AND ABSENCE OF LEGAL STATUS

The Roj and Al-Hawl camps have been operating since December 2018. ISIS fell in March 2019 after its defeat by the U.S.-led international coalition and lost its last stronghold in Baghouse in Syria. Since then, people have remained stranded in overcrowded camps under inhumane conditions, and the international community has not yet found a viable solution to address ISIS fighters and their associates. There is an ongoing debate on this subject in the United Nations and other international organizations, such as the OSCE and European Union. Many legal analyses have been conducted on main solutions under international law. There is an intense international debate, and the central imperative advocated is repatriation, prosecution, and rehabilitation at home.

The United Nations has been a persistent advocate for repatriation, saying that Member States have the primary responsibility for taking back their nationals.[29] The UN mandates and experts called upon Member States to repatriate their citizens and guarantee due process and a fair trial. At the same time, UNITAD, UNOCT, UNMA, and other international ad hoc bodies, such as the International Mechanism on Syria and the Syrian Constitutional Committee, have been working hard to collect evidence and work with victims to make it possible to bring ISIS fighters to justice for committed war crimes and genocide. However, at the moment, there is no clarity and unity on where and how ISIS male fighters should be tried. Women and children are special categories and should be repatriated and treated individually on a case-by-case basis.

The legal status of women and children in the two camps in Northeast Syria is unclear. They do not possess the legal rights of victims of war and are considered neither refugees nor internally displaced persons due to the armed conflict. According to the International Crisis Group, the horrific conditions in camps result from the ambiguity of the legal status of women and children: they are neither formally displaced persons, nor prisoners, nor conflict detainees. This ambiguity led to a blurred division of "who precisely was ultimately responsible for providing essential services and protecting basic rights (such as access to legal counsel) among the U.S.-led coalition, the YPG, and various UN agencies."[30] The services a refugee or internally displaced persons' camp could usually receive have been poor and inconsistent for ISIS associates.

Women who were wives of ISIS fighters vary greatly, and there is considerable variation in levels of their radicalization and committed crimes. As the UN Secretary-General stressed, women in Al-Hawl and Roj camps can be "facilitators, supporters, and perpetrators of crimes, while also being victims of violence, trafficking, and other human rights violations."[31] States should implement careful screening and build gender-responsive risk assessment, repatriation, and rehabilitation policies. As International Crisis Group noted, since these women have lived in camps for months and years, the Kurdish forces have monitored and observed their personalities and behaviors.[32] The SDF assessed some women in the camps and created catalogs. Although its lists and registers might be incomplete, states may be able to use them to identify and evaluate profiles of women before repatriation, prosecution, and rehabilitation.

The main question on the international community's agenda is what to do with the wives and children of ISIS fighters. Where should they go, and how should they be rehabilitated and reintegrated? How can male fighters held in prisons in northeast Syria be brought to justice? There is an ongoing debate, but the main conclusion is that repatriation remains the most viable solution. However, the question of repatriation continues to be fraught for many countries. Despite the UN and OSCE's efforts, many States are still reluctant to take their citizens back. In the meantime, the camps' poor conditions push many women back to the radical ideology, since they are disillusioned with the idea that their home countries will repatriate them. Meanwhile, the Al-Hawl and Roj camps have become dangerous environments for incubating future generations of terrorist groups, and as more time passes, the more this danger rises.

RADICALIZATION AND HARD-LINERS AMONG WOMEN

The situation inside the two camps is volatile. The young woman from Kyrgyzstan currently living in the Al-Hawl camp told me via WhatsApp that she is afraid for her security. "There are very aggressive women in the camp who are still associated with ISIS. They shout 'Dawliyat Bakiya' every day, which means 'ISIS is forever.'" "They watch us, and if they suspect that you are no longer loyal to ISIS ideology, they will come and punish you," she told me. She stressed that these aggressive women had already burned the tents of several women who contradicted them. According to residents of the Al-Hawl camp, the Kurdish guards carry small electric shock devices and sometimes shoot in the air to calm down this kind of aggression, but not always do they manage to prevent it. "At the very least, I know exactly that this mafia burned tents of two women to punish them for not wearing their veil," she told me.

Radicalization is present in these two camps, especially in Al-Hawl. During the interviews, women in the camp told me that some women go from tent to tent to invite them to group conversations. These women urge other women not to abandon the ISIS ideology, declaring that a new caliph will come to free them. These women have never dreamed of repatriation while other disillusioned ones think of it every minute. "They invited me several times to join their gatherings. I know it; they will brainwash me and insist that I stay here with ISIS. I did not tell them that I did not want this. If they find out that I am disillusioned, they will come after me. So I kindly explained that my child was sick and very small. So they are hoping that I will join them later. But I do not want to be brainwashed again; I want to go home and to be normal," a woman from Azerbaijan told me during the interview conducted via Telegram. She is hoping her country will repatriate her.

The situation in the Al-Hawl camp is indeed tense. The SDF guards stated to the Independent that some women in the camp were learning how to build mines. Kurdish forces also discovered a short, but deep tunnel in the camp heading towards the fence.[33] This suggests that some women in the camp may plan to escape and are seeking ways to do so. Radical women, who refer to themselves as the morality police of ISIS, are enforcing sharia law in the Al-Hawl camp, and have burnt the tents, beaten other women and carried out brutal killings of other residents of those who refuse to follow their ideology. At least ten women have been killed, including a fourteen-year-old Azerbaijani girl who was strangled to death for not covering her face. The SDF warns of an increase of radicalization in the camps and children are being raised there in accordance with the radical ideology of ISIS. "This means that a future generation of terrorists are being held here, which will pose a threat to the Middle East as well as the international community," the SDF representative stated.[34]

The longer they stay in camps, the higher radicalization will mount. Women who remained loyal to the ISIS ideology formed cells inside camps, and those who lost their hope of being repatriated have started to rejoin them. This militant band of women is led by women from Egypt, Morocco, and Tunisia, but some European women appear highly radicalized. I interviewed women who told me that European women sometimes chanted to return their men, saying their previous life in ISIS was better.[35] Women that stayed until the last ISIS-occupied city of Baghouse were particularly loyal to ISIS and did not wish to leave until the last moment. One of the women I interviewed told me that she cried while heading to the Kurdish camps. She explained that she cried from the pain of being defeated. "My whole life was collapsed. Our dawla (meaning *a state*) collapsed, and I was hurt thinking it did not exist; we were defeated. When we arrived, I was shocked to see the huge camp full of people. They knew that there would be refugees and prepared everything to welcome us," she told me during the interview conducted via WhatsApp. After living for thirteen months in the camp, she feels better, but she is unsure about returning to her home country. "I do not want to spend my whole life in prison. I would prefer to receive asylum in a third country," she told me.[36]

The Syrian Democratic Forces also warns about the danger of the camps saying the temporary facilities constitute a ticking bomb for international peace. Mr. Bedran Ciya Kurd, the representative of the SDF in Hasaka province of Syria, expressed the following view during our interview:

> There are large numbers of radical ISIS women in camps. The children in these camps are raised according to the radical ideology of ISIS, which means a future generation of terrorists that will pose a threat to us as well as the international community. Therefore, the international community should assume its responsibility by building fortified prisons with modern technology, helping us to separate the radical women from the less radical ones, and opening rehabilitation centers for women, schools for children, and recreational facilities until a solution is found to this big problem, which needs to be addressed in coordination with the international community.[37]

The Kurdish forces face daily challenges to guard camps and maintain security. Sometimes guards are attacked by aggressive women. Dozens Kurdish soldiers were stabbed by women in the foreigner sections of Al-Hawl. The SDF representative stated in our interview:

> The situation in Al-Hawl camp is tough, especially in the section of the foreign ISIS families. The radical women are still implementing Al-Hissba laws (a set of harsh laws implemented by ISIS police during ISIS reign) that resulted in summary executions and burning of tents. In addition, attempts to escape the camp happen daily, some of which succeed due to the weak fortifications and monitoring techniques and the limited number of guards compared to the large area of the camp.

Women brutally attack both security guards and residents of the camp. Researchers reported how the male security officer, taking ISIS women to the market in Camp Hawl, was stabbed in the back by one of the extremist ISIS wives.[38] The women who attacked, shouted that they had no fear of bullets. Some women refused to be repatriated or hid when their government retrieved them. According to the research conducted by the International Center for the Study of Violent Extremism (CSVE), when Kazakhstan's delegation arrived in Al-Hawl to repatriate its citizens, four Kazakh families hid and refused the offer to be sent home. The camp administration of Al-Hawl confirmed how these Kazakh families hid to escape repatriation. "They are the most radical families. They are waiting for Baghdadi. It is not a camp anymore; it is an academy for the youth. They recruit here," said the camp official working in Al-Hawl to CSVE researchers.[39]

The longer women stay in camps, the more they will be radicalized due to the pressure from radicals and dire conditions. Furthermore, women are afraid to behave differently and do not dare to remove niqabs and veils. ISIS ideology looms over the camps, and some hardliners control their behavior. Some women told me they are afraid to share their feelings with other women because there is too much espionage. "I trust nobody here. I am afraid that tomorrow everyone will know about my feeling or plans. I sit and cry at night. I talk to Allah and ask him to help. Only Allah's mercy will save me. I trust nobody. Neither my government nor United Nations will save me; please do not talk about their efforts. We are traitors for them," expressed a woman who does not wish to indicate her country and name.

FOOD SUPPLY, MALNUTRITION AND CROWDFUNDING

Women living in two camps receive a monthly box containing food, but it is not enough. "In the box, there is 1 liter of oil to cook, lentils, sugar, and rice. We never eat meat or eggs. Children want to eat chocolates or something sweet. So the box that we receive per month is just to keep us alive, so we do not die from starvation," a Russian woman told me. More positively, families receive baked bread from the distribution center each day and sometimes even cooked meals. However, it is not enough. Thus women in camps try to earn money. There is a bazaar in the territory of the camps where women sell their handmade cookies and cakes. Young boys make money by fixing tents or digging ditches around camps to prevent rain floods. Several women organize classes for children in Math, Russian Alphabet, and Quran reading. Women informed me that they pay 1 dollar for each class. Women who have the time and capacity try to earn as much money as possible.

Women living in the camps generally have about three to five children each, with a minimum of two children. The whole day they cook and take care of their children. Women use two types of stoves: one to cook and one to heat tents in the wintertime. Several women I interviewed preferred to speak at night, as they did not sleep during the cold nights of winter. "I am afraid of fire," said one of them. "I have to keep an eye on the stove, which works with kerosene. Moreover, there is a possibility of explosion due to overexertion. I cannot switch it off; otherwise, my children will freeze. So the stove works through the night, and I keep an eye on it," she told me. There were several fires in Al-Hawl involving exploding stoves at night where sleeping children died. In April 2020, there was a tragedy in the Roj camp. The cooking stove exploded, killing one woman and injuring two others. After such tragic accidents, some women stopped sleeping at night. Women receive ten liters of kerosene from the Kurdish forces, hardly enough for two days, after which women buy fuel in the bazaar of the camp.

Women I spoke with expressed constant hunger in the camp. One woman from Azerbaijan told me:

> Kurds give us rice, lentils, bread, and canned food. They all are very bad quality. We miss a lot eating meat, vegetables, and fruits. Sometimes we buy them in the market here, but prices are much higher than in Syria. We try to earn money to buy vegetables or chocolates for children. I make cakes to sell, but Kurds permit us to use the cooking stove that works with gas for only three hours per day.

Many women in the camps found the means to earn money before self-isolation due to the coronavirus. They cleaned the houses of wealthy Iraqi families or sold their homemade cookies and hamburgers. It seems that Iraqis and Syrians in camps have better living conditions and hire foreigners to clean, bring water and wash dishes.

Cooking at home and selling handmade food in a bazaar also become risky. On 13 May 2019, several families contracted a food borne illness from homemade hamburgers in the camp Roj. Four little girls had a high temperature and were brought to the hospital in Hasakah. After this incident, the Kurdish forces imposed an official ban on private cooking and selling in the territory of Roj. However, food poisoning and diarrhea are widespread in two camps and are not only caused by homemade hamburgers. Some women told me that the food distributed by the Kurdish forces would sometimes contain worms, and the precooked food they distribute provokes diarrhea among children and swollen bellies. One woman whom I interviewed was confident the food had some toxic components. She told me that as soon as her son eats the distributed meal by the camp administration, he falls sick.

Another Kyrgyz woman I interviewed told me that she is afraid to die of a heart attack.

> I cannot sleep at night; the whole night, I think about my future and how I will look in the eyes of my parents. I left for Syria without telling them. I know that my mother is crying a lot because of me. She had a serious problem with her heart, and further, I added more sorrow to her soul. I do not know if I can hold out any longer or not live here. I want to escape from here, but there are mines around camps. I do not want to die now when I am very close to returning to my country.

She stressed that they need more food, especially meat and vegetables. "When Uzbekistan repatriated their citizens, Uzbek women left some food for us. My children and I were lucky to have more food for a month," said the Kyrgyz woman in Al-Hawl.

However, several months later women in Al-Hawl and Roj camps have mastered crowd funding through the Internet. They opened digital banking through QIWI, Yandex, Bitcoin and Webmoney. Every month they receive financial assistance worldwide and distribute them among habitants of the two camps. I have observed Telegram channels created by Russian speaking women in Al-Hawl. They publish monthly photos reporting how the money was distributed. They post photos of women and children who received the aid closing their faces. On 9 February 2021, they posted photos saying that forty families in Al-Hawl each received 50 USD. On 15 November 2021, they reported that 237 families received each 50 USD. On 21 December 2021, they reported that 140 families in Al-Hawl each received 50 USD. This kind of crowdfunding through online platforms is almost systematic. Sometimes they announce crowd funding for sick children or women. They also instruct people how to send money securely, explaining from which country should be used Bitcoin or QIWI.

VOICES OF WOMEN IN THE CAMPS: WE ARE DYING HERE

I have contacted women in both camps conducting interviews for an extended period. The interviews were conducted for a period of fifteen months in total in 2020 and 2021. Women were stressed whenever a new season approached. The weather conditions in northeastern Syria are harsh. After being blackened and burned by hot weather in the summer, women were usually afraid of winter approaching. Their tents are not adapted to the winter conditions. In February 2020, women were shocked by the heavy snow covering their tents. Many were freezing and were surprised by the snow, which rarely falls in Syria. They sent me videos and photos of extensive snow in the territory of the camps. While their mothers were worried about the freezing weather and tried to push out snow from their tents, children started playing in the snow. Some who had never seen the snow or might have been missing it were pleased. They began building snowmen and sliding through snowed ice, laughing and having fun. Women told me that their children found optimism in such a surprise of the frosty weather despite the freezing tents. I saw children playing and enjoying the snow in a just-recorded video by women in the camp. Women smiled and observed their children, but later joined them and started playing in the snow.

It is indeed tough to withstand weather cataclysms in the desert. Most of the time, tents fall from the pools of water or are destroyed by heavy winds. Of course, many women in Roj and Al-Hawl dream of sleeping in regular houses with walls. "Every night, I think what a happiness it would be to fall asleep in a normal house. Before, I wanted to live in a big city and a nice apartment, but now I would love to live in a small house in any village in my country and be happy. Living in a tent here, you realize how important it is to have walls and roof over your head," the Kyrgyz woman in Al-Hawl told me. She stressed that her tent is very old, having been used by six other families before her. She bought it simply because she lacked the financial means to purchase a new one. "In winter, when I cook, and we start eating, the meal starts freezing immediately. In the summertime, it is always 40–50 Celsius hot here and feels like sitting in a frying pan," she told me.

In mid-April 2020, the Russian woman in camp Roj sent me some pictures of her children. His son was playing by sculpting tents, arms and tanks with mud. "He was born in Syria and had no idea that people could live in normal houses. He just has never seen them. Since his birth, we have lived in ruins and have always been running from one place to another to flee the fighting," she told me. She is determined to leave Syria to live in a third country. She wants her children to become ordinary citizens with a peaceful life. "I need to educate my children. Without education, they will be lost in this world. What I understood here is that only education will give them more stability and respect," she told me. Her two sons are intensively learning Math, Russian Alphabet, and Quran reading. A woman in the camp organizes private classes for children in her tent. She pays 300 Syrian lyres per hour for each subject. She told me that the teacher organizes separate courses for girls and boys. In each group, there are about seven or eight children.

Another Russian woman dreams of returning to Russia and living with her grandmother, who is serving time for financing terrorism in Russia. "My grandmother sent me some money so I could return home with this money. I received it but could not find a way to escape ISIS territory. Nevertheless, the local law enforcement agencies in Russia decided that sending money to her granddaughter is financing terrorism. She is very old and now in prison because of me." Her grandmother, who unconditionally loved her granddaughter, sent her last savings hoping that it would save her life and she could finally return to Russia. However, her decision was fatal. The Russian authorities arrested and charged her with financing terrorism. However, she could not escape ISIS after receiving the money as her grandmother had hoped. She bought a television for her children, who now watch cartoons in the camp. They are lucky to be in Roj rather than Al-Hawl, which allows them to have electricity and live in better conditions.

She says:

> I talk a lot about my grandmother to my children. I tell them that we will live with her in the future and both sons will have bicycles. Our grandmother will cook for us delicious food that we have never eaten here in Syria. She is the best mother in the world who was ready for everything to save her granddaughter. I want to be with her for the rest of my life and take care of her. I want my children to love her as much as I love her.

This woman lived in Roj and said that they are lucky to be in this camp living in better conditions. Their tent is sturdier, and they have a concrete floor, but there is nothing to entertain or educate the children. "My children play with other children around. They play only war games: they capture each other and imprison them. They make guns from wood and shoot each other. They pretend that planes are flying and going to bomb; they hide. They have never seen other things in their whole life, so they imitate what they had seen here in Syria in their games," she told me.

In the Al-Hawl camp, some orphan children live alone in their tents with neighboring women, who keep an eye on them. Recently, a woman passed away, and her two small children were left without parental care. Women in the neighboring tents consulted one another, and one of them took them to her tent under her care. Some siblings live alone. Four children from Azerbaijan, whose parents died in Syria, live in their tent alone in Roj. Their uncle, who is currently in Baku, frequently calls them. He is in contact with a Russian woman who agreed to take care of them. "My sister died in Syria, and now I am fighting to bring back her children. I will take care of them. My sister was not radicalized. We had a tough childhood, and later she also had a difficult life. Now I analyze and understand that she just wanted to change her life, to escape the grievances and trauma she had," he told me. His sister found a little boy in ruins in Mosul and adopted him. She named him after his uncle. During the interview conducted via WhatsApp, the Azerbaijani man told me the following. He did not wish his name to be publicized.

> She named him after my name, and he is now five years old. I want to adopt him too. Now the four siblings are living alone. Before, they were living in

> dire conditions, but we reached out to the Red Cross and managed to involve them. The oldest of my cousins is only twelve years old, and she takes care of everything. She is very serious and understands everything. She saw war and now takes responsibility for her brother and sisters. I am very thankful to women who live in neighboring tents. They manage their situation every day to see if they have food and if they are not sick. If there is something [of concern], they tell me immediately.

I contacted him in ten months, and he still was hoping to bring the children back. However, Azerbaijan has not made any positive steps toward repatriation of children and women.

I interviewed seven women living in Al-Hawl who were citizens of Kyrgyzstan. All of them wanted to return to Kyrgyzstan and were waiting for repatriation. After the repatriation of Kazakh women, they hoped that their country would do the same. Their parents united and advocated for their repatriation by giving press conferences and protesting near the White House in Bishkek. Kyrgyz women in Al-Hawl told me that they are afraid of their security in the camp, as their tents might be burned down or be beaten by violent and radical women. "Kurdish forces can free us for money. They have already freed some people who paid them. It is about ten thousand dollars. However, my parents do not have such bigh money. But of course, I want to be repatriated by our government, so everything is state-organized. Uzbekistan did not charge women; hence, all of them are free. I would be grateful also if our country did the same. I did nothing wrong here. I stayed at home and took care of my three children," the Kyrgyz woman told me.

In general, women in the camps have no access to Internet and using mobile phones is forbidden. The Kurdish forces frequently check the tents to find forbidden stuff, including phones. But women manage to hide their phones and connect to the Internet at night. They call their relatives in their home countries, while waiting for hours. There is a long queue to use a phone. But the most striking thing is that there are women who master social media. They created Telegram channels and actively post on them on different issues including Umma, infidels and Muslim community. Many posts are about their life in the camp. "Finally, today we received the kerosene. It is almost three years Kaffirs (meaning humanitarian organizations—author) providing us with kerosene without interruption" posted the administrator in Telegram. Another post was about ice. "Finally, the car brought ice to the camp. It is very hot in the desert and impossible to live without ice. We need to put ice into water otherwise it gets hot and impossible to drink." In this post, women call international organizations as kaffirs. They still live in with rejectionist mindset and call humanitarian organization as infidel. One can read frequently such posts based on religious mutated concept on their Telegram channels.

Among other festive dates, they celebrate only Ramadan. I have noticed also majority of them even do not celebrate birthdays of children. Each Ramadan they posted photos. On 20 July 2021, they published photos from the celebration of Ramadan. They posted that twenty-three sheep were bought and their meat distributed among families. Children received toys and sweets.

THE DIARY OF SABINA: WHAT IS IT LIKE TO BE A FUGITIVE?

I spoke with Sabina (a pseudonym), who lives in the Roj camp with her five children, for several days through WhatsApp. She answered my questions whenever she had free time, usually in the evenings. She speaks Russian and Arabic. Sabina was usually very busy cooking and taking care of her five small children; thus, our conversation lasted several days. In contrast to the other women, she reached out to me herself, as she wanted to tell me about her life. She is from Russia, married to a Dagestani man. Her story started in Egypt, where her husband was studying. She got married when she was seventeen. Her parents forced her to marry him because he was religious and believed to be trustworthy and good. Her husband's social circle, including his mother and siblings, truly believed that Muslims should travel to Syria and save Muslims there from infidels. So, they travelled from Egypt to Syria with their two babies. She told me that she would never return to her life in Syria. "I saw death and famine. When we suffered, I was hoping that the man behind the idea of the caliphate was dead. I hoped. Because it could be unjust that he is still alive," she told me. It appeared that Sabina wrote a diary while living in the camp. She sent me twenty pages of her diary through WhatsApp. She writes in Russian her innermost thoughts, some of which are piercing. She offered her permission to share some moments of her diary. In her sentences, one sees how she struggles to find answers with endless thoughts about her future. At the same time, her trauma is deep, and she does not know how to address it. Indeed, she feels lonely with nobody nearby to help her. She wants to change her life, but does not know how. While she was recording her answer on her telephone, I could hear how she shouted at her children. She used to shout very hard. I could feel how she was tired and psychologically exhausted. She was living in her small tent with her five children. They were small. The little one is almost two years old, and the oldest is seven years old. She told me she wanted to escape her children and hide somewhere not to see them. Her diary will talk for her and tell you more about her feelings.

> 09.04.2020. It is not easy to be someone who does not care about what is happening around you. It is a fight with myself. I am tired of swallowing grudges

and smiling. Then pretend that you do not care about what other people have said to you while sitting in loneliness and realizing that you are completely alone and hiding the pain you have in your soul. Every evening of this month, I understand that I am completely alone. They smile, they show me that they are glad, but when they gather together in the evenings - they do not invite me. I am not a burden. I am not a parasite. But I need communication with people of the same color as me. Nevertheless, flowers with a color that would bloom from the same seedling as me do not exist yet.

16.12.2019. The weather is becoming overcast and dull. With the changes of this weather, my soul is turning to hell. Days are passing unnoticed. Yesterday was Friday, and I just looked around, and again it is Friday. As if I am lost in a time machine. My whole life turned upside down. Where are my feelings, my goals, and my inspirations? I just exist. I sleep, get up, move around and sit. One day replaces another day. People walk around back and forth. My children seem to be living on their own. I feel as if I have not given birth to them. Where is that woman who loved her children? Where is that woman who took care of and cherished her children? Where am I stuck?

20.12.2019. I sleep because I need to forget my life in the camp.

24.02.2020. Each person has their transition point, which is their grave. Not everyone will find peace in it. Their grave will be an ambush for some people who do not follow Islam. Our religion is a compass that should be followed carefully. For those who did not look at the compass and did not follow instructions given to travelers and who led a frivolous life, their grave will be an ambush that will lead to prison. Nevertheless, those who carefully followed the compass will return to their permanent home, where they will rest and enjoy life. Their grave will be like a five-star hotel with all conditions where they can take a break. Take care of yourself! Never close the compass or even put it in your pocket. Otherwise, you will be lost.

15.03.2020. The longer I live here, the more I understand how worthless and insignificant life has become here. I am no longer surprised by even the most astonishing things. Life has become gloomy and dark. Relations among people are always tense without trust in each other. You try to love people, but reality makes you hesitate and doubt. Life is just fleeting by, and you do not notice. You meet people, you want to trust and rely on, and you want to think that you feel more confident with them because they will support you. But you just turn and hear from your back how they laugh at you and start whispering. They smile, look around and throw stealthy looks at you. And you are confused again. What to do? Whom can this explain to me? Nobody. Because again, I am talking to myself. I frequently find myself to be the only companion to talk to. It is ridiculous! And again, I am entering to myself. I am living but no longer here!

14.04.2020. I am lost in an Islamic State space and falling into the abyss. And it is dark here. But I see glimpses of light far away from me. I know that not everything has been lost. I will stand up; I will get out. However, I regret the time I have spent here for nothing. Inshallah, I need to return to my Sunni and Sharia. I need to take care of my children and myself. But it is so hard. It is easy to fall down but hard to get up. Easy to fall asleep, but hard to wake up. I always do something first, then rethink and analyze what I did. Why? Why do I start thinking when it is too late to change something? But it is me! I am crazy and loony! I am sick. If I remain alone, I am going crazy.

20.04.2020. Every day I think about what I experienced here in Syria. My thoughts throttle me. All my ambitions have come to an end. All my dreams were crushed. Is there enough eloquence to tell you what I have been through? Can I catch the rhythm of the soul to sing about how I feel? No, it is too beautiful and telling. It is too painful and too joyful. Should I tell you about the laughter hiding the pain or about tears that showed happiness? What exactly should I tell you? Where do I start?

18.03.2020. Life for me is like tea. If you do not add sugar, tea is not tasty. It is hard to swallow, and there is no joy from it. It is impossible to drink if you add too much sugar and become unhealthy. That is why you have to add sugar to your life in moderation to the best of your taste, and so it cannot harm your health and well-being.

15.02.2020. Usually, at night while everyone is sleeping, I do not sleep. I am lying and dreaming. Sometimes dreams take me far away. Sometimes a whole life passes before my eyes. I unwittingly cry, laugh, smile, get angry and relax. Dreams give you strength and hope. But do not forget that dreams do not come true because they are far from reality. Dreams and hope are two different things. If you do not make an effort to realize your dreams, it means you are wasting time. But hope always stays with you. Even if you die, you will have hope. Living in this camp, I realized that I should hope more for Allah's mercy and spend less time on dreams. After all, I still have so many tasks unrealized. For example, I used to dream about learning Turkish somehow in the future, and now I have started to realize this dream, and I will soon succeed. Inshallah.

26.04.2020. Even in Baghouse, when I was sitting in the two square meter cell, I felt free. I was free. Here in the camp, even though there is vivid life going around, the mesh of the camp is pressing me. It is crushing my soul and psyche. I want freedom. I am dying here among my memories. Even those years of life when I saw blood and death seemed better because I had freedom. Nobody controlled me, and I was not afraid of anyone. I need to stop thinking seriously; otherwise, I am close to becoming mad.

29.04. 2020. I sleep not because my body needs to rest. I sleep to forget what is going on around me. I sleep not to see faces around and to hear their problems. Please wake me when my time comes. I sleep because I want to oversleep my depression. I sleep to oversleep this interval of my life and wake up when it is over. Wake me up when my spring is here.

30.04.2020. I am tired of tents. When I was jailed, I was pleased. I said, "Finally, I have walls." Walls can protect you from the sun that burns you, from heavy wind, rain, and the cold. Living among walls, you feel protected. But when you live in a tent, you are so vulnerable. You are not protected. Even a small blade can ruin it. But I hope to Allah's mercy. Everything in this life is temporary, and I hope these days will pass. I believe that after suffering, next comes relief. If I continue like this, suicide is not far.

17.04.2020. Maybe we will return home exhausted after this long journey, and finally, in that home, our body, heart, and mind will be reunited. In this difficult journey, there is a compass. This compass should lead and bring us to our home. Our home is our religion. Sometimes that compass can appear false, but sometimes it is real. A real compass will bring us to our religion. But sometimes, even a real compass is unable to bring us home. Because people do not know how to follow it. It is a huge mistake if you think having the compass in your pocket is enough. A compass can be possessed by both the poor and rich, but only a select few will know how to follow the compass, and only they will reach their home.

26.01.2020. The more I think about my life, the more I am afraid of my thoughts.

18.03.2020. I close my eyes, and I see his silhouette. I cannot forget him no matter how much I try. I thought I would easily forget him because of how he offended me. But my heart has already forgiven him. I miss him a lot. I could not say too many words to him. I could not do for him too many things. I miss him. I do not need other men. Yes, I want to be alone. I could even say that I feel sick of men. I want to live on an uninhabited island. I also want to go to Korea; I do not know why. I do not know the true reason, but I want to see it. My soul is saying that I need to go to Korea.

30.03.2020. I want to grow up eventually. I want to be a mother caring for and loving her children. I want to hug them and kiss them. I want to protect them. But when I sit at home next to them, things change. I want to escape. I am tired of them mentally and physically. I am broken. I am lost in myself. I need to find myself. I try to hold on to it when I find something in myself. Not always, it turns out. I cannot keep it, and it escapes from my hands. I tell myself, if you want to become the same person, then be better. Why have you lowered your hands? Why have you thrown yourself into the abyss? I feel myself to be such a doily or doormat without will or purpose. My goals change every day. My days are also the same as my mood; that changes every minute. I am telling myself I am strong; I can. But truthfully, I cannot even change a small part of myself.

17.05.2020. Do you know what it is like to live the life of a fugitive? It is a life where you must turn to see that nobody is chasing you. Our life is full of fear. When I was in ISIS territory, I had to turn around to see if death was coming to me. Now I have to watch over my shoulder to see if people want to hurt me. People around me want me to go astray. They want me to be broken. But I just want to have a normal life. I want to have walls and windows. I want to have a door that can be locked. I want a kitchen with a dining table. I want an ordinary stove to cook without fear that it can explode at any moment. I want a wardrobe with beautiful dresses. I want a separate room for children to play in without disturbing me. I want a table for children where they can do their homework. I am very tired of living in a tent where you cannot even hide from the heat of the sun.

12.09.2019. A person might have several homes. One home where the person finds education and knowledge, one home where their body is, and one home where their heart is. And you do not know which one is your real home. Once you have left that home, you do not realize if that was your true home. You struggle to return there, but the road has grown and become difficult. It is hard to find the right way to reach it. Sometimes you find the right road but do not recognize it. We do not know if we will return to our real home. Maybe we will be jailed and sentenced to death. Then there will be endless suffering as we will be tortured but not die.

Sabina's diary says a lot about her life. She takes the radical ideology as a compass that should be followed carefully. At the same time, she struggles to manage her loneliness and psychological problems. Even though she wants her children to live a normal life, she told me that she wishes to live in a caliphate. While she admits that the Islamic state was a mistake and a total failure in her diary, she still dreams about a caliphate. "I want all Muslims to live in their state. Secular states always pressure us, and there is no justice for us. But I do not want to have ISIS again. They betrayed us," she told me. She informed me that she would continue writing in her diary. She believes that she has a talent with a pen and likes to call herself a writer. She wants to return to a normal life and publish a book in the future about her life in the Middle East. Sabina believes that the Middle East, to which she refers to as the land of Sham, is a blessed land. "I wanted to live in Sham because it is a land Allah blessed. There is hadith about Sham in Islam, so it has its miracles. For example, some women had been told by doctors that they would never have children. They arrived in Syria and became pregnant," said Sabina.

She and her husband entered Syria with their close relatives: her mother-in-law, sister, brother, and her husband's uncle—all of them with their families. In total, the group numbered about thirty people, including children. In the beginning, they lived in Um-Haratan.

> We, three families, lived together in a big house. The house belonged to a rich family who fled due to the war. So there was everything inside. We even had a big pool in the house yard. We had everything and enjoyed life. I even learned how to swim for the first time in my life. At that time, I thought we would be living like that; I never thought we would see death and violence.

Now she is alone in the camp with her children. Both her husband and mother-in-law were killed in Baghouse. She does not know the whereabouts of some of her relatives, except that her other sister is in the Al-Hawl camp. She does not want to return to her country. She dreams of travelling. She told me that she might prefer to travel across the world. "I do not know why but I want to go to Korea; my soul is calling for it," she told me.

Speaking with women in camps Al–Hawl and Roj extended mixed feelings of compassion and fear about the capacity of states to manage their return. I felt a danger because some of them still stay loyal to the ISIS ideology. Some women seem completely incapable to take control over their destinies and unable to think and understand how far the situation is serious. They still do not realize outcomes of their decision to go to the Middle East. However, some of them provided the impression that they could reintegrate and return to their normal lives. These women understand that they made a critical mistake by going to Syria and never intended to cause harm. They merely sought a better life. It was heartbreaking to see how they await repatriation and hope their government eventually retrieves them, as Kazakhstan and Uzbekistan did. Some women are afraid to return to their home countries and hope to be tried in third countries. Others wish to stay in the Middle East. To sum up, the contingent in the camps is manifold and varicolored. It is impossible to generalize as each woman has her own story, which is very different. But their children are the most vulnerable group that demands immediate and urgent action.

CONCLUSIONS

Almost three years have passed since ISIS was defeated and I started conducting interviews with women who live in Al-Hawl and Roj camps. They are spending their third or fourth winter in the desert. They might be dangerous; they might be naïve and brainwashed. But they are all products of our society, and we need to deal with them. States should take responsibility for their citizens. Their further actions will depend on how we will treat them.

Speaking with women in camps Al–Hawl and Roj extended mixed feelings of compassion and fear about the capacity of states to manage their return. I felt a danger because some of them still stay loyal to the ISIS ideology. They are a ticking time bomb for international peace. The more days spent together in these two camps, the more they become angry and radical. Women in Al-hawl call their sons "our lions" and frequently write in their Telegram channel, "our lions are growing up and will restore our dignity." Women in camps are active on the internet and use social media. They urge Muslim men worldwide to free them from captivity and fight for the future of a caliphate. Indeed, the current situation is about future peace. If the international community fails to manage this situation efficiently, the future generation of terrorists will grow out of these camps.

NOTES

1. Bethan McKernan, "At Least 750 Isis Affiliates Escape Syria Camp After Turkish Shelling," *The Guardian,* October 13, 2019. https://www.theguardian.com/world/2019/oct/13/kurds-say-785-isis-affiliates-have-escaped-camp-after-turkish-shelling.
2. International Rescue Committee, "Al Hol Camp At 'Breaking Point' As Another 12,000 Women and Children Arrive In Just 48 Hours," Press Release, March 8, 2019, https://www.rescue.org/press-release/al-hol-camp-breaking-point-another-12000-women-and-children-arrive-just-48-hours.
3. International Rescue Committee, "Al Hol Camp at 'Breaking Point.'"
4. International Rescue Committee, "Al Hol Camp at 'Breaking Point.'" *The New Yorker*, April 4, 2019, https://www.newyorker.com/news/dispatch/how-trump-betrayed-the-general-who-defeated-isis.
5. Bedran Ciya Kurd, interview by the author in April 2020.
6. Jane Arraf, "Visiting Imprisoned ISIS Fighters" *NPR*, December 8, 2019. https://www.npr.org/2019/12/08/786039731/visiting-imprisoned-isis-fighters.
7. Bedran Ciya Kurd, interview by the author on 12 April 2020.
8. The interview with the official from the Ministry of Foreign Affairs of Turkey was conducted by the author. He asked to remain anonymous.
9. Arraf, "Visiting Imprisoned ISIS Fighters."
10. Interview with Bedran Ciya Kurd was conducted by the author, ibid.
11. Bedran Ciya Kurd, interview.
12. Richard Hall, "British ISIS Prisoners May End Up in Iraq, Where Death Sentences are Handed Down Without Due Process," *The Independent,* February 2020. https://www.independent.co.uk/news/world/middle-east/isis-iraq-international-law-prisoner-deaths-trial-a9311556.html.
13. Fionnuala Ní Aoliáin, interview by the author on 12 April 2020.
14. The interview with the official from Ministry of Foreign Affairs of Turkey was conducted by the author. The official preferred to remain anonymous.

15. Nadim Houry, "The 'Unreturned': Dealing with the Foreign Fighters and Their Families Who Remain in Syria and Iraq," quoted in *Militant Jihadism: Today and Tomorrow*, by Pektas Serafettin and Leman Johan, (Leuven (Belgium): Leuven University Press, 2019), 67.

16. Also known as the principle of *non-refoulement* in international human rights law.

17. UN Security Council, "Tenth Report on the Threat Posed by ISIL."

18. Residents of the camps in northeast Syria, interviews by the author via Telegram and WhatsApp in March 2020.

19. Aaron Y. Zelin, "Wilayat Al-Hawl: Remaining and Incubating the Next Islamic State Generation," *The Washington Institute for Near East Policy*, October 2019, https://www.washingtoninstitute.org/uploads/Documents/pubs/PolicyNote70-Zelin.pdf.

20. Bedran Ciya Kurd, interview by the author in April 2020.

21. United Nations Office for the Coordination of Humanitarian Affairs (UN OCHA), "Syria: Humanitarian Response in Al Hol Camp, Situation Report No. 5—As of 5 July 2019," July 6, 2019. https://reliefweb.int/report/syrian-arab-republic/syria-humanitarian-response-al-hol-camp-situation-report-no-5-5-july.

22. UN OCHA, "Syria: Humanitarian Response in Al Hol Camp."

23. Human Rights Watch, "Syria: Dire Conditions for ISIS Suspects' Families," July 23 2019. https://www.hrw.org/news/2019/07/23/syria-dire-conditions-isis-suspects-families.

24. Human Rights Watch , "Syria: Dire Conditions for ISIS Suspects' Families."

25. Syria: Dire Conditions for ISIS Suspects' Families, *Human Rights Watch*, 23 July 2019.

26. The interview was conducted in Russian by the author in March 2020.

27. "Women and Children First," International Crisis Group.

28. Anne Speckhard and Ardian Shajkovci, "Waiting for the Return of the Islamic State Caliphate among ISIS Enforcers in Syria's al Hol, Ain Issa and Roj Camps," *International Center for the Study of Violent Extremism*, September 3, 2019. https://www.icsve.org/waiting-for-the-return-of-the-islamic-state-caliphate-among-isis-enforcers-in-al-hol-ain-issa-and-roj-camps-in-syria/.

29. UN Security Council, "Tenth report of the Secretary-General on the Threat Posed by ISIL (Da'esh) to International Peace and Security and the Range of United Nations Efforts in Support of Member States in Countering the Threat," Counter-Terrorism Committee, March 4, 2020, S/2020/95. https://undocs.org/S/2020/95.

30. International Crisis Group, "Women and Children First: Repatriating the Westerns Affiliated with ISIS," *ICC Middle East & North Africa*, November 18, 2019, https://www.crisisgroup.org/middle-east-north-africa/eastern-mediterranean/syria/208-women-and-children-first-repatriating-westerners-affiliated-isis.

31. UN Security Council, "Tenth Report on the Threat Posed by ISIL" & "Women and Children First," International Crisis Group.

32. UN Security Council, "Tenth Report on the Threat Posed by ISIL."

33. Richard Hall, "Tunnels, knives and riots: This Syrian camp holding thousands of Isis wives is at breaking point," *The Independent*, 9 December 2019.

34. Bedran Ciya Kurd, interview.

35. Euronews, "European Children of ISIS, Special program of Euronews," available at http://prevention.kg/?p=5053.

36. She lives in the Al-Hawl camp and preferred to remain anonymous.

37. Representative of the SDF, interview by the author in April 2020.

38. Speckhard and Shajkovci, "Waiting for the Return of the Islamic State Caliphate among ISIS Enforcers."

39. Speckhard and Shajkovci, "Waiting for the Return of the Islamic State Caliphate among ISIS Enforcers."

Chapter 5

Women's Roles in ISIS and Gender-Based Assumptions

Women in terrorism is not a new phenomenon. Throughout history, women have been involved in terrorist groups both actively and passively. In general, as Cragin and Daly (2009) posit, "twenty-two different terrorist and insurgent groups incorporated women into their day-to-day activities as well as political and military leadership structures."[1] They examine women's roles in terrorist organizations such as Hamas, Hezbollah, Chechen separatists, LTTE, Red Brigades, Al-Qaeda, PKK, and Palestinian Islamic Jihad. However, ISIS had reached the exceptional level of recruiting women and making them travel to the Middle East to live under the caliphate. As a UN report highlights, ISIS's success in recruiting women has been remarkable in several ways, including the geographical diversity of the women and the highest unprecedented number of women and children recruited. As UN researchers state, the world faces new policy challenges that "have emerged as a result of this unprecedented level of mobilization."[2] Bringing women and children to the Middle East was an important and salient feature of ISIS and other terrorist groups.

Since ISIS had a global appeal that aimed to challenge the existing political order, it needed to create an image of an authentic Islamic state. Women and children were necessary for its state-building project. However, women were not only a demonstration of that image but an important actor playing a significant role within the caliphate. First, it was a political appeal to the rest of the world that meant that the Islamic State was real, and it started having a real shape by having inhabitants including women and children. Second, the fact that entire families were arriving and joining was a demonstration of the power of ISIS, which attracted thousands of women and young girls across the world. Women have become a political tool to recruit more people. As Lahoud (2014) highlighted, even when women got arrested, they did not stop contributing to jihadist ideology. "The jihadis use women's imprisonment as a recruiting tool to highlight Muslim men's lost honor and awaken feelings of chivalry in their psyche by calling on them to join the jihad."[3] There is a tendency in scholarly literature and media coverage to minimize women's roles in jihadism. However, the fact that women did not fight on the battlefield alongside male fighters should not undermine their role in ISIS and terrorism in general. First, women gave political power to ISIS for its state-building project by creating an image of a whole society with women and children. As Cragin and Daly rightly suggested, women had been rarely called political vanguards of terrorist organizations in history by being appointed to leadership roles. However, there are examples where women have become operational leaders and guerrilla fighters throughout history.[4] Even though ISIS had a distinct patriarchal hierarchy and did not appoint women to high-ranking positions, women had organizational, recruiting, disseminating radical ideology, and facilitating roles within the caliphate. Women were also involved in military operations in the role of suicide bombers.

In general, women's roles under ISIS are less visible than men's, even though their presence has been depicted widely by the media. In general, ISIS benefited from women's presence at a large scale as they participated in many ways. As ICCT expert notes, "women have most frequently taken on supportive and facilitative roles."[5] Once they reached the Middle East and lived under the caliphate, each woman contributed to the common goal by participating in propaganda, recruitment, supporting their jihadist husbands, and indoctrinating their children. Even though women's roles frequently have been "overlooked, downplayed or considered of secondary importance,"[6] we cannot underestimate their role in jihadism. The presence of women made ISIS powerful, giving legitimacy and sending a powerful message of intimidation to the rest of the world.

There is a debate among scholars about women's agency under ISIS. Women's agency has been buried mainly by gender-biased assumptions, and media and scholars tend to sensationalize the presence of women in terrorism. In general, scholars underscore that "there is growing evidence that in recent years women are playing a more significant role in terrorism."[7] As Berko and Erez highlighted, women have been involved in terrorist groups in the Israel/Palestinian territories of Gaza and the West Bank, Russia/Chechnya, Sri Lanka, India, Turkey, and most recently Iraq and Jordan. Terrorist groups also increasingly rely on women to execute terrorist operations. My empirical evidence suggests that women played different roles but heavily contributed to the ISIS doctrine, mainly by being family keepers, caregivers, recruiters, propagators and most importantly by being responsible for minds of children. Women were responsible for bringing up children accordingly with the ISIS ideology and indoctrinate them from the early age. Thus, when countries address the issue of returning women from Syria and Iraq, each case should be considered individually as some women might be victims. However, while some women were deceived and had no intention to join ISIS, other women played an essential role in ISIS, acting as suicide bombers, logisticians, recruiters, and facilitators.

WOMEN'S CONFLICTING IMAGES IN ISIS

Women who traveled to Syria and Iraq have a conflicting image. In the context of ISIS, women have had "hypervisibility" and have become "central to the fighting and coverage of the conflict in Syria and Iraq."[8] Usually, women have two different images during conflicts throughout history. The first perception is that women are peace builders and always stand for peace and can be victims of violence committed by men. The second image of women is that women participate in conflicts and perpetuate political violence (Sjoberg and Gentry, 2007). While in other conflicts, women's stories, images, and roles were invisible, and women who joined the Islamic State have drawn too much attention from media, research institutes, and international actors. Women and children have been mainstreamed from when they traveled to the Middle East, their experiences in the caliphate, and living under the Kurdish forces.

There have been several narratives with gender-stereotypical assumptions. First is the victimization of women and picturing them as helpless and choiceless. Media news and reports have featured women as captives and slaves held by ISIS. At the same time, media outlets and even research reports tend to sensationalize the presence of women by calling them "ISIS brides." This is a second reductionist narrative that has minimized the role of women to marriage and sex. According to Sjoberg and Gentry (2008), the domination of sexual narrative in descriptions of women's violence and terrorism "serves to undermine women's agency in their violence" and "obscure investigation of women's actual motives."[9] Women's motives and real stories have been buried under the narratives of sex. Even approaches to women in ISIS reveal how the world shows an unequal treatment of women and men, how gender hierarchy is still important, and how women's roles have been reduced to their femininity and biological nature. Journalists and scholars should stop imposing the so-called "erotomania" label on women in ISIS, portraying them all as sex-crazed (Sjoberg and Gentry, 2013). My empirical evidence, interviews with repatriated women and women living in camps, has rejected this assumption. Women who went to Syria and Iraq had other incentives and grievances, and sexuality has no link to their decisions to join ISIS. Such a reductionist approach will further limit deradicalization processes and reduce the understanding of why these women have chosen radical paths.

There is no similar approach to the presence of women and men in ISIS. Women's motivations and role in ISIS have been regarded through a gendered prism. This narrow vision has implications for the prevention of terrorism and the development of policies. This narrow view and these gender-biased interpretations limit the examination of women's incentives and actions. As Alice Martini notes, "this process prevents fully grasping the phenomenon and, consequently, to provide an effective response to radicalization dynamics."[10] Sensational headlines and research and media articles about women who joined ISIS and other terrorist groups are biased. As Laura Sjoberg states, women in conflicts receive gendered attention, "where the gender stereotypes litter stories told about those women and their political contexts."[11] However, more research needs to be conducted to understand the context, grievances, cultural norms, and religion-based pressures on women that force them to make such decisions.

Women were exposed to recruitment in different contexts by having complex and wide-ranging motivations. However, the most salient context in Central Asia is the dependability on men, as many of them followed the decisions made by their husbands. That dependability is two-fold: women have no economic independence and obey their husbands under religious dogmas. They blindly believed that life in the Islamic state would be better. I have interviewed women who traveled to Syria and Iraq from Russia, Azerbaijan, Uzbekistan, Kyrgyzstan, Tajikistan and Kazakhstan. My empirical evidence suggests that the search for belonging, attempt to escape trauma, family conflicts and pain, and the promise of appropriate living conditions lured women. Most women wanted to escape poverty and live in a big house with beautiful household goods. I agree with scholars who observed that these women "are, as stereotypically expected, nonviolent and apolitical." [12]Women are mothers and feminine beings who care about their family's well-being and want better living conditions. I agree that "women's femininity is a way into manipulating them" (Sjoberg, 2017). I have concluded that women were mainly manipulated and misled due to their gendered nature and specialized roles as mothers and wives. However, at the same time, women believed that building a caliphate was tangible and realistic. They believed and were lured by the utopian idea to build an Islamic state.

Women I interviewed mainly married early and already had several children in their twenties. As other experts highlight, my female respondents also were "at their twenties are simply revolutionizing a utopian politics."[13] Women from developing countries in the post-Soviet space, whom I interviewed, wanted to escape both their socioeconomic problems and emotional sufferings such as psychological pressure, pain, and family conflicts. However, young women and girls, especially those living in Europe and annoyed with the rising instances of Islamophobia, decided to choose "something more adventurous and thrilling."[14]

SUICIDE BOMBING, PLOTTING, AND PROPAGANDA

Women present a particular group that should be treated carefully. Some women committed crimes, such as killing people, torturing and beating other women, while some were trained to become suicide bombers. Indeed, it would be imprudent to treat all women as victims. According to Cunningham and other scholars, approximately one-third of all suicide attacks carried out between 1981 and 2007 involved women. Since 2005, there has been a marked increase in women's participation in these attacks.[15] ISIS also trained women to carry explosives and conduct suicide attacks. Even though female suicide bombing is not an innovation and was "started by the Kurdish terrorists in Turkey in 1996–1999 and made popular by Palestinians from January 2002"[16]; Al-Qaeda and ISIS have benefited from women's participation in terrorist tactics.

Previous studies have highlighted women in ISIS were radicalized and committed an extensive range of crimes, such as torture, by joining ISIS's moral police. In particular, the so-called Al-Khansaa Brigade of ISIS, which served as female morality police, committed severe violence against other women.[17] Women from the Al-Khansaa Brigade were ruthless. Their goal was to punish those who violated the rules. As Khelghat-Doost states, "the members of this brigade, who are selected mainly from citizens of Middle Eastern states, undergo military and police training for several weeks before starting their missions."[18] There is also evidence that women were trained to commit suicide attacks successfully.

In general, the overall approach has been to victimize women in the context of religious dogma that reduces women's activity and sees men as leaders. However, regarding women only as victims and ISIS brides is a limited and simplistic vision. ISIS utilized women as education and health care workers and as military combatants. Thus, we need to be mindful that ISIS challenged the conventional understanding of women's roles in jihadism. Their participation is not limited to cooking, giving birth, and indoctrinating children. Women have also been "involved in plotting and executing terrorist violence."[19] There are cases where women committed suicide attacks. In Kazakhstan, which repatriated more than 700 women and children, the media featured a Kazakh woman who blew herself up in Syria.

Women were constantly being forced to become suicide bombers. Some women agreed to execute such an act, after trauma or loss. Several Kazakh women, whom I interviewed, said that women took that decision as a last chance to join their loved ones.

"I saw and also heard that usually women who lost their children agreed to be a martyr. They wanted to join their children in Jannah. They lost any hope to be happy, because they did not want to live without their children. We also were told that Allah will reward for such a death, but only now I learned from theologians here that God says the following: 'Do not kill yourself, and God is merciful to you.' We thought that we are doing everything for the mercy of Allah, but turned out to be not true," the Kazakh woman told me. There are cases where women were convinced by their own husbands to become a suicide bomber. The Kazakh woman told me the following:

> In 2014, the siege began and our life became a living hell. We were surrounded by the Kurdish forces and bombed from air as well. One of those difficult days, my husband brought a suicide belt home and asked me to put it on. He told me that I must detonate it when the Kurdish soldiers got very close. "You should not surrender and never let them to capture you," he told me. He wanted me to commit suicide for the cause, but at that time I was pregnant. In that moment I thought about my baby, and in my mind I was totally against the idea. Being pregnant, how can I commit suicide? I had to think about my baby. When I recall my life in Syria, I understand that I was living in hell where I had to decide—die now or die later.

She was repatriated as part of Operation Zhusan with her two children and is now trying to rebuild her life in Kazakhstan.

There was one reported incident in Syria where a Kazakh woman detonated a suicide vest, but before doing so, she had entrusted her two sons to another woman. The Ministry of Foreign Affairs in Kazakhstan located these two Kazakh boys and looked for relatives to take them in. The government had tried to show this case in a positive light by highlighting the story of the "Kazakh woman who saved her two sons."[20] There were no details about why the woman decided to kill herself in that manner. She did not send any messages to anyone before committing suicide. She may have been trained to become a martyr in the eyes of ISIS or she may have done so under duress. At the same time, many women were apparently desperate to return to their home countries but afraid of being shunned by society. According to experts, they may have chosen to die instead of facing that shame upon returning home.

"I don't know details if a Kazakh woman committed suicide in Syria or not. If even this happened, we never know what kind of motivations she had. Many returnee women told us that they wanted to commit suicide, not because they were radicals but due to despair and hopelessness. They were tired of fighting every day to survive. They lost their husbands, lost their children. They were afraid that they will be sentenced if they return. Some women were feeling guilt that they went to Syria. Many women wanted to escape and return. We have information that three to four Kazakh women were killed by ISIS for their attempt to run away," said Alim Shaumetov, a director of the foundation Akniet in Kazakhstan.[21] Indeed, many women in Syria wanted to escape their sense of desperation and, as some told me, to fall asleep and never wake up.

Wives, Mothers and Caregivers, but Indoctrinators

Women under ISIS played a crucial role as a caregiver to both fighters and their children. The most importantly, women played an important role by giving birth to the future generation of jihadists—children—and indoctrinating them. The ISIS doctrine needed children to become a future generation of jihadists, indoctrinated and trained from their childhood to fight for the caliphate. Thus, women were responsible for indoctrination of future generation of the terrorist group. Thus, women under ISIS were forced to be married and give birth to as many children as possible. If a husband dies, ISIS places a woman immediately into the widow house, which is a common guest house for all widows. Widows had a right to mourn their husbands for four months, after they needed to marry again. They were placed into such house where they had dire conditions and many internal conflicts with other women. "The widows house is a like a prison. You are constantly guarded and live with hundreds of women who have each several children. They specially created with harsh conditions so women decide to leave this house. There is no electricity, no water and very little food. You can leave this place only if you marry. Thus, women had to remarry. When four months passed, men start coming to you to see you and you can agree to one of them" said one of the Kazakh women, repatriated from Syria. "I had to remarry twice. My Kazakh husband died, then I married to Azerbaijan man, after his death I had to marry the Arab man. But I saw other women who married more than ten times," she said. Each woman who joined ISIS, married several times and have children from different fighters. In this way, as Seran de Leede points, "mothers bring forth the next generation of fighters."[22] Another woman from one of the Central Asian countries told me that she had to marry three times. "I wanted to be secure. If you don't have a husband, you cannot go out. ISIS pays only if your husband is involved in the battle, otherwise you will be dying in the widow house without food. So my husband died in six months after our settlement in Syria, then I had to marry three times: to Kazakh man, to Dagestani man, then to Arab man. Otherwise, I could not survive, as the marriage was only solution for survival" she said. Another woman who spent six years in the Middle East, told journalists that she had seen women who married nineteen times.[23] Among female returnees in Kazakhstan and Uzbekistan, some women are very young but have already three of five children. They had to give birth almost every year spent in the Middle East.

Almost all women who gave the interview to me told me that their duty was to stay at home with children and take care of them. However, the most important part of their duty was to bring up children accordingly with the radical ideology by indoctrinating them. Women taught their children to read Quran but also to talk about the ideology to embrace necessary concepts such as tawhid, takfir, jihad, hijra etc. Subsequently, even four-to-five-year-old small children already knew the radical ideology and see the world through their prism. Children were taught that doing jihad against infidels is necessary and Allah will mercy them for jihad. They also were taught that to be a part of Islamic state is duty as Muslims need to undertake Hijra and relocate. Children in Kazakhstan, Kyrgyzstan and Uzbekistan repatriated from Syria and Iraq, were fully indoctrinated. Women played crucial role in poisoning children`s minds and entrenching in them the radical ideas. Chapter 5 of the book looks closer on the mindset and behavior of children, who were born or taken to the conflict zone, and now repatriated to their home countries.

KAZAKHSTAN AND UZBEKISTAN: MANIPULATED AND MISLED WOMEN

Many women I interviewed or whose profiles I analyzed stated that they had no idea about the actual situation in the conflict zones and that there was a war going on. They could not imagine that ISIS would use them as human shields and force them to remarry each time their husband died. Among returnees in Kazakhstan and Uzbekistan, sixty percent of the women had initially followed their husbands to Syria. Sometimes these women shared their husbands' extremist motivations and followed willingly, but many women simply obeyed, feeling that they had no other choice. Many of the women only had a basic education. 60–70 percent of the women from Kazakhstan, Uzbekistan, and Russia I interviewed or whose media story I analyzed, had married early at seventeen, eighteen, or nineteen. They had no financial or professional prospects of their own. They never worked before going to Syria and always stayed at home.

Many women, while blindly following their husband's wishes, did not think about the consequences of going to a conflict zone. The absence of critical thinking is salient feature among them. Their husbands promised them a better life and the opportunity to receive the mercy of Allah. They followed their husbands because they believed that Muslim women should obey their husbands. Other women were coerced into traveling with their husbands, who threatened to leave them without financial support and without a place to live if they did not comply. There are examples of husbands selling all the family property in Kazakhstan and declaring that the whole family would be going to Syria. Women blindly followed their husbands without taking the consequences for their little children into account.

The women in Central Asia who followed their husbands were economically dependent on them. They often did not have further educational qualifications and had never worked. As such, they had no prospect of soon becoming independent by acquiring an income source for themselves. They feared that it would be difficult to feed their children if they were to stay in their country alone. Some women stayed in their home countries for five to six months, then headed to Syria to join their husbands. Cases of female returnees have shown the importance of educating girls to enable them to think critically, to express their views, and have the means and capacity to say no. Anar, who was living in Nookat in Kyrgyzstan, told me it was difficult to be left with two children after her husband left for Syria. "I had no money. My children were hungry. I agreed to join my husband in eight months because he told me that ISIS pays 100 US dollars per child and 400 dollars per adult each month. He lived with other people in a grand villa. When he sent me the video from Syria, he lived in a two-story, very nice house. The furniture also looked very expensive. My husband was telling me that we would be rich there." Her husband died in Syria, and she is currently in the Al-Hawl camp hoping for repatriation.

Many young women simply disappeared with their husbands, leaving their parents shocked to discover the truth for themselves. I met the mother of Kamilla, a Kyrgyz woman currently trapped in the Al-Hawl camp in Syria. Her mother lived in a small village near Osh and took care of her grandchildren. Kamilla's mother recounted: "My husband has passed away recently. He died suffering from the grief that he could not return his daughter from Syria," she said. Kamilla calls her mother from time to time, begging her family to find a way to allow her to return home. Her parents approached the Red Cross, police, and special services of Kyrgyzstan, but nobody could help. "I heard that the Kurdish forces ask for a big sum of money for each person. If I had such money, I would go to Syria immediately to bring her home," said her mother.

Kamilla's story began in Turkey. She got married when she was nineteen. Her husband traveled to Turkey first, and after several months he invited Kamilla to join him.

> It was August of 2015. My daughter left for Turkey thinking that they would work and live there. We kept in touch on the phone for two months. Everything was normal. Then they just disappeared—no phone calls. We were very worried. Once at night, she called and said, "Forgive me, if you can, I cannot talk. I am in a very faraway, distant place." We tried to call her back, but it was useless.

> Then we learned that she called from a Syrian number. We understood that she was in Syria.

After several months, Kamilla started calling her parents again.

> We wanted to see her, and once, we insisted on video chatting. Her husband was holding the phone. She was dressed in black, and her face was covered. We could see only her eyes. Her voice was very slow and teary. We asked to show her face, and she looked at her husband as if to ask permission. Her husband revealed her face for three seconds and then covered it again. We wanted to know where they were, what they were doing, but all questions remained unanswered as her husband forbade her to say anything.

Kamilla could not talk to her parents for an extended period. One day, she called and informed her family that her husband had been killed. Only after the death of her husband she had the opportunity to speak about what had happened and why she had gone to Syria.

"My daughter did not know that they would go to Syria. She thought that her husband would be working in Turkey and earn good money," Kamilla's mother continued. Ten families lived in Istanbul together in a dormitory building, all from Central Asian countries. One day, a big bus arrived, and the families were told to get on the bus with their children to go to an Iftar dinner. Kamilla's husband, aware of the real situation, insisted that they bring clothes for the children. A few hours into their journey, they understood that they were not going to an Iftar dinner but were on their way to Syria. They moved to Raqqah, where her husband later died. After his passing, Kamilla was obliged to marry his brother so that she would not be forced to marry other fighters. In 2019, he died in a bombing raid, and she lived in the ruins of the city for six months. Finally, when Kurdish forces came to Raqqa, she was taken to the camp in Al-Hawl after being wounded during the battle with Kurdish forces: "The bullet hit her back, and she was bleeding but had to walk the entire way to reach Al-Hawl camp. Upon her arrival, doctors took out the bullet from her back. She recovered, but now she cannot move her right hand properly," said her mother.

There are some other reasons than economic why women were obedient on their husbands. Psychologists in Kazakhstan who worked with female returnees explained why women obediently followed their husbands—the emotional attachment to their children and husbands. They feared that they would destroy or lose their families by refusing to go. Many women did not take the time to read and find out more information on the real situation in the Middle East. They were led to believe that there was no armed conflict in Syria and that the caliphate would provide them with a morally supportive neighborhood and the material needs in a socially just society. However, according to Lola Shakimova, expert-psychologist in the republic information-explanatory group under the Ministry of Communication and Public Development of Kazakhstan, there was also the impact of religious radicalization. "Some women had lived with their husbands under Sharia norms. Their husbands demanded full obedience from them, referring to Islam. Their husbands, who already had radical ideas in their minds, wanted women to follow these two principles: 'If you please your husband, you please Allah,' and that 'the Gates of Paradise open to a woman only if she goes there with her husband.'" Lola Shakimova highlighted that psychological attachment and the religious dogma about total obedience of women to their husbands were two driving factors for women who followed their husbands.

Young Girls at the Crossroads without Education

After conducting interviews and analyzing profiles, I identified a particular group of young women and girls. They were recruited between the ages of sixteen and twenty-five. Usually, this group dropped out of college or university studies or did not undertake studies and had no concrete idea of what to do with their lives. These young women were an easy target for terrorist recruiters precisely because of their lack of education. They were targeted by recruiters through the internet, usually by handsome men who showed a romantic interest and made promises about being a trusty husband to them and living together happily with the mercy of Allah.

The Kazakh woman who had just returned from Syria sat in the yard of the rehabilitation center in Aktau. Her four children were playing around her. She wore a hijab and always looked down. What do you dream about? It seems like a very simple question, one that can be answered even by a small child. But she answered, "I don't know. I never thought about it."[24] Her answer says a lot. She got married when she was sixteen. Now she is twenty-three and back from Syria with her four surviving children, all born from different ISIS fighters. Women who were recruited and joined terrorist groups in Syria and Iraq lost many things. They lost their dreams, their friends, their normal lives, and many skills. They turned into zombies. This woman lost her fifth baby in Syria to starvation. "We lived without food for one month in Baghouse, so my little baby died from starvation. She was only one month old," she said.

Another tragic story is about Arman. His two daughters, sixteen and eighteen years old, went to Syria from Kyrgyzstan. "It started with my eldest daughter, who had started talking to a man on the Internet. The guy was from our city but had disappeared a long time ago. We thought he might be working in Russia or Turkey, but it appeared that he had been radicalized abroad and traveled to Syria. He was one of the main recruiters, sitting on the Internet and brainwashing young girls," said Arman. His eldest daughter had studied in school with this man. To this day, Arman regrets not having stopped his children from departing to Syria. Arman still does not understand how he could have let each family member go to Syria, following each other one by one. He finds himself asking what mistakes he made as a father and how he missed opportunities to stop them. "Now, I cannot look people in the eyes. I feel so ashamed. Not only one but two of my daughters departed to Syria. Then my wife wanted to save them and bring them back, so she also went. My life turned to hell." Arman's story is marked by particular hardship because his family members remain stuck in Syria, his daughters, his wife, and his little son. They survived the conflict and currently live in the Roj camp in Syria. "They are alive but very exhausted. Now they are living in a camp. My son is four years old. My wife was pregnant when she left for Syria. I have never seen my son. He was born in Syria," says Arman.

Arman's story started in 2014. One day, his daughters declared they would begin to wear a hijab. "My eldest daughter asked me: "Papa, we want to wear the hijab. What do you think?" I asked: "What is it? How does it look?" I did not have a clear understanding at that moment. I knew that it was something like a handkerchief, but for Muslims. She showed me a photo of it. It was black! I was shocked. I said, "No, never, you are not going to wear this kind of black hijab; we are not religious fanatics." However, Salima and Jamila insisted, and one day, both appeared at home wearing a hijab. Arman and his wife were forced to accept it, but they did not know the two girls were in the hands of recruiters who had already begun influencing their thoughts and behavior.

One day both girls started reading Namaz. "At the beginning, they read it twice per day, then it progressed to reading it five times a day," says Arman. This came as a shock to Arman and his wife, as the family had not previously been religious. "No, I cannot say that we were practicing Islam. Not at all. I was just working. I was always at work and had no intention to practice Islam. I never thought about this," he said. Salima was eighteen at the time and was working at a beauty salon. Jamila was only 16. Everything appeared relatively normal. However, although somewhat normal for their respective ages, both girls spent too much time chatting and texting on their phones.

"They came home, ate, and went to their rooms. When I think back, now I recall that both were addicted to their smartphones. They used to spend each evening chatting and texting on the Internet. Maybe they were connected on WhatsApp or Facebook; I do not know. But they were constantly talking to someone. Even at night, I remember my wife use d to go into their room and ask them to go to bed. Otherwise, they would stay on the Internet until three in the morning. We thought they were chatting about girl-related things, such as love, fashion, or chatting with friends. We had no idea about the recruitment."

On February 13, 2013, Arman's eldest daughter took a flight from Bishkek to Istanbul. None of the family members were aware of this; they believed she was visiting her grandmother, who lived just a few miles away. The recruiters in Bishkek accompanied her to board the plane. "We saw on the airport video that she was with someone. My daughter later told me that she did not know who it was. He came by car and took her to the airport but never spoke to her. He kept silent and was even trying to hide his face. My daughter was told to wait in the corner of two streets in Bishkek for the car. So, she waited, and eventually, the car came." She reached Istanbul, where she married this man. They then crossed the border and entered Syria, where the man had previously stayed.

Arman's second daughter continued to read the Namaz and wear the niqab. She remained silent and continued to spend time on the internet. One day she ran away from home. Arman later learned that she was in contact with her sister with the agreement that she would eventually follow her. However, she was only sixteen, and she could not travel alone from a legal point of view. The recruiters had a solution to this. She was first kept locked in a house in the outskirts of Bishkek without a phone for two months. A Kyrgyz man provided her with food and living necessities. He refused to give her access to her phone and continuously ignored her demands to call her parents. After two months, the man said that she had to marry him to go to Syria to join her sister. At first, she refused, but eventually, she agreed. They married in Bishkek and flew to Syria through Kazakhstan. "My daughter told me that they boarded the plane without any problems. She was only sixteen at the time, and she said the man had all the necessary documents with him," says Arman.

Several months later, Arman's wife declared she would go to Syria to bring back her two daughters. Once, during a meeting with the special services of Kyrgyzstan, she met an Uzbek woman who went to Syria and brought back her daughter and grandchildren. She was determined to do the same, declaring to Arman: "Nobody can stop me, so do not even try." She left for Syria leaving her husband with their youngest daughter. One positive aspect of this story is that she reunited with their two daughters in Syria. The girls were married twice to ISIS fighters after their husbands died in armed conflict. They had each given birth to two children. They had relocated to five different cities looking for shelter and eventually reunited in camp Roj in Syria. Arman desperately continued his attempts to bring them all home to Kyrgyzstan. However, the sad news came in August 2021. Arman passed away from a heart attack after desperately fighting for his family. His heart could not bear the grief and suffering he had had for several years.

Another story about a young girl starts in Russia. Karina was living in Moscow with her parents. After graduating from school, she did not apply to start university. She started wearing a hijab when she was seventeen. "I did not want to study in Moscow, but I wanted to go to Arab countries and study Islam in-depth," she said. When she turned eighteen, Karina disappeared. Having traveled to Turkey without informing her parents, she had met a man on the Internet who spoke to her about an ideal and utopian life under the caliphate. He promised to marry her and live there with her. "He sent me videos, where everyone was wearing the hijab and Muslims lived happily. I saw very beautiful houses where they sat and shared meals. I decided that I wanted to live in the caliphate. Not to mention, he was very handsome, so I fell in love," said Karina. She took a plane to Istanbul, but the man did not meet her. Instead, several other people met her at the airport. She spent several nights in Gaziantep, then crossed the border. "Dozens of other people I met in Gaziantep and we all were taken to Al Shadidi, where hundreds of Kazakhs lived. I had to marry one of the Kazakh men there. In two years, he was killed. I was left with my baby. Then I married again to a fighter from Azerbaijan. However, he died in three months. I had to marry again, this time to an Arab fighter," says Karina. She gave birth there to her second child. The situation started to become very dangerous. Her Arab husband agreed to allow her to escape but refused to help her find the means. She knew that she would have to pay money to locals to reach the Kurdish forces. "I paid 8,000 US dollars to the agent who earns money by accompanying people. Luckily, I had the money. We walked thirty hours through mountains and the desert and reached the Kurdish forces," said Karina. She was only eighteen when she went to Syria by simply following the instructions of the unknown man in Internet. While living in Al-Hawl, she wears black niqab and told me that she will be dressed in this way always. She knows that her country does not want to repatriate its citizens, but she wants to reach Turkey and stay there. "Sometimes I want to escape, but there are mines around, and the Kurdish forces will also kill me if I try to escape."

There are many stories where young women and girls went to Syria to marry men they met on the Internet. The psychologist in Kazakhstan, Lola Shakiomova, calls this phenomenon the syndrome of the "Dagestani lover." These women sought to receive the love, attention, and affection they lacked in their lives. Lola Shakimova, who worked with returnee women to understand their psychological difficulties and help them recover, explained the phenomenon of "a Dagestani lover." This syndrome is about young women and girls who usually have emotional vulnerabilities, feel isolated, and lack attention and love from their inner circle. They attempt to find a husband through social media channels. "The 'virtual lover' was a recruiter with rich knowledge about gender psychology and psychology of communication. He easily identified what his target wished to hear and what kind of dreams and aspirations she had. He adjusted his behavior to portray the ideal image of a man, according to the apparent wishes of the partner, and encouraged a stable psychological dependence," said Lola Shakimova. This is not only about finding a husband, but also about seeking compensation for the deficit of love and attention in their lives.

The recruiter would ensure the targeted woman made up her mind to agree to unite with him, even in a conflict zone. She would become dependent on communication with him as a source of comfort and support. She would forget everything else in her life and become preoccupied with her virtual lover. This sense of romantic attachment would be strengthened by presents, financial support, and the promise of creating a happy family under the caliphate. These women and girls would not have known what kind of trap awaited them. It was rare that the women would meet the same handsome man once they arrived in Turkey or Syria. Usually, recruiters used photos of handsome men in their social media accounts and stayed behind the computer screen. Sometimes women and girls would talk to them through video chats, but they did not dare meet online. Text messages appeared to be enough for them; they seldom tried to confirm the man's identity in the profile photos. Many young women simply disappeared one day. Once they reached Syria, they were forced to marry any of the other ISIS fighters. The promise of true love was quickly forgotten, as women in ISIS were used as the source of the next generation of fighters.

Escaping Trauma and Hostile Environments

Many women who went to Syria experienced significant psychological distress stemming from conflicts, hostile environments, and personal traumas. They wished to escape these hostile environments and forget their traumas, which typically had gone untreated. They thought the utopian idea of the caliphate would be a refuge from their previous experiences. Going to Syria seemed, for some women, to be a unique chance to change their lives and to live without conflicts and traumas. According to psychologists who worked with repatriates in Kazakhstan, most female returnees had suffered from different traumas before going to Syria.

"Many women had a history of childhood trauma, such as having a troubled family or divorced parents, rape, or an 'ugly duck' model in the family. Some of them had psychological problems at a later stage in their lives. Alcoholic husbands or drug abusers, endless conflicts with other family members, exposure to domestic violence, and lack of support from her parents and other family members. Some women had several divorces, and some were victims of a social circle with radical religious ideas," said Lola Shakimova.

Women I interviewed spoke about the hostile environment they wished to escape from. They were humiliated, marred with conflicts, and faced judgments every day. Larisa was a Russian woman who converted to Islam when she was nineteen. She had married a religious man from Dagestan when she was twenty-two. However, their life had been challenging, as her husband's parents did not want to accept her. "Our life was full of conflicts every day. His parents pressured me to divorce. The very first reason I decided to go to Syria was that I wanted to escape that life," she recounts. Larisa emphasized that she wanted to escape their village's hostile and conflict-prone situation. In Dagestan, people often attempted to falsely accuse one another with the local police and bribe the police to avoid being sent to prison. "For example, for someone who is very religious and with a beard like my husband, people could plant arms and explosives in their home. This is usually done jointly with the police. Then they arrest the person and demand money. Witnessing what was going on in our village, I was afraid that this could happen to my husband as well," said Larisa. They heard about Syria from other people who had already left the village and reached Syria. They started sending them videos. "The caliphate looked very nice. They lived in big houses. All of them were Muslims, and nobody was going to condemn you. Everyone was kind and nice," she emphasized. "We decided to go. We sold the one precious thing in our home—our car. We bought tickets and told my husband's family that we need to visit my grandmother. First, we went to my grandmother to say goodbye. I hugged my grandmother and said, 'I think we will never see each other again' because I knew that it would be difficult to return," said Larisa. Her grandmother cried but did not stop them. These days Larisa is living with her two sons in the Roj camp in Syria. Her husband is alive and is in a detention center run by Kurdish forces near Hasaka.

Women also wanted to escape pain, conflict and trauma in their previous lives. Domestic violence is another source of terror for family members, with some experts referring to it as "intimate terrorism." Domestic violence is widespread in many countries, especially in families where a woman does the child-rearing work at home. "I divorced my husband but he continued chasing me. He was very violent and used to beat me when he is drunk. So I decided to join my friend who was leaving to Syria. I took my son with me as my husband wanted to take away him from me" said one of the women in Al-Hawl. She married twice in Syria and now is living in the camp with her three children. In general, domestic violence is widespread in many countries. Home isolation during COVID-19 has exacerbated the violence that many men impart against women in different countries. The UN has expressed great concern over domestic violence that augmented during the lockdown in all countries. The United Nations has called for urgent action to combat the worldwide surge in domestic violence. "I urge all governments to put women's safety first as they respond to the pandemic," Secretary-General António Guterres wrote on Twitter.[25] Women suffer from violence at home from their husbands or psychological violence from other people in their inner circle. Consequently, women bear long-term effects on their mental health especially, when these traumas remain largely unaddressed.

After having personal conversations with women who joined ISIS, what was evident was that many women became disillusioned about an Islamic state. If many talked about the lack of justice in their society before departing to Syria, the injustice inside the caliphate built by ISIS and other terrorist groups was far worse. After living under ISIS, their hopes were ruined. "I was hoping to find their respect, belonging, and comfortable life. However, the leaders above us did not care about our feelings. I understood that in one year spent in Syria. I could have escaped immediately, but it was impossible," Elmira told me, who is from Kyrgyzstan and was living in Roj camps at the time of the interview. Women also told me that the local population mistreated them. A Russian-speaking woman living in Al-Hawl told me:

> I lived in Raqqa and then in Shedaddi; even in these cities, Arabs maltreated us. In the streets and bazaars, they used to call us "ajnabi," which means non-Arab or a foreigner. At the beginning, I did not pay attention but later understood that they meant to humiliate us. Saying "ajnabi" was a signal that they should not sell good products to us. We, non-Arabs, were receiving the worst food or starving. By the end, they did not tell us that the products would be in short supply; they lied to us, and foreigners were starving while Arabs had all the stock. And the same mistreatment is here in the camps. Syrians and Iraqis are treated better than us.

Another woman currently living in the Roj camp echoed the sentiment that local Syrians and Iraqis mistreated foreigners. A Chechen woman living in Al-Hawl told me:

> We came here to help them thinking that it was our duty to help Muslims. But they considered us to be vicarious and excessive. In Baghouse, Arabs had food and products but hid them while we were starving. My brother was wounded. So, as he was wounded, he was provided with food. He saw huge stockpiles of products and asked why they were not distributing them to the people. They told him, "these ajnabis—non-Arabs—should leave, then we will start to distribute food and products." He came home shocked. From the beginning, our men from Caucasus and Asia were put on the front line to die. Our women had always been mistreated. When I came to camp Al-Hawl, the Arab women asked me, "What are you doing on our land?" I said, "We came to help you because you begged us to come." They told me that they never invited us to come and help. I was so disappointed.

She seemed disillusioned with the initial sense of belonging and the idea of having an Islamic state sold to her by recruiters.

Another Russian woman living in the Roj camp at the time of our conversation also stressed the true injustice she saw during her time under the Islamic State:

> Many women here from Kyrgyzstan, Azerbaijna, Russia, Tajikistan, and Kyrgyzstan, we talk to each other and discuss why we came to the Middle East. In many countries, we saw injustice, poverty, and political pressure. But what we saw here is flagrant injustice. We did not expect that the idea of having a just society would turn out in the opposite. ISIS created a community where killing was normal. I saw death and blood. They treated us, women, like animals.

At the same time, she also wanted to highlight the racism she saw inside the so-called Islamic State:

> I thought we would have a state where all Muslims are equal. No, they treated Iraqis better at first, then Syrians started dominating. However, we foreigners who gathered from each corner of the world did not become a part of that community. We remained classified as non-Arabs. It was so painful for me. From the beginning until the end, they treated us as unwanted guests who could only serve them. They never showed us respect.

My empirical evidence suggests that some women who currently live in the camps are deeply disappointed with the idea of building an Islamic state. Their dream now is to return to their home countries while their mind and perception of the world are deeply plunged into the patterns of the radical ideology. However, if you observe the social channels created by women in Al-Hawl and Roj, the majority of women are still dreaming about a caliphate. They are deeply radicalized and live with the mind that fully grasped the idea of tawhid and takfir. Radical women do not plan to return to their home countries. Some women told me they prefer to get asylum in a third Arab country or Turkey. However, states should work with those disillusioned, as their reintegration processes might be faster and easier. Kazakhstan's experience, where more than about thirty women are involved as volunteers in rehabilitation and deradicalization processes, is an excellent practice to learn. The women who saw atrocities of ISIS can be goodwill ambassadors to prevent radicalization and to explain that terrorist groups such as ISIS are evil and have nothing to do with Islam. Using voices of female returnees can contribute to deradicalization and prevention of religious extremism.

Returning with Tunnel Thinking and Survivors' Instinct

Having conducted dozens of interviews with female returnees in Kazakhstan, my impression was that most of them seemed very tired, tired of everything. Tired of their children being born in Syria from different husbands, tired of public attention, tired of being between two realities: what they had seen in Syria and life after repatriation. I did not see the light in their eyes, eyes which were deep but empty. They seemed lost and, even after returning to Kazakhstan, they had not been able to find themselves. They remained at a crossroads thinking about whether to go right or left. They were afraid of society, public judgment, the future, how to earn money, how to raise and educate their children. They were afraid of that responsibility. It seemed too much for them. However, some women might have changed in a positive way as the quite long period of time passed since the interviews were conducted.

Many women who lived in Syria and Iraq had four or five children, and have taken some children to the conflict zone with them and given birth to several others there. According to psychologists, an absence of maternal feelings was apparent in some of the repatriated women. "At the beginning, they had a very cold and mechanical attitude towards their children, but this does not mean that they were bad mothers. It is connected to the violent context they came from. They lived in Syria; seeing so much violence and blood that their feelings became blunt. Dull maternal feelings suggest a self-protective reaction to their grief. Some of them lost their children or husbands but remained cold and restrained simply because it is a protective reaction. They had to survive in Syria by overcoming many things every day and the mechanism of psychological protection simply kicked in," says Gulnaz Razdykova, a well-known psychologist in Kazakhstan. Yes, they were disconnected from their maternal feelings, but there were clear reasons for that. Some women who lost their children accepted their fate with kind of honor, referring to Allah's will, and so did not cry, nor mourn. Olga Ryl explained that women, exposed to cruelty and violence, usually disconnect from their caring and loving feelings. "If we put aside the religious beliefs of these women, in general, women who experience domestic violence struggles with their maternal feelings. They struggle to properly exercise their maternal duties and lose any sense of positive feeling toward themselves. The women returning from Syria lived in deadly conditions and had to survive. So that's why it is understandable that their maternal feelings got blunted," said Olga Ryl.[26]

The rehabilitation specialists recognized that the women had a survivor's instinct and tunnel thinking, and worked with them accordingly, taking into account all of their symptoms. "Most mums could not protect their children. They could not even react properly to the needs of their children since they did not know how they should be addressed and met. That's why we started working on building relationships and ties between mums and children," said Olga Ryl. The rehabilitation center in Aktau organized classes for children and mothers together. According to Olga Ryl, the goal was to teach the mothers to do homework with their children. If in the morning there were classes for the children, in the afternoon they had classes where the mothers learned to support the children with their homework.

Lola Shakimova, a psychologist under the Ministry of Communication and Public Development of Kazakhstan, worked with returnees from the beginning. She stressed that the women were severely psychologically distressed when they arrived. "The women who returned from Syria had severe post-traumatic stress disorder. They had very high levels of anxiety. They were afraid of the future and they felt unstable. Each of them had depression. It is because they saw violence, death and lived in fear all the time," she said.[27] Of course, from the moment of their arrival, the specialists noticed particular thinking and behavioral patterns. "Insularity, isolation and black-and-white bipolar thinking. We could see the deep religious immersion that leads to fanatical behavior," said Gulnaz Razdykova. The majority of women were dressed in black from head to toe, wearing a black niqab and some even had black gloves.

During the initial sessions with psychologists, the women did not talk much, presumably because there had been too much tragedy in their previous life in Syria and Iraq. They bore multiple traumas. Psychotherapists worked with them to unleash and then treat these traumas. When the women started talking, each session saw many tears. According to Gulnaz Razdykova, the first step to deradicalization was the women's refusal to continue to wear black niqabs, and thereafter, a decrease in the level of fanatical behavior was evident. They started wearing brightly colored hijabs. Some of the women confessed that they felt uncomfortable in such colors at first. "I lived in Syria for seven years and the whole time I dressed only in black. These bright colors are beautiful, but I feel very strange in them," said a woman sitting in the rehabilitation center in Aktau.[28]

After several weeks, the women became more curious about their surroundings and started learning about local life. Some women asked questions about new norms or trends that had come about during their absence from the homeland. They expressed concerns like, "Do you think that society will accept us? Do people condemn us? What will be their reaction be when they see me on the street? Can I wear a hijab on the street?" The psychologists and theologians tried to answer each question carefully and offer them some level of comfort.

In order to reintegrate fully, the women would have to ideally learn how to communicate and socialize with the wider Kazakh society. However, the psychologists noted a problem with the socialization as the returned women felt comfortable communicating with each other, but struggled to communicate with other groups. Following their time at the rehabilitation center, the returnees continued to seek each other out and call each other for support. It seems they felt safe only relying on women who have shared the same experiences in Syria. Psychologists in Kazakhstan working with returnees believe that this kind of behavior is indicative of ongoing post-trauma symptomatology.

COMPLEX PROFILES AND MIXED FEELINGS

Women who joined ISIS have complex profiles. They can be divided into several groups depending on their level of radicalization, while it is indeed very hard to generalize. However, after analyzing profiles and interviews conducted with women in Central Asia who joined ISIS, I have identified several groups. First group is "hardliners," who strictly follow ISIS's rules and still hope that ISIS will be revived. For instances, several Kazakh women refused to be repatriated and stayed in the camps. One Kazakh woman, after being repatriated and placed into the rehabilitation center in Kazakhstan, hid the radical ideology materials among children's toys. There are women among female returnees in Kazakhstan who strictly follow the ISIS ideology and reject the values of the contemporary society. At the same time, in two camps—Al-Hawl and Roj, there are hardliners who are still propagating the ISIS ideology and urging other women to stay loyal. The second group of women are those who are disillusioned with ISIS and about the idea of a caliphate, but deeply embraced the Salafi-Wahhabi ideology. They usually followed their husbands and share his religious beliefs. However, these women are ready to integrate but still cannot get detached from the radical versions of tawhid, takfir and jihad. Theologians and psychologists have been working with them to help them to embrace Islam in its true sense. The third group of women who realized that the radical ideology is not Islam and stepped back from the mutated version of the religious concepts. Janara, who was repatriated from Syria to Kazakhstan with two children, described her days in Syria as hell. Before she had to fight to survive in the conflict zone, she had a period of religious awakening. During her first two years in Syria, she began to realize that the ideology which she had been encouraged to believe, was the wrong interpretation of Islam.

Janara said,

> During the first two years, my husband was involved in the combat operation but I stayed at home. That was during the very quiet period when we had food and no bombings at all. Everything seemed in order, but I started having doubts about the religious ideas they kept planting in our minds. I started comparing

> them with the Quran and other hadiths and I soon understood they were interpreting them in the wrong way. I started suspecting that we were following the wrong ideology and that the caliphate we had dreamed of and believed in was not right.[29]

Now she still practices Islam but in Hanafi Mazhab that is being practiced in Central Asia. She had individual and group sessions with theologians in Kazakhstan who helped her to understand Islam.

The third group consists of women who were deceived and forced to travel due to different circumstances. They are the victims of recruiters who used their vulnerabilities to lure them. They were driven by false promises such as marriage or well-paid jobs. Usually, this group was immediately disillusioned but faced impossible circumstances in attempting to escape. "We arrived in Jarablus, and then we reached Raqqa. On the third day, it was clear that I had made a huge mistake. I wanted to return immediately, but my husband told me they would kill us if we try to escape. There was a door to enter but no door to exit. I dreamed every single day of escaping from ISIS," a Kyrgyz woman living in the Al-Hawl camp told me. She added that ISIS deliberately spread rumors about punishment in home countries. "I was also afraid that I would be jailed in Bishkek. Arabs told us there is brutal torture in prisons for joining the caliphate, such as piercing needles under your nails. And they also told us that we would be charged with betrayal of the homeland, which usually resulted in the death penalty. So, we were told that instead of the death penalty, it is better to die for jihad," she told me.

In Kazakhstan, some returnee women immediately took off their niqabs and hijabs once on the plane back to Kazakhstan and never put them back on. There are women who rejected radical ideas immediately and returned to a normal way of living almost straight away. However, they were in the minority. According to the Ministry of Foreign Affairs presenting at the 2020 Vienna conference, thirty-one women out of 156 rejected a radical ideology and deradicalized as hoped.[30] Some of them followed a moderate practice of Islam and some returned to an ordinary secular way of life. Several of these women became volunteers working with returnees and assisting the rehabilitation program. I met two Kazakh women who work as a volunteer in the rehabilitation program and also travel with the Kazakh government to speak in international conferences. I met them in Geneva and Vienna. Both spoke in front of the diplomats and international experts reflecting on their experience of being repatriated.

While many women seem to be ready to be rehabilitated and reintegrated, they remain shrouded in the radical ideology. They apply religious understanding to each aspect of the life. For example, Jihad against infidels seem legitimate for them and they believe that their husbands who died in Syria are in Paradise. One woman, whose two husbands both ISIS fighters were killed in Syria, mentioned that both of them are in heaven. The most striking development is that some of the repatriated women got remarried in two years after being returned to Kazakhstan. They remarried to religious men in Kazakhstan as second or third wives. There are cases, when two female returnees are both the wives of one man. They call each other "sister" and one agreed to have another as a second wife of her husband. Another pattern is that they never register their marriage in state institutions, as they consider their religious ceremony of marriage to be legitimate. Why they did decide to remarry? Remarriage is a kind of refuge for them. They do not want to take responsibility, as these women always had been dependent economically on their previous husbands. Their religiosity has also played a role. Finding a husband who shares his religious beliefs is also important factor for them. They agree to be a second or third wife and agree to bring their children into such environment.

Women who joined ISIS are active on social media. Female returnees in Kazakhstan have their own WhatsApp groups and due to the pandemic psychologists have worked with them on Zoom. What is remarkable is that female returnees try to stay in touch and prefer communicate among each other. They feel comfortable in the company of returnees as they have common past experiences and also shared religious beliefs. Those women who are still held in Al-Hawl and Roj, though with difficulties but manage to use Telegram and Whats app. They constantly communicate with repatriated women to learn about their new life in home countries. Even though it is challenging to pay for Internet, they manage to have one phone serving to several women. Observing WhatsApp and Telegram profiles of the women who were living in the camps in Northeast Syria, I wanted to understand what about they think and how they think. Almost all of the women only shared religious texts and pictures in their statuses on WhatsApp and Telegram. They shared photos of women in niqabs and some citations from hadiths and ayahs. One can observe reading them, how deep the religious ideology is planted in their minds. One woman's status said, "Oh, Allah, I am ready to suffer if the eventual destination is Jannah." The message could be understood as accepting the difficulties she faced in Syria with continued hope to ascend to heaven. The next message that struck me was about Ummah, meaning the community of Muslims. The message was the following: "Ummah needs strong men who will devote their lives to help its religion and to protect weak Muslims. Ummah does not need crying ones in the Minbar." I understood this sentence to be about foreign fighters, but I could be mistaken. Another woman wrote in her status the following sentence: "Oh, Allah, do not replace us and use us for the victory of your religion." A woman from Russia posted a photo of boys praying and wrote the following: "Our lions are growing up and they will defend our Ummah." What struck me is that women never posted regular messages, for example, about their children or how they missed their parents or home countries. I was expecting to see texts of being homesick, but never seen them. None of them posted such texts or photos, sharing exclusively religious topics.

CONCLUSIONS

ISIS managed to spread a powerful message to the world through the presence of women and children, the message that an Islamic state will remain as a threat to the existing state system. The family jihad is a new phenomenon that has many implications for terrorism and global politics as the presence of women and children can convey several things. First, women have complex grievances that characterize their everyday lives and gender-based pressures from society. Women's roles in jihadism should be studied in-depth, beyond gender-biased assumptions. Policymakers, state officials, and researchers should stop downplaying their participation in ISIS governance. We cannot exclude that they were forced to comply with ISIS once they started living under ISIS. However, women contributed heavily to maintain ISIS governance and spread its ideology. Women played diverse, large-scale supporting roles to maintain an Islamic state, recruit other women with their children, and disseminate radical ideology. Thus, it would be irrational to generalize and treat all women as victims. Countries should be ready to repatriate women and children, but most importantly, work with these women to deradicalize and reintegrate them. The lessons learned from women repatriated and those still in camps in northeastern Syria are two-fold. First, we need to get clear answers on why women traveled to the Middle East and joined terrorist groups. Why have they decided to put their children at risk? What are the real motivations behind these choices, and what were the precipitant factors? Countries need to uncover and understand these grievances and their push and pull factors. The second lesson is that religious extremism will be present and will continue to challenge states. The family jihad can reoccur any time in the future, and it means that states should adopt more policies to address women's grievances. Women in terrorism are not anymore invisible or less important than men. Terrorism and family jihad have destroyed and will continue destroying "the stereotypical expectations of women as pure, innocent, and nonviolent."[31] Societies should wake up, and governments need to take seriously that women's involvement in terrorism is not deviant anymore. Women may remain nonviolent but contribute heavily to the mission of terrorist groups even by their role as supporters of their husbands, mothers, and wife. Based on the interviews and observations, my research concludes that women have vulnerabilities that make them open to the radical ideology. First, women need to get access to education and become economically independent. Second, early marriage is still a serious problem in many developing countries. Girls are forced to marry at fifteen or sixteen, without a chance to education. I remain convinced that terrorist groups will continue to exploit the nature of women as caretakers and nurturers as an operational tactic in recruitment of other women, indoctrination of children, and spreading fear. As long as societies regard women through gendered stereotypes, terrorist groups will continue to exploit that assumption for their interests. Thus, I agree with the conclusion that "terrorist leaders simply view women logisticians, recruiters, and suicide bombers as additional weapons in their arsenal."[32] As Caron Gentry argues, gender is threaded throughout the study of terrorism. "Women are often seen lacking political rationale, which implicates how their agency is understood."[33] The main conclusion is that women's agency in terrorism should not be ignored or downplayed.

NOTES

1. R. Kim Cragin and Sara A Daly, *Women As Terrorists: Mothers, Recruiters and Martyrs*, (London, Praeger Security International, 2009), 104.
2. UN CTED, "Gender Dimensions of the Response to Returning Foreign Fighters, Research Perspectives," UN CTED Trends Report, (2019).
3. Nelly Lahoud, "The Neglected Sex: The Jihadis' Exclusion of Women from Jihad," *Terrorism and Political Violence* 0;1–23, 2014, DOI: 10.1080/09546553.2013.77251.
4. Cragin and Daly, *Women As Terrorists*, 93.
5. Seran de Leede, "Women in Jihad: A Historical Perspective," ICCT Policy Brief, September 2018, 8.
6. Leede, "Women in Jihad," 8.
7. Anat Berko and Edna Erez, "Gender, Palestinian Women, and Terrorism: Women's Liberation or Oppression?" *Studies in Conflict & Terrorism*, 30(6), 2002, 493–519. doi:10.1080/10576100701329550.
8. Laura Sjoberg, "Jihadi Brides and Female Volunteers: Reading the Islamic State's War to See Gender and Agency in Conflict Dynamics." *Conflict Management and Peace Science* 35, (3): 296–311.
9. Laura Sjoberg and Caron E. "Gentry, Reduced to Bad Sex: Narratives of Violent Women from the Bible to the War on Terror," *International Relations* 22(1): 5–23, (2008), [DOI: 10.1177/0047117807087240].
10.Alice Martini, "Making women terrorists into 'Jihadi brides': an analysis of media narratives on women joining ISIS," *Critical Studies on Terrorism*, 1–20, (2018), doi:10.1080/17539153.2018.1448204.
11. Sjoberg, "Jihadi brides and Female Volunteers," 296–311.
12. Sjoberg, "Jihadi Brides and Female Volunteers," 296–311.

13. Debangana Chatterjee, "Gendering ISIS and Mapping the Role of Women," *Contemporary Review of the Middle East* 3(2), (2016), 201–218. doi:10.1177/2347798916638214.

14. Chatterjee, "Gendering ISIS and Mapping the Role of Women," 210.

15. Cunningham, K.J, "Cross-Regional Trends in Female Terrorism. Studies in Conflict and Terrorism," (2007) 26, pp. 171–95 and Tunde Agara, "Gendering Terrorism: Women, Gender, Terrorism and Suicide Bombers," *International Journal of Humanities and Social Science* 5, no. 6(1), (2015).

16. Tunde Agara, "Gendering Terrorism: Women, Gender, Terrorism and Suicide Bombers." *International Journal of Humanities and Social Science* 5, no. 6 (1), June 2015.

17. Joana Cook and Gina Vale, "From Daesh to 'Diaspora': Tracing the Women and Minors of Islamic State," *International Center for the Study of Radicalization, King's College London*, 2018.

18. Hamoon Khelghat-Doost, "Women of the Islamic State: The Evolving Role of Women in Jihad," *Counter Terrorist Trends and Analyses* 8, no. 9 (2016), 21–26.

19. Seran de Leede, "Women in Jihad: A Historical Perspective," ICCT Policy Brief, (2018), 7.

20. Interviews of Kazakh officials sourced from the media and several media articles about the case on Kazakh media.

21. Shaumetov, interview.

22. Leede, "Women in Jihad," 5.

23. Women are forced to marry 19 times: Central Asian woman spoke about her six years spent in Syria, Sputnik Tajikistan, 14th May 2019.

24. National Security Committee of Kazakhstan, "official video from the rehabilitation center," available at: https://youtu.be/pDfABGYAYaA.

25._Amanda Taub, "A New COVID-19 Crisis: Domestic Abuse Rises Worldwide," *New York Times*, April 14, 2020, https://www.nytimes.com/2020/04/06/world/coronavirus-domestic-violence.html.

26. Olga Ryl, interview.

27. Shakimova, interview.

28. From the official video produced by the National Security Committee of Kazakhstan.

29. Janara, interview by the author via WhatsApp, and her name has been changed upon her request.

30. Yerzhan Ashikbaev, "Official speech by Mr. Yerzhan Ashikbaev during a side event at the Vienna conference on foreign fighters organized by OSCE and UNOCT," 11–12 February 2020.

31. Laura Sjoberg, Grace D. Cooke and Stacy Reiter Neal, *Introduction in Women, Gender, and Terrorism*, (University of Georgia Press, 2011).

32. Cragin and Daly, "Women As Terrorists: Mothers, Recruiters, and Martyrs," 117.

33. Caron E. Gentry, "Gender and Terrorism," in *Women, Gender and Terrorism*, (University of Georgia Press, 2011).

Chapter 6

Children of ISIS

Brought to or Born in the Conflict Zone

Thousands of children were taken to the conflict zones by their parents and thousands more children were born under ISIS in Syria and Iraq. There is no exact number on how many children lived under ISIS, as there is no headcount or registration conducted neither by the Syrian Democratic Forces nor international humanitarian organizations. International organizations estimate that currently about 43,000 children have been held in Al-hawl and Roj camps. The majority of them are Syrians and Iraqis, and about 8,000 are from third countries. In total 1,460–1,525 minors (22–25 percent) have now returned to their country of departure (or the country of their parents).[1] This number may include repatriated children by Kazakhstan, Uzbekistan, Kyrgyzstan, Tajikistan, Russia, Kosovo, the U.S. and several European countries. International organizations estimate that about 43,000 ISIS-linked children have been held in Al-Hawl and Roj camps. According to the U.S. State department, about 16,000 children were born in Syria and Iraq under ISIS and other terrorist groups. This number was announced by the U.S. state official during the OSCE conference in Vienna held on 11–12 February 2020.

Should children be considered as victims? Small children can automatically be categorized as victims as they are incapable of taking decisions on their own. However, boys who have attained the age of thirteen to fourteen, may have already acquired combat skills. As Renard and Coolsaet (2018) argue, the return of these children will present a number of serious challenges—social, psychological, and educational. "While they are essentially perceived and treated as victims, a small minority of them could develop into a security threat."[2] No state can treat children as terrorists or criminals after their repatriation. However, if a teenager shows signs of deep radicalization or has committed crimes in the Middle East, the state should choose a tailored approach to deradicalize and rehabilitate him. Renard and Coolsaet have given a concrete example from Belgium where four children were taken away from the custody of their parents, who were returned foreign fighters, and entrusted to childcare institutions due to signs of continued radicalization.[3]

After having interviewed psychologists and social workers who worked with returnees in Uzbekistan and Kazakhstan, listening to stories of repatriated children and their conversations with journalists and social workers, I came to the conclusion that children were heavily affected by the radical ideology. They had no choice, but to only perceive the world through this radical ideology. Children faced indoctrination and training starting at an early age, while boys were sent to the military training camps from the age of nine. Thus, they grew up with the black and white mindset based only on religious dogmas dividing the world into Muslims and "unbelievers." The primary concepts that were planted in their mind were tawhid, takfir, hijrah and Jihad. The latter was taught as a main life-long goal. A teenage boy, who was repatriated to his home country in Central Asia and living in an orphanage, said to the social workers: "We have a good life now eating good meals, having toys and books because God rewarded us for doing Jihad. We will depart to Jihad if the God calls us." Another boy, whose parents died in Syria, lives with his grandmother after his repatriation. He also sees people of another religion as enemies. "Non-Muslims are our enemies and we have to fight these infidels," he repeats. His grandmother has been making huge efforts to convince him that it is not true. Several social workers and psychologists in Kazakhstan and Uzbekistan were told by children that they are kaffurs. Children's first words were after repatriation that they are facing infidels. One of the coordinators of the rehabilitation program in Kazakhstan is a Russian woman. One boy told her directly: "you are kaffir, because you are not Muslim." Children perceived their home country as a place that is full of infidels as a result of indoctrination that lasted for several years in the Middle East. Some children spent six years there, some four years.

Children under ISIS were deprived of education. They never went to school and never learned school subjects. ISIS organized religious schools and training camps. Both of them were mainly only available for boys. Religious schools are meant to brainwash children, teaching them the Arabic language, Quran lessons, and strict interpretations of Islam that focus on radical jihadi Salafist ideology. Children were indoctrinated from an early age by learning that their homeland is an Islamic state and non-Muslim nations are their enemies. Girls under ISIS were taught to respect and obey their husbands and their life-long goal is to serve the Islamic state by giving birth and raising as many children as possible. ISIS prepared girls to marry as soon as they reach puberty, but in some cases even from ten years old. There are girls of thirteen to fourteen years old in Central Asia that are repatriated with their babies. They were raped or married off, all while being twelve to fourteen years old.

ISIS treated girls in a horrible manner and its worse crimes were committed against girls and women.

There are many challenges states have to deal with when it comes to minors. They are undocumented and DNA tests should be organized to identify their biological parents. Legal guardianship is also a difficult task, as relatives hesitate to accept them. In many cases, the repatriation efforts raise a question of separation from their parents, when they are the ones who they should stay with in the custody in the Middle East. However, separation will exacerbate children's trauma, thus European states repatriated mainly orphans from camps, but in a small number. However, for those children who have been held in Iraqi prisons, separation can be a better option. The inhuman conditions in the cells are worse than the conditions in camps. Hundreds of women from third countries were sentenced in Iraq for joining ISIS[4]. Minors have been held in the Iraqi prisons together with their mothers who were convicted of terrorism charges. Approximately two thousand children had been held in Iraqi prisons before several countries repatriated their children including Tajikistan, Kazakhstan, Kyrgyzstan and Russia. More than one thousand children are still being raised in crowded and unsanitary prisons cells. According to Cook and Vale, "two hundred foreign infants have reportedly been born inside one Baghdad prison alone."[5] The Iraqi courts sentenced not only male fighters but women and children too. Human Rights Watch estimated that Iraqi federal authorities and Kurdish authorities had detained around 1,500 children in Iraq at the end of 2018, and at least 185 children of foreign nationals were convicted and sentenced to prison terms under anti-terrorism laws by mid-2019.[6] About thirty children in jails in Irbil informed Human Rights Watch that they were tortured to obtain confessions. Children were beaten with plastic pipes, electric cables, or rods, subjecting them to electric shocks, or using painful stress positions. "Many of the children said they had little or no actual involvement with ISIS but confessed simply to stop the torture."[7]

Iraq took very harsh punitive measures by punishing children, including those who did not participate in combat operations but were cooks or stayed home taking care of their small siblings. This approach will have a profound negative impact on Iraqi society stigmatizing families. Human Rights Watch experts warn that the detention and prosecution of children may also foster future grievances in Iraqi society. One seventeen-year-old boy told Human Rights Watch, "kids detained based on fabricated testimonies. Once they are released, they might take revenge on the government and the people who took them to prison."[8] The international community has been urging Iraq to end the detention of children and prioritize their rehabilitation and reintegration. States should also accelerate efforts to repatriate children from Iraqi prisons who are living with their mothers. But some women are refusing to give their children back to their home countries. For example, seventeen Tajik women refused their children to be taken back to Tajikistan last year when Tajikistan repatriated eighty-three children. As a consequence, their children are still living in the Iraqi prisons with their mothers who are serving their terms.

On 17 December 2020, psychologists in Kazakhstan sent me a video of the Kazakh repatriated children singing and celebrating the Independence Day of Kazakhstan. What I noticed is that the children have changed a lot. Last year they were completely different. Now they smile and their eyes are shining. Meanwhile, other children are still living in Al-Hawl and Roj camps under violence and indoctrination, not to mention the lack of access to medical services and education. Every single day spent at the camps is damaging their health and mind. Children who were repatriated received a chance to get education and to be rehabilitated. The earlier they will be repatriated, the easier it will be to work with them. As one of the U.S. officials told me, children are changing fast. "Two years ago, we saw a boy, he was a six-year-old. This year he is at Roj camp, he is eight, and now he is different. Because he started thinking and judging the world according to what is around him." Children are growing up. Repatriation is the only solution for children to save them and help them return to normal life.

INTERNATIONAL NORMS TOWARD CHILDREN IN ARMED GROUPS

States have legal obligations to protect and save children. The Paris Commitments to Protect Children from Unlawful Recruitment or Use by Armed Forces or Armed Groups illustrates a number of state obligations concerning the protection of children who have been victims of armed conflict. The Paris Commitments clearly state that children who have been utilized by armed forces must be treated "in accordance with international humanitarian law, with special consideration of their status as children."[9] The Paris Commitments clearly spell out that children should be considered "primarily as victims of violations against international law and not only as alleged perpetrators."[10] According to the main Conventions on children's rights, states should act in the best interest of children. The Convention on the Rights of the Child affirms the basic right to life for every child, including the duty of the states to uphold the right to life, as well as the right to survive and develop. The right to develop specifically states that children should be able to grow up in an environment that doesn't negatively impact their physical and mental well-being.[11] Further, the Convention clearly articulates the need for all states to put the best interests of children at the forefront of any of their actions.[12] The Convention on the Rights of the Child makes it clear that states are obligated to ensure the well-being of children, including securing their survival, access to healthcare, and access to education.

The children of foreign ISIS fighters are currently being deprived of access to healthcare and education, which is severely threatening their ability to survive. The OSCE's *Guidelines for Addressing the Threats and Challenges of "Foreign Terrorist Fighters" within a Human Rights Framework* notes the shift away from the practice of the "best interest of the child" denoted in the Convention:

> The UN Convention on the Rights of the Child (CRC) is the most widely ratified human rights convention, with almost universal ratification by 196 states parties. The cardinal principle reflected in the CRC, and across international and regional standards, is that the primary focus should be on acting in the "best interest of the child." However, in practice, as noted by the United Nations Interregional Crime and Justice Research Institute (UNICRI), in counterterrorism the focus appears to have shifted towards children being potential threats. This approach risks neglecting the "best interest of the child."[13]

The Optional Protocol to the Convention of the Rights of the Child on the Involvement of Children in Armed Conflict builds on the obligations of states regarding the rehabilitation and reintegration of children who have been victims of armed conflict. The Optional Protocol was drafted due to a need for further "international cooperation" concerning the "physical and psychological rehabilitation and social reintegration of children who are victims of armed conflict."[14] The Optional Protocol further affirms that states must work to cooperate on preventing activities that would disallow the rehabilitation and reintegration of children.[15] Moreover, the Optional Protocol outlines the obligations states have to reintegrate and rehabilitate children. This is a duty that states must undertake to ensure the protection of children as well as their future security. Children who are not able to return to their states of origin, and instead remain isolated in camps, not only risk significant health and mental health issues, but also radicalization, further endangering the state and the wider international community. In this vein, the OSCE's Guidelines state, "While the challenges are considerable, states should take all possible measures to give meaningful effect to children's rights." There is a strong legal background that obliges states to protect children and consider them as victims. Thus, many European states softened their positions and started repatriating children from Syria but in a small number. States such as France, Denmark, Belgium; Germany, Switzerland and the Netherlands repatriated dozens of orphan children. The experiences of Kazakhstan, Kyrgyzstan, Uzbekistan, and Tajikistan are unique. They repatriated a large number of children. Kazakhstan repatriated 680 women and children and I have been lucky to have access to returnees in Kazakhstan and also have read many media materials in Russian and Kazakh that had given me a good opportunity to have empirical evidence.

KAZAKH CHILDREN BROUGHT TO OR BORN IN THE CONFLICT ZONE

A seven-year-old boy sat on the bed at the rehabilitation center in Aktau, Kazakhstan in the video produced by the Kazakh authorities. The social worker approached the boy and gave him some multicolored pens. The boy looked excited and started to draw something. The social worker asked whether he knew about colors. He answered "No." Then, the social worker showed him, "This pen is red, this is green, this is yellow."

> —Did you ever have colored pens in Syria?
>
> —No. Only once, but I lost them.
>
> —What are you going to draw now?
>
> —A boat on the water.
>
> —Do you know what color water is?
>
> —It is dirty, muddy.
>
> —No, water is not dirty, it is very clean here. Tomorrow, we will go to the sea, the Caspian Sea is just nearby, so you will see that the water is not dirty here. The dirty water was in Syria.[16]

The boy continued drawing as he was revealing many new things after returning to Kazakhstan during the operation Zhusan. The Kazakh government repatriated more than 500 children from Syria and Iraq in 2019 and 2020. A majority of the children went to school and are well integrated.

The majority of the returnees in rehabilitation were children, most of them born in Syria and Iraq. One of the missions that ISIS demanded from women who joined them was to give birth to as many children as possible. Typically, each woman gave birth to between three and five children. Sixty-five percent of returnees in Kazakhstan are children and Operation Zhusan brought back about 500 of them. The youngest was seven days old and the oldest was sixteen years old. Instead of playing and enjoying their childhood, these children went through the horrors of war. When they played with each other, they would pretend to play by imitating the things they had seen—shooting, kidnapping, and arresting each other. That was the kind of life they had lived in Syria and Iraq.

One ten-year-old Kazakh boy returned alone from Syria during Operation Zhusan. He was separated from his parents during the bombings and was left alone in the streets. He was not sure if his parents were still alive or had been killed. He had crawled out the ruins and could not find his family. He joined some other Arab boys and lived as a street boy amongst the ruins of collapsed houses for two years. As bombs continued to fall, he ran from one city to another. He walked through northern Syria and along the border of Iraq. Finally, he reached the Kurdish camps and found some Kazakh women. The Kazakh women recognized him because they knew him and his parents, and he was repatriated alongside them. He was a very serious boy who spoke Arabic fluently. Fortunately, he was reunited with his mother when she was repatriated during the following phase of Operation Zhusan. She had also been thinking that her son was most likely dead. The mother and her son now live together in their home city in Kazakhstan.

Another Kazakh boy was fifteen years old when he went to Turkey with the goal to reach Syria. Now, he is eighteen years old and back in Kazakhstan. He confirmed that he was forced by his parents to go with them to Syria. "I did not want to be there. I wanted to escape and return. I even tried to run away once, but I was captured," he said. He was charged along with other men for his involvement in terrorism and sentenced to eight years imprisonment. He was trained in the so-called *Muaskar* in Syria, which is a military training camp for teenagers. "When I arrived in Syria, they wanted me to become a suicide bomber. I refused. They insisted, but I was resistant. Then they sent me to *Muaskar* anyway. We lived there in caves and were trained how to shoot. In the evenings, we had lectures about their ideology and watched propaganda videos. I was punished many times for disobeying. Twice, I was buried in the ground for disobeying," he said.[17] He does not know the whereabouts of his mother and sister. The last time he saw them was in Syria in 2017, and then they never met again. His father was supposedly imprisoned in Syria by the Kurdish forces.

The time spent in Syria left an appalling imprint on the children both taken to Syria or born there. A fifteen-year-old girl returned to Kazakhstan with her one-year-old baby. Currently, she is working in a beauty salon and taking care of her child who is now two years old. Another girl, thirteen years old, also had to marry whilst in Syria. Her mother told social workers that she decided to marry her off to one of the ISIS fighters because she was afraid that she might become a victim of rape otherwise. For a mother, it was a difficult decision, but she felt she had to marry her off for her own safety. Another fourteen-year-old girl did not want to go to school after having been repatriated, as she was taught in Syria that school education is against her religious belief. It took six months for social workers and psychologists to convince her to study at school.

Children returning from Syria did not know how to read as they never went to school in the traditional sense. ISIS indoctrinated them with their ideology and forced them to read the Quran and then to learn distorted concepts such as tawhid, takfir, jihad, and the caliphate. Even children as old as ten and eleven did not know the Kazakh alphabet because they had no opportunity to study it. Periodically, the children were sent to *madrasas* whilst in Syria, but they were mainly expected to read the Quran at home. The important factor was indoctrination at home. Their mothers taught their children to see the world through the prism of the Wahhabi-Salafist ideology. Children were intensively taught to read the Quran at home, and they also had group lessons with other families. A nine-year-old boy, who returned to Kazakhstan alone and was reunited with his grandmother, spoke to journalists. He explained why he went to Syria. He said confidently that they went there for jihad. His grandmother said the terrorists brainwashed her grandson. She tried to explain to him that those who do not read Namaz but believe in God are not infidels or *kafur*s. "I asked him, 'I do not read Namaz, am I also a *kafur* to you?' 'No, you are my grandmother,' he answered. I explained that those people are also someone's grandparents."[18] Many children perceived other people as infidels and the Islamic state to be their home.

ISIS would usually take boys away from their mothers as soon as they reached nine or ten years of age. The boys were usually taken to visit religious *Muaskar*, where they were trained and indoctrinated into radical ideologies. Those who reached the age of ten, were considered soldiers to be trained in a military *Muaskar*, a training camp for boys. In 2016, ISIS produced a video wherein Kazakh boys appeared with arms and called out to kill *kafurs*. Three Kazakh boys who appeared in the propaganda video were later killed during drone attacks. The repatriated children told Kazakh journalists they knew these boys from the video who were trained in the *Muaskar* camps and how they later died.

The children who were returned to Kazakhstan started attending school. However, the government had to deal with many legal challenges prior to this. Firstly, the children, who were born in Kazakhstan, had returned without any identity documents, so the government had to restore all their birth certificates. Then, they started registering them at schools and kindergartens in their hometowns. For children who were born in Syria, the government had to undertake DNA testing to confirm that the children actually belonged to the Kazakh families who claimed them. These children returned to Kazakhstan with a certificate of repatriation to their homeland. Subsequently, the government attended court hearings for each of the children, after which birth certificates could be issued for them.

The children attended normal schools with other Kazakh children. After working with psychologists, the mothers had agreed to remove their daughters' hijabs, so that girls and boys could go to school dressed like their peers. After several months, however, the psychologists learned that some of the women had reverted to forcing their daughters to put on hijabs. The children had not been able to resist their mothers and some of them were attending school in religious attires. Many girls returned from Syria still wearing hijabs and are under the strict control of their mothers who still want to follow all religious attributes imposed in the Middle East.

One positive skill common to all the returned children was that they were multilingual. They spoke Arabic, Russian, and Kazakh. Some of them even spoke some French because they had played with French-speaking European children in Syria. On the other hand, the children were behind in all aspects of their learning. They could not read, they could not do basic calculations, and they did not even recognize colors. As such, the children were going to school, but all of them had to join classes for younger children. Fifteen-year-old Kadyr should have joined at the ninth level, but he was studying in the fifth class with eleven- to twelve-year-old children. Twelve-year-old Assem should have been with the fifth level class, but she joined second year alongside eight-year-old children. ISIS did not want children to be educated but brainwashed, trained to shoot, and become suicide bombers. Children participated in executions and were married off as teenagers.

The psychologists who worked with the children every day at the rehabilitation center conducted various tests. Psychologist Lola Shakimova said that during projective drawing tests, the children used only black and gray colors, indicating a depressive condition. "The children had delayed speech development, socio-pedagogic neglect, and some of them suffered from cognitive and neurological difficulties associated with congenital dementia, also known as oligophrenia," said Lola Shakimova.[19] These pathologies were understood to result from the conditions under which the children had lived during the preceding several years. Women had given birth in basements without any medical assistance or access to medicines. They were starving and malnourished during pregnancy and some of them lived several months in the trenches without access to clean water or food.

According to the attending psychologists, the children had not been given enough affection, physical contact, love, kindness, or harmonic-moral education. All of the children had returned to Kazakhstan depressed and shut down. The children were very hesitant in their manner and highly sensitive to loud noises, especially the sound of airplanes. They had survived hundreds of bombings in Syrian cities. Since there is an airport in Aktau, airplanes were flying overhead once or twice a day. The children would start crying and trying to run away from the sound of the airplanes, with some of them even running into their rooms and hiding under the tables and beds. The psychologists who worked with the children repeatedly explained that they were safe in Kazakhstan and that there was no war and no bombings to be afraid of.

What was striking among the children was how compassionate the older children were towards their younger siblings whom they looked after. As caregivers for their siblings, they reacted to their needs very quickly, presumably since there had been many threats in Syria and the older children had learned to be prudent. The children had, of course, been left alone at home, especially during times when their parents were fighting or looking for food. Mothers, who were trying to provide food for the children amidst the bombings, would leave them alone while they went to find food and water. After returning to Kazakhstan, the older children retained their protective instincts and took care of their younger sisters and brothers. According to psychologists, this sense of compassion was very important for furthering family ties and adaptation to new circumstances.

There is a scheme for working with female returnees and children developed in Kazakhstan. The author of the handbook—Yulia Denisenko, is an independent expert on countering violent extremism and deradicalization. She stressed in her scheme that the majority of women wanted to believe in a miracle that was expected to come after experiencing difficulties in their lives. "Naively believing in such a miracle was successfully sent by recruiters as a 'fast food.' The side effect of such naïve belief is a dependency on illusion, practically the same as dependence on drugs and alcohol," said Yulia Denisenko during the interview.[20] Yulia stressed that rehabilitation and reintegration of small children would be smooth compared to adults and older children.

"Rehabilitation of small children is possible but only if they are surrounded with love and care. There are older children who were indoctrinated and still remain radicalized, but they are a minority. The majority of repatriated children are under four to fives years old, so we have a greater chance to raise them normally and prevent their radicalization. However, there is a risk that they will have psychological and physical pathologies in the future as a result of experienced violence and malnutrition. But each case is individual and there is no universal way to treat them," said Yulia Denisenko.

Kazakhstan repatriated children from Iraq who were living in Iraqi prisons with their mothers, who were convicted of terrorism charges. On 27 November 2019, as part of Operation Zhusan, Kazakhstan evacuated fourteen children, eight girls and six boys from Iraq. The oldest of them was ten years old and the youngest was one and a half. Only two of them were born in Kazakhstan, the other twelve were born in Syria or Iraq. According to Stanislav Vasilenko, the Kazakh authorities had undertaken DNA testing before repatriating them to be certain of their heritage. "First, we found their grandparents, aunts, and uncles and took DNA tests. We then sent their results to Iraq and compared both results to ensure that they were our children," said Vasilenko.[21] These children had been living in an Iraqi prison in terrible conditions since dozens of Kazakh women had been sentenced in Iraq for terrorism offenses and had been detained together with their children. "In one cell, there were forty women plus their children. They ate twice a day and were given only rice and water. As such, when presented with the opportunity, the mothers signed the document giving their consent for the children to be repatriated without hesitation," said Daniyar Baybekov.[22]

The separation of children from their mothers was a heartbreaking moment that occurred in Iraq. "We had a soul-destroying and heartbreaking moment near the prison in Iraq when the mothers had to say goodbye to their children. Everyone cried. Our social workers and lawyers also cried at that moment. But we had to save the children as they were living in deadly conditions in the prisons. Now they are in Kazakhstan and are living with their grandparents or other relatives," said Yerzhan Ashikbaev.[23] Indeed, this is a heartbreaking moment as nobody knows if the women who were sentenced in Iraq will see their children again. After landing at the airport in Kazakhstan, the siblings held each other's arms and did not let them go. "They had walked every day in Iraq and Syria, holding onto each other. Over several years they held each other for fear of losing one other. This psychological aspect showed that they lived with the feeling that they were at risk of losing each other at any moment. The children were aware of this risk and this is the big tragedy," said Yerzhan Ashikbaev, Deputy Minister of Foreign Affairs, during the side event in Vienna.

Children in Syria witnessed executions too. ISIS used to make the children watch the beheadings in their propaganda videos. Two brothers, Abdul and Aman, returned from Syria and were lucky not to have been placed in the military *Muaskar*. They periodically went to religious lectures where they were taught radical ideas. Their father worked as an *Idari*, a guardian of the widows' house called *Mukar*. He was armed and had to monitor the widows and accompany the women if they needed to go somewhere. He was killed while he was transporting several women from one *Mukar* to another. The car they were traveling in was hit by a bomb and no one survived.

The two brothers told Kazakh journalists how they once played with their father's gun in Syria. One of them accidentally pulled the trigger. The bullet ricocheted off the concrete floor, hitting their mother in the leg. Luckily, she was taken to the hospital in time and survived the wound. The brothers also told journalists how they once witnessed an execution in the street. "We saw the body of the executed person with a hole in his head. They said that he was a *djesus*—a spy. I was not afraid of the bombings, but for the first time I was really shocked at seeing the body of an executed person," said Abdul.[24] Both of them witnessed many bombings. "You sit at home and hear a bomb flying down. By the sound, we could already recognize whether it was artillery, aircraft, or a drone bomb. If we were home, we hid under the porch. It was very dangerous to run outside. We needed to immediately run away from the place where the shells hit because five minutes later, they would usually bomb there again. And it was also necessary to have time to drag away the wounded," Aman recalled.[25]

In the final throes of the siege, the weakened terrorist groups tried to escape to the surrounding cities and deliberately transported women and children to use them as human shields. Consequently, Kazakh women and children had to move from one place to another. Their final destination was the town of Baghouse. The women and children were trapped in the city while the Syrian Democratic forces were fighting to take over the city and defeat ISIS. The women and children recalled these days spent in Baghouse as some of the most difficult, during which they were left without food or shelter. "We were living without any shelter under the open sky. It was raining endlessly and many children died from the cold and starvation," said Aida Sarina, a Kazakh returnee to journalists.

Operation Zhusan brought back approximately forty orphaned children. They were adopted by grandparents or other family members in Kazakhstan. The most challenging part was finding relatives who could adopt them, particularly since siblings often had different fathers. Most of the time grandparents were unaware of how many new children had been born in Syria, which was why Kazakh authorities had to use DNA tests to convince grandparents to adopt children. Some grandparents took the children of their sons who had died or had been imprisoned in Syria. A Russian woman, who lived in the Al-Hawl camp, convinced the Kazakh government that she gave birth to four children belonging to Kazakh fighters. She insisted them to be taken to Kazakhstan and to be given to the relatives of her two husbands. After completing DNA tests, the four children were brought to Kazakhstan and given to two different families.

Some orphan children were taken care of by other Kazakh women in Syria for several years. Despite the horrible conditions, they kept feeding and protecting the children as well as they could. Nazgul, a Kazakh woman, brought back eight children, four of whom were orphans. She had managed to reach the Kurdish camps with all eight children and had taken care of them there for four months. "The oldest of the children was sixteen years old. He spoke good Arabic and could drive a motor, so he helped me a lot. Early in the morning, we used to go to the streets and look for food. We starved a lot, but we survived. Sitting in the camp, I repeated to them, 'Children, we have to return to Kazakhstan, we should stay alive, so we will hold each other by the hand and go together all the time,'" she recalls. Another woman, Aida Sarina, found a Kazakh boy in Syria and brought him back with her when she was repatriated. The boy now lives in Kazakhstan with his grandmother.

CONCLUSIONS

About 20,000 children were born in the Middle East under ISIS and they have never seen normal life. Other thousands of children were brought to the conflict zone by their parents. Children saw brutal crimes, were beaten, raped, and forced to learn Quran and radical ideologies, while being deprived of their childhood. These children were taught to imagine a world only with the Islamic state and still don't know that there is an entire world exists full of joy where they can enjoy life by going to school, having books and toys. The Russian woman living in the Roj camp sent me a photo of her son playing by sculpting tanks, arms and tents with mud. The boy has no idea about normal life living in a normal house and having books and toys. Currently, 70 percent of the two camps in Northeast Syria are populated by children. They should be a top priority for repatriation. Even though older children may remain radicalized, there is a chance to save their minds. What is striking in children's indoctrination is how they see the world and how they think. They were taught to see the world through the prism of the Salafi-Wahhabi ideology. They divide people into Muslims and infidels. However, we can still save their minds. Thus, the earlier we repatriate them the more chance for rehabilitation and returning them to the normal life. There is a big difference between repatriated children in Kazakhstan and those who are still in the desert in Northeast Syria. Kazakh children go to school, they started to understand that living in a homeland is completely different. They do not divide people into Muslims and non-Muslims. Many of them started to forget about the bombings. Some children are fully integrated and receive good marks at school. Several videos were published where returnee children were singing and celebrating Kazakhstan's Independence Day. Now they know that they have a homeland and their government saved them by repatriating them. I hope they will remember that and will return their gratitude by being responsible citizens. At the same time, children who are living in Roj and Al-Hawl camps are still exposed to brainwashing and indoctrination. They are living without access to medical assistance, food, and education. Radicalized women call their sons lions and say "our lions are growing and will restore our dignity." The main task of states should be to save the minds of children, even from their radicalized mothers. Otherwise, the world gets hundreds of Usama ben Ladens. Repatriation of children should be done for the sake of international peace.

NOTES

1. Joana Cook and Gina Vale, "From Daesh to Diaspora II: The Challenges Posed by Women and Minors After the Fall of the Caliphate," *CTC Sentinel* 12, Issue 6, (2019).

2. Thomas Renard and Rik Coolsaet, "From the Kingdom to the Caliphate and Back: Returnees in Belgium, in Retûrnees: Who Are They, Why Are They (Not) Coming Back and How Should We Deal with Them?," *Egmont Paper 1010*, (2018), 37.

3. Renard and Coolsaet, "From the Kingdom to the Caliphate," 37.

4. News24, "Iraq sentences 616 foreigners for ISIS links in 2018," https://www.news24.com/news24/World/News/iraq-sentenced-616-foreigners-for-isis-links-in-2018-2018123.

5. Joana Cook and Gina Vale, "From Daesh to Diaspora II, ibid.

6. Human Rights Watch, "Everyone Must Confess: Abuses Against Children Suspected of ISIS Affiliation in Iraq," (2019), https://www.hrw.org/sites/default/files/report_pdf/iraq0319_web_1.pdf.

7. Jo Becker, "ISIS Trials Don't Deliver Justice—Including for Children," *Human Rights Watch*, (2020), https://www.hrw.org/news/2020/01/31/iraqs-isis-trials-dont-deliver-justice-including-children.

8. Human Rights Watch, "Everyone Must Confess."

9. The Paris Commitments Commitment 9, "The Paris Commitments to protect children from unlawful recruitment or use by armed forces or armed groups: Consolidated Version," (2007).

10. The Paris Commitments Commitment 11, "The Paris Commitments: Consolidated Version. The Paris Commitments to protect children from unlawful recruitment or use by armed forces or armed groups: Consolidated Version," (2007).

11. Article 6, The Paris Commitments.

12. Article 3, The Paris Commitments.

13. OSCE: Office for Democratic Institutions and Human Rights, "Guidelines for Addressing the Threats and Challenges of "Foreign Terrorist Fighters" within a Human Rights Framework, (2018), 69, https://bulaninstitute.org/wp-content/uploads/2020/04/Guidelines-for-Addressing-FTFs.pdf.

14. OHCHR, "Optional Protocol to the Convention on the Rights of the Child on the involvement of children in armed conflict," (2000).

15. OHCHR, "Optional Protocol to the Convention on the Rights of the Child on the involvement of children in armed conflict: Article 7," (2000).

16. The episode is from an official video produced by the National Security Committee of Kazakhstan about the everyday life of returnees at the rehabilitation center in Aktau.

17. Aqjaiyq TV, "Returnees from Syria: A Long Journey to Home," TV program produced by Aqjaiyq TV, (2009), he was interviewed in the prison by journalists of Aqjaiyq TV, the full video available at: https://www.youtube.com/watch?v=M7q_LRQsNKY&t=197s.

18. Aqjaiyq TV, interview conducted by Kazakh journalists and published by Aqjaiyq TV, (2009), TV program available here in Russian at: https://www.youtube.com/watch?v=M7q_LRQsNKY&t=197s.

19. Lola Shakimova, interview by the author.

20. Interview with Yulia Denisenko was conducted by the author.

21. "Kazakhstan evacuated fourteen children from Iraq," *Cabar,* 29 November 2019, translated by the author from Russian, available at: https://cabar.asia/ru/kazahstan-evakuiroval-14-detej-iz-iraka/.

22. "Kazakhstan evacuated fourteen children from Iraq," (2009).

23. Yerzhan Ashikbaev answered questions during the side-event organized by Kazakhstan on the margins of the Vienna conference in 2020.

24. Askar Djaldinov, "Hostages of a caliphate," *Newspaper Vremia*, 26 July 2019, translated by the author, available at https://time.kz/articles/risk/2019/07/26/zalozhniki-halifata.

25. Askar Djaldinov, "Hostages of a caliphate."

Chapter 7

State Policies to Deal with Returning Fighters and Their Associates

From the outset of the conflict in Syria that started in 2011, countries had struggled to stop the outflow of people to Syria and Iraq. However, several years later they saw many foreign fighters marching back home. As of 2014, some states had already received voluntary returnees who were disillusioned and managed to escape the conflict zone. Since 2018, when ISIS began to crumble in Iraq, the international community has been faced with the impasse of how to deal with returning foreign fighters. But the real difficulty came later, after the fall of Baghous, the last stronghold in Syria. While foreign fighters and their associates, captured in the territory of Iraq, immediately fell into the authority of the Iraqi government, the fate of those in Syria remains unclear. As ISIS's territory shrank, fighters were moving gradually toward northeast Syria, together with their wives and children. After the fall of ISIS in Syria, all of them fell into the custody of the Syrian Democratic Forces (SDF), which is a non-state actor. This presents an acute policy problem, as members of the terrorist groups are held in a territory without a state authority. Thus, there is no legitimate power to bring them to trial and states have struggled to find an adequate approach on how to deal with captured fighters and their family members. The two main issues are how to bring foreign fighters to justice for their crimes committed in Iraq and Syria and what to do with their family members trapped in northeast Syria.

The international debate continues to unfold and several options have been discussed, such as trying the accused in the country where their crimes took place, repatriating and prosecuting in home countries, creating an ad hoc tribunal, and transferring all fighters to Iraqi prisons. At the same time, some states have put administrative measures to use, such as stripping citizenship and a temporary ban on entering their home countries. The UN and other international actors have urged states to repatriate their citizens, stating that countries have to comply with their obligations under international law. The UN and international lawyers have advocated and urged states to repatriate at least children and women. Nevertheless, several states such as the US, Kazakhstan, Uzbekistan, Tajikistan, Kyrgyzstan and Kosovo, have repatriated their citizens from Syria, but only about ten countries have repatriated a small number of children.

The issue of dealing with returning foreign fighters shows complexity because of two reasons. First, both the scale of global travel to ISIS-held territory by fighters from over sixty countries and the substantial percentage of women and children who joined them were unprecedented. The international community had never witnessed the mobilization of foreign fighters at this scale. We had never seen small children and women traveling to conflict zones to join terrorist groups. The second complication stems from fighters trapped in the territory of northeast Syria, which is administered by the Autonomous Administration of North and East Syria (AANES) and the Syrian Democratic Forces. This lack of state authority is a source of ambiguity states refer to when they refuse to repatriate or take other concrete actions. Many states maintain a firm position that former ISIS fighters and their associates should be brought to justice on the territory where they committed their crimes. However, in northeast Syria, there is no state authority to bring them to court and no tribunals where evidence, concerning the committed crimes, can be presented. States do not consider the SDF to be a legitimate negotiating actor; thus, other options have been considered, such as creating an ad hoc tribunal or transferring all captured foreign fighters to Iraqi prisons. However, the judicial system of Iraq has shown to be inadequate and Western countries cannot hand over their citizens to a system operating under such deficits.

IRAQ AS A HOST COUNTRY WITH DEFICITS

The first solution to address ISIS fighters is to bring them to justice in the country where they committed their crimes. Thousands of foreign fighters have been taken to court in Iraq where the judicial system has many deficits. In Iraq, a legitimate government and state authority has been in place, allowing the court hearings to immediately begin following the defeat of ISIS. In 2018, Iraq retook control of large portions of its territory that ISIS had seized four years ago. After the defeat of ISIS, Iraq immediately began hunting down and arresting ISIS fighters and their associates roaming its territory. Since 2018, about 10,000 ISIS fighters captured in the territory of Iraq have been tried in Iraqi courts. In 2018, as Amnesty International highlighted, there was a sharp spike in the number of death sentences imposed in Iraq. "In Iraq, the number quadrupled from at least 65 in 2017 to at least 271 last year."[1] This rise in death sentences is presumably directly connected with the trials of ISIS fighters.

Among thousands of cases treated in local courts against individuals linked to ISIS, there are also hundreds of women and children. Iraqi and Kurdistan Regional Government authorities have arrested thousands of children on the suspicion of an ISIS membership. Human Rights Watch estimated in its report that approximately 1,500 children were detained in Iraq, including at least 185 foreign children.[2] All of them have been convicted on terrorism charges and sentenced to prison in Iraq. Human rights law, both on a national and international level, prohibits the sentencing of children and instead prescribes rehabilitation and reintegration. Governments should seek alternatives to prosecution and detention should be a measure of last resort for the shortest possible duration. Children taken by their parents to conflict zones should be approached as victims. Most were forced into training camps and compelled to acquire combat skills. It is inhuman and illegal to capture minors and to charge hundreds of children with terrorism offenses based on supposed links to ISIS. About thirty children that are in jails in Irbil informed Human Rights Watch that they were tortured to obtain confessions. Children were beaten with plastic pipes, electric cables, or rods, subjecting them to electric shocks, or using painful stress positions. "Many of the children said they had little or no actual involvement with ISIS but confessed simply to stop the torture."[3]

Iraq took very harsh punitive measures by punishing children, including those who did not participate in combat operations but were cooks or stayed home taking care of other children. This approach will have a profound negative impact on the Iraqi society stigmatizing families. Human Rights Watch experts warn that the detention and prosecution of children may also foster future grievances in Iraqi society. "One seventeen-year-old boy told Human Rights Watch, 'You have many kids detained based on fabricated testimonies. Once they are released, they might take revenge on the government and the people who imprisoned them.'"[4] The international community has urged Iraq to end the detention of children and prioritize their rehabilitation and reintegration. The Iraqi government should amend its counterterrorism laws to end the criminalization of membership in terrorist organizations for children under the age of eighteen, as children are not capable of apprehending such decisions on their own.

Many deficits are present in the judicial system of Iraq, which has been labeled by human rights defenders as "Guantánamo East" for its inability to guarantee fair trials.[5] UN experts monitored over 600 trial hearings against ISIS suspects in Iraq, including forty-four hearings against children. The courts did not distinguish between those who were commanders and responsible for violent crimes and those who took on a smaller role, such as cooks;

most defendants were charged for their ISIS affiliation and many of them received a death sentence.[6] UNAMI experts noted that trials were focused excessively on confessions, which may have been acquired through the practice of torture, which has been widely documented in Iraq.[7] The limited access to legal representation and frequent allegations of torture consisting of violations of international obligations and the right to a fair trial, UNAMI notes.

The UN mandates also warned about profound fundamental deficits in trials that have taken place in Iraq. Fionnuala Ní Aoláin, UN Special Rapporteur, informed me during an interview that there are profound concerns about the quality and fairness of the trials in Iraq. "Individuals are often charged without access to lawyers and in many cases, it is clear that individuals may have been subjected to torture and inhumane and degrading treatment prior to giving evidential statements, which are then unreliable. The trials themselves have been short, sometimes less than ten minutes particularly in cases of the death penalty. It's very clear that the Iraqi judicial system is struggling to implement those trials fairly," Dr. Ní Aoláin stated.[8]

Iraq, as a sovereign state, has a full right and obligation to bring ISIS fighters to justice as the terrorist group seized its territory, exploited natural resources, and killed innocent people. Iraq also played an important role in defeating ISIS and capturing fighters. Iraq has been very active in cooperating with the international community by closely working with UN mandates and commissions. However, it sought to deal with foreign fighters hastily and court hearings have been overly short, in some cases only lasting for fifteen minutes. The conviction of ISIS fighters has revealed deficits in the judicial system and the ways in which the Iraqi court system disregards basic human rights norms.

TRANSFERRING FROM SDF CUSTODY TO IRAQI PRISONS

Many states hold the position that ISIS fighters should be tried in a territory where they committed crimes. Especially, Western countries have been advocating for the option to try them in Iraq. Seven European countries held internal negotiations to discuss the option of transferring their citizens from the custody of the SDF to Iraqi prisons. However, these negotiations were discontinued after being criticized by the UN and international experts. France was a leading country seeking to have its citizens remain in the Middle East, and Iraq was the only state to try them. The French government visited Iraq several times to negotiate the details of the deal.[9] Many European countries have already faced terrorist attacks on their soil and consider returning fighters as a security threat. "Except [for] Germany, no other European country is interested in the return of their citizens accused of being Daesh members," said Hisham al-Hashimi, an Iraqi researcher who briefs officials on jihadi group dynamics. "Western countries don't have a policy for jihadi returnees, they are not ready for their arrival. . . . And if they get a death penalty in Iraq, they will be thankful," he said.[10]

EU countries are very reluctant to bring back their citizens and some diplomats consider the option of repatriation to be akin to self-harm. Seven European countries considered a similar position of trying its citizens in a host country and began working on a framework to do so beginning in June 2019. These officials had several talks with the Iraqi government to reach a deal to try European fighters in Iraq. Iraq in turn was also interested in the deal and requested millions of dollars in financial compensation for taking European fighters. According to media reports, Baghdad asked European countries, including Belgium, the UK, and France, to pay two million euros for each foreign combatant tried on its territory.[11] The seven EU countries may have discreetly discontinued the negotiations with Iraq due to the financial burden of the deal. Iraq also requested 100 million euros to construct a high-security prison and additional compensation of 10 million euros. Although this information has not been officially confirmed, media reports disclosed that Iraq demanded a very high price.

FRANCE'S TACIT ATTEMPTED DEAL WITH IRAQ

On 2 June 2019, the court in Baghdad heard the cases of eight French fighters, appearing in yellow jumpsuits and plastic slippers in court. French diplomats, UN observers, and journalists were present to observe the hearing, where the fighters were charged for joining a terrorist group and taking part in combat operations. One French fighter looked to those sitting in the courtroom and said "If anyone from the French embassy is present, I'm asking you to take care of my case and bring me back to France." But diplomats kept silent as they were merely there in an observational capacity and had no right to intervene. Seven of the twelve French fighters, who were captured by Kurdish forces earlier that year, were handed over to the Iraqi government.

On the same day, seven French men were sentenced to death and on the following day, the court of Baghdad sentenced another three French fighters to death.[12] France did not make any efforts to repatriate them but was present there to observe the court hearings.

France has the largest number of ISIS fighters compared to other European countries but has only repatriated about ten orphan children from Syria.[13] In total, it is estimated that about 2,000 French nationals traveled to Syria and Iraq.[14] A 2018 report from the International Centre for the Study of

Radicalization at King's College estimates that parents brought up to 460 children into ISIS territories.[15] France made the critical mistake of covertly negotiating the transfer of eleven French fighters captured in Syria to Iraq, all of whom were sentenced in an Iraqi court to death by hanging.[16] The French government and President Emmanuel Macron faced criticism for this, as France is staunchly opposed to the death penalty.[17] One of these critics, Agnes Callamard, the United Nations Special Rapporteur on Extrajudicial, Summary or Arbitrary Executions, expressed her concern by stating, "there are serious allegations that the sentences were handed down following unfair trials, with the accused having no adequate legal representation or effective consular assistance."[18] She called on the French government to repatriate all French fighters sentenced in Iraq and to try them at home. The French Foreign Ministry responded with a statement saying, "adult French nationals, men and women, having joined (ISIS) to fight in (Iraq and Syria) . . . should be tried nearest to where they committed their crimes."[19] However, France softened their position later on.

French high-level officials paid several visits to Iraq to discuss a judicial framework that would enable French fighters, that were held in Syria, to face trial in Iraq. France, which has experienced calamitous terrorist attacks on its soil, appears to have no compassion, even for women. Jean-Ives Le Drian, French Minister for Foreign Affairs, told journalists that those who traveled to Syria are not tourists. "The French women who went to this region in 2015 knew what they were doing. They aren't tourists. They are fighters against France and must face trial (in Iraq) if possible," he said.[20] However, France had to soften its position and stopped actively advocating the transferring of fighters from Syria to Iraq after facing additional backlash from the French community. An open letter from forty-five French lawyers with fierce objection was published in the media, titled: "It would be a huge disgrace for our country." They condemned the French government for relegating its own citizens to the death penalty in Iraq rather than repatriating them. The lawyers referred to the French constitution, which bans the death penalty, and considered the government's inaction to stop the trials in Iraq over French fighters an act of hypocrisy.[21] After facing harsh criticism at both the international and national level, it seems that France has ended its active engagement with Iraq, but there has not been an official update as of yet.

Generally speaking, France is a country highly concerned about religious radicalization. As President Emmanuel Macron stated, the country is fighting against Salafism and religious fundamentalism. "I want to be very clear about this: This is a problem in our country."[22] After the October 2019 terrorist attack at the Paris Police Headquarters, President Macron called on the French people to be vigilant in looking for radicalization signs in fellow citizens "at school, at work, in places of worship, close to home."[23] France experienced several deadly terrorist attacks in the last decade and thus systematically confronts any threat of violent extremism. France has serious arguments to put on the table against returning foreign fighters, as some of these deadly attacks were carried out by returnees. Several suspects connected to the November 2015 Paris attacks are also reported to have spent time in Syria with ISIS before returning to carry out the attacks.[24]

However, France should reconsider its approach when it comes to minors. France has the third-highest proportion of foreign ISIS minors, between 24–37 percent, equating up to 700 children, half of which are under the age of five.[25] So far France has repatriated fewer than 100 children of its total 700.[26] Hundreds of French children languish in the camps held by the Kurdish forces. On 30 May 2020, the New York Times reported that a seven-year-old French girl was on the verge of dying if she did not receive urgent medical care.[27] As a result, in April 2020, France sent a medical jet and flew her to Paris for treatment, leaving her mother, two brothers, and twin sister in Syria. The urgent repatriation of the little girl, which was an exception due to her health conditions, demonstrated that France could negotiate with the SDF if necessary and retrieve children easily if the French government desires to do so. The French government has been brought to court several times for its unwillingness to repatriate women and children.[28] In mid-2019, a lawsuit was filed before the European Court of Human Rights on behalf of the grandparents of two French children who are held in Syria. The suit claims that the current conditions in the camps is leading to inhumane treatment and exposure to dangerous diseases. The lawsuit also referred to Art. 3 of the European Convention on Human Rights, which states that "no one may be deprived of the right to enter the territory of the state of which he is a national."[29] In July and September 2019, lawsuits were filed against Foreign Minister Jean-Yves Le Drian by family members of several children and their mothers held in Syria for his refusal to repatriate them.[30] However, despite the ongoing trials and pressure from the international community, the French government has not significantly changed its position on repatriation.

STRIPPING CITIZENSHIP IS A DELUSION

The 9/11 attacks were a turning point in the use of deprivation of citizenship as a counterterrorism tool. Western countries, mainly the U.S. and the UK, began using denaturalization as a security measure as a part of the War on Terror. States began revoking citizenship from terrorist suspects, and later from foreign fighters who traveled to conflict zones. The national legislation of many states already contained special provisions about the revocation of citizenship for acts that undermine national interests, including terrorism activities. It is usual practice for states to have such provisions, but they had rarely been used in modern times. According to the Global Database on Modes of Loss of Citizenship, 130 countries around the world have such norms in national legislation, including nineteen European countries.[31] However, since 2014, some states have amended it to specify traveling abroad to join terrorist groups. Nonetheless, not all states employ this practice, and stripping citizenship as a punitive measure is practiced mainly by Western countries.

United Kingdom was one of the first countries that enacted administrative measures for joining terrorist groups abroad and began denaturalizing foreign fighters.[32] The UK not only targets individuals with dual nationality, but singularly British nationals too, while other states only revoke the citizenship of those who hold dual nationalities. In fact, the policy of the UK renders its citizens stateless. The UK adopted the Counter-Terrorism and Security Act in 2015, which includes Temporary Exclusion Orders. The document bans the re-entry of British citizens to the UK for up to two years where there are concerns regarding threats to security.[33] Although these norms have been evaluated as incompatible with the European Convention on Human Rights by the National Council for Civil Liberties, the UK has moved ahead.[34] The subsequent Counter-Terrorism and Border Security Act of 2019 introduced, as a new offense, entering or remaining in select areas designated by the Home Secretary.[35] Furthermore, the government has insisted prosecutions be brought in the region where offenses are alleged to have been committed.[36]

Another document that cements the denaturalization of British citizens is the 2014 Immigration Act. The Act includes section 66, which stipulates deprivation of citizenship for actions seriously prejudicial to the vital interests of the UK. This provision allows the Home Secretary to revoke naturalized citizenship, as long as doing so is conducive to the public good and authorities have reason to believe the concerned individual will have the ability to be naturalized elsewhere.[37] The British government took such measures from the initial return of foreign fighters to its soil and the BBC, the Guardian and other media outlets had already made such cases public.

No official numbers have been made public on how many British men are held in custody in Syria or Iraq, but we can assume that most of them may have already been stripped of their citizenship. There are several cases journalists have made public. Brothers Aseel and Nasser Muthana were interviewed in prison in Syria by a journalist in December 2019. Neither of them was aware that their citizenship had been revoked.[38] Shamima Begum, who left for Syria when she was fifteen years of age, was stripped of her citizenship in February 2019. She wanted to return home, but the British government declared that Begum could claim Bangladeshi citizenship due to her family heritage.[39] Despite the Bangladeshi Foreign Minister stating this was unacceptable and that she would face the death penalty if prosecuted there, Ms. Begum's appeal regarding her UK citizenship was denied in February 2020.[40]

Other countries that have revoked citizenship or denied entry of their citizens in the conflict zones are Australia, the U.S., France, Canada, Bosnia and Herzegovina and the Netherlands. In 2017, the Netherlands revoked the citizenship of four Dutch men who went to Syria and sentenced each of them to prison for six years, but in absentia. The Dutch government adopted administrative measures against foreign fighters, including denaturalization and stripping passports. The Dutch government may issue entry bans against individuals originating from a non-EU background and declare them as "undesirable foreign nationals." Since March 2013, these measures have been used against fifteen individuals.[41] Finally, the Netherlands can also refuse or revoke the residence permit of non-EU citizens constituting a threat (resulting in expulsion).[42] Australia amended its legislation in 2017, allowing the government to revoke the citizenship of individuals having joined a foreign army or terrorist organization outside of Australia. In December 2018, the government denaturalized the most wanted ISIS fighter who held dual citizenship and was born in Australia. The man was captured by Turkish forces and has been in captivity near Gaziantep. A diplomatic disagreement arose between Australia and Fiji when Australia revoked an individual's citizenship, referring to his Fijian nationality.[43] The Australian government issued a statement on this case and stated that dual nationals who choose to be involved in terrorism will be stripped of their Australian citizenship.

Belgium announced in its legislation in 2012 to strip those with dual citizenship of their Belgian citizenship if convicted of serious crimes, including terrorism. In January 2020, six foreign fighters with Belgian-Moroccan nationality, who left for Syria, were stripped of their Belgian nationality.[44] All of them were already tried and sentenced in absentia in 2015. Among the six people stripped of their Belgian nationality was Fouad Akrich, a former student in Deurne. Akrich's family said he was brainwashed by Sharia4Belgium, and that he ran away from home in 2012 to travel to Syria. The Brussels Times reported that he was captured in Turkey with his wife and detained, but that his whereabouts since then are unknown. Denmark also criminalized acts of terrorism, financing terrorism, and participation in unlawful military organizations. Persons convicted of committing an act of terrorism may lose their Danish citizenship unless this loss renders them stateless.[45] Denmark has revoked the citizenship of returnees too. In March 2017, a Danish-Turkish man was sentenced to six years imprisonment for joining ISIS and was simultaneously stripped of his Danish citizenship. He will be expelled to Turkey upon completing his sentence. Denmark had used these measures once before in June 2016 for a Danish-Moroccan citizen and became one of the first countries to exercise such power for a returnee. The United States also refused the request of a woman born in New Jersey, Hoda Muthana, to return to the country. She left to go to Syria in 2014 and is currently detained in a camp in Syria with other women who are linked to ISIS. Her family brought a lawsuit against the US government to try and force her repatriation, but this was contested in court. The judge ruled in favor of the government arguing that, when she was born, her father, who is from Yemen, had diplomatic protection and as such, she was not entitled to US citizenship at birth, despite having been issued a US passport.[46] Yet generally, the citizenship of US-born citizens is guaranteed by the Constitution of the United States and cannot be revoked.

In 2015, after the Paris terrorist attacks that killed 130 people, France declared a state of emergency that lasted for two years. France has been considered as the main target of ISIS in Europe and the French government has therefore enacted very strict rules. Currently, the French government may issue expulsion or entry bans against potential or suspected foreign fighters and can revoke or confiscate their passports. In the French Civil Code, there is a provision concerning the stripping of citizenship of naturalized citizens convicted of treason or terrorism, but such measures have only been used thirteen times since 1996. However, dual national French citizens cannot have their French citizenship removed by authorities for the sole reason of being identified as a threat to national security. In the aftermath of the November 2015 attacks, the French government sought to make changes to be able to revoke citizenship, but the proposal was found controversial and was dropped in 2016.

Why does denaturalization not work? Mainly because states do not eradicate the threat of terrorism merely by stripping citizenship. Fighters will still remain in facilities in the Middle East. Abandoning them signifies neither fighting against terrorism nor bringing foreign fighters to justice for their crimes. Abandonment contributes to further radicalization and moreover diminishes the possibility of tracking their actions. Fighters move into illegal and underground existence, making it difficult to detect and monitor terrorist plots. It is important to remember the destiny of Bin Laden who was left stateless and continued to operate terrorist schemes underground. Foreign fighters stripped of their citizenship will acquire a new goal: to enact revenge and prove their existence. States must prioritize bringing to justice at home and rehabilitation and reintegration instead of abandonment and rejection.

Stripping citizenship does indeed have the short-term effect of conveying a symbolic message to the populace. This action, in fact, may lead to awakening and allowing serious considerations to spread among the public that, "people who have reneged on their obligations as citizens are no longer entitled to the protection of the state."[47] Concurrently, in European countries where Muslim communities feel fragile and marginalized, stripping citizenship could be understood as a selective approach. Muslims may perceive their citizenship to be conditional and conclude that the state may abandon them. Such a discriminatory approach will only further escalate the feeling of isolation and may come with the ramification of spreading discontent among communities.

The principal concern is that revoking citizenship violates international norms. Deprivation of nationality results in statelessness and this violates the state's obligations to reduce it under international law. States should respect UN resolutions and treaties including the UN Convention on the Reduction of Statelessness. Deprivation of nationality leads to statelessness where the individual in concern does not possess or immediately acquire another nationality. In the case of foreign fighters, European countries have primarily revoked the citizenship of those who hold dual nationalities. However, in many cases, we have seen that the other state also rejects to recognize them as its citizen. The UN recommended Member States to ensure that such deprivation is not arbitrary. States should "establish procedural standards, notably issue reasons in writing and grant the right to a review by a court or an independent body."[48] Most importantly, states must avoid deprivation of nationality based on discriminatory grounds, in particular on grounds of race, color, gender, and religion. If states follow distinct policies for Muslims and non-EU nationals, while having softer policies for EU citizens, this can be considered as a discriminatory approach.

To sum up, denaturalization is simply an act of states escaping their responsibility. The deprivation of citizenship removes the state's responsibility towards its citizens to protect and prosecute while guaranteeing due process. It is also irresponsible behavior in terms of international peace. If an individual poses a danger to other states, the state is responsible for capturing and bringing the purported suspect to justice. However, abandonment and leaving fighters stateless is a direct threat to international peace. The lack of repatriation, prosecution, rehabilitation, and reintegration will only lead to further radicalization. Western states have taken an approach that "citizenship is a privilege, not a right," a concept first used by Hillary Clinton in 2010 and then followed by European partners.

SENTENCING FIGHTERS IN ABSENTIA

Many states have sentenced citizens in absentia who went to Syria. Their terms ranged from six to fifteen years for joining terrorist groups and disseminating propaganda. Foreign fighters, having learned of their sentence, decided not to return to their home countries. The ultimate goal of a trial in absentia may be to avoid the return of these foreign fighters. EU-leading countries such as the UK, Belgium, the Netherlands, Denmark, and France have already conducted at least two or three cases of trials in absentia. In Germany, the national legislation prohibits prosecutions in absentia based on an 'immediacy principle' that requires individuals to be present in court. The Sharia4Belgium terrorist organization, officially disbanded in 2012, reportedly sent seventy of its members to Syria by March 2013 through peer recruitment. In 2014, Belgium sentenced thirty-seven members of the Sharia4Belgium organization in absentia for up to fifteen years, though it was claimed that some of them had already died in Syria. In 2015, Belgium also sentenced four women in absentia to five-year prison sentences for joining ISIS.

US POLICY AND EFFORTS FOR REPATRIATION

In 2019, the US was the first country to initiate the repatriation of foreign fighters and called on other states to bring their citizens back from Syria. President Trump, in February 2019, called on European states to repatriate 800 foreign fighters to their respective countries of origin following their capture by US and Kurdish forces. "The United States is asking Britain, France, Germany and other European allies to take back over 800 ISIS fighters that we captured in Syria and put them on trial. The Caliphate is ready to fall. The alternative is not a good one, as we will be forced to release them," Trump wrote on Twitter. "The US does not want to watch as these ISIS fighters permeate Europe, which is where they are expected to go. We do so much, and spend so much time for others to step up and do the job that they are so capable of doing," he continued. The statement was issued when the SDF captured around 800 fighters, 600 women, and over 1,200 children, from dozens of countries. These people were the first advent of ISIS fighters and associates to surrender during the Kurdish-led offensive against ISIS. However, Trump may not had known that in the days following the fall of Baghouse, thousand more people would be flooding into the camps and prisons. After the fall of Baghouse, which was the last enclave of ISIS, about 50,000 people headed to camps in the following forty-eight hours. Since then, camps and prisons in northeast Syria have been on the verge of collapse due to a large number of people.

President Trump could have done more if he had used more diplomatic tactics. As the President of the United States, he failed to build a constructive dialogue with European leaders. His angry posts on Twitter should have instead centered around consistent diplomatic efforts. "Would you like some nice ISIS fighters?" he asked French President Emmanuel Macron at the NATO summit in December 2019.[49] Mr. Macron, vexed by such unexpected behavior during the high-level meeting, replied, "Let's be serious." This dialogue between the two Presidents circulated in the media during the week of the summit. President Trump might have been displeased by the silence of EU countries, he should have nonetheless behaved as a U.S. President and followed a more diplomatic approach. In international relations, threatening other countries seldom works and may worsen the situation. President Trump delivered several public speeches during which he threatened EU states that he would release foreign fighters into Europe. He stated that if Europe does not take them, he would have no choice but to release them into the countries from where they came. Of course, these kinds of speeches had a tendency to corrode the diplomatic efforts of the Trump administration.

The Trump administration proposed that high-value fighters could be transferred to and detained at the controversial Guantánamo Bay prison. Administration officials, including State Department deputy spokesperson Robert Palladino, stated that, while repatriation remains the first priority, high-value detainees, including members of the ISIS leadership could be sent to Guantanamo Bay. However, no fighter was sent. The US government continues to appeal to the duty of countries to repatriate their citizens. US Deputy Coordinator for Counterterrorism Christopher Harnisch reiterated the moral and security imperative of repatriation. "There is a moral and security imperative to repatriate our citizens, bring them to justice, and ensure that they never return to the battlefield . . . leaving your citizens in squalid camps in the desert or overcrowded prisons without charge, or worse yet, stripping citizens of their citizenship, shows a complete and utter disregard for human rights," said Mr. Harnish at a conference in Vienna.[50] The United States repatriated twenty-seven American citizens, including men, women, and children. "With this week's repatriations, the United States has brought back every American supporter of ISIS known to be held by the Syrian Democratic Forces against whom we have charges," said John C. Demers, Assistant Attorney General for National Security.[51]

The United States has been the only country ringing the alarm bell for over two years about the urgent need to repatriate children and about the dire living conditions in camps and detention facilities for women. The US government played a crucial role in convincing and assisting the repatriation operations of Kazakhstan, Uzbekistan, Kosovo, Tajikistan, Russia, and other states that at the very least brought back children. As Mr. Harnish highlighted, the collective inaction of states is planting the seeds for a future generation of terrorists. "One year ago, we met a seven-year-old boy, who was held in the al-Hol refugee camp. He has since turned eight years old and missed a year of primary education that he could have attended somewhere in his hometown in Europe or the Middle East or Central Asia. Instead, he received another year of indoctrination by ISIS. If we don't act now, he will eventually reach the fighting age and will be ready to carry the torch for his father," said Mr. Harnish at the Vienna conference on 12 February 2020.

There is an ongoing debate on whether repatriation remains the most effective way to address foreign fighters and their associates. European states, which oppose repatriation of adults, often refer to the absence of consular services in northeast Syria, noting that the lack of such services makes repatriation impossible. However, the US has been guaranteeing for states such access to foreign fighters and their family members, and the SDF, moreover, has never refused such requests by states. There is openness for direct engagement. The only related refusal has been in regards to children who were requested to be repatriated without their mothers. Several European governments previously intended to repatriate some small children but separating them from their mothers. The SDF refused to separate children from their mothers, referring to their internal norms and the fact that these women had not yet been brought to court. Regarding the absence of consular services, Special Rapporteur Fionnuala Ní Aoláin stated during an interview that states play a double game.

Ms. Ní Aoláin underlined the following during an interview conducted in April 2020:

> Practice has shown that many of these states are in direct contact with the camp authorities. We know that there had been significant and well-documented reporting that the security services of these states have been present in the camp and have been engaged in negotiations and discussions with a non-state actor. So, it seems that if you are willing to engage with a non-state actor regarding security measures, you could also step up in another way, that is, in a way to safeguard your citizens.

The examples of other states that have successfully repatriated their citizens have proven that repatriation can be undertaken by any state. Moreover, the cases of Kazakhstan, Uzbekistan, Kyrgyzstan, Tajikistan, and Kosovo have shown that states will have an opportunity to assess each case, prosecute jihadists where necessary, interrogate returnees to learn more about ISIS methods and plans, and build rehabilitation programs for women and children. Neither the US nor Iraq can become the world's jail for foreign fighters. States of origin should take responsibility for their nationals. Given that conditions in Syria could continue to deteriorate and the Kurdish forces may lose control over camps and facilities, European countries should seize any opportunity to remove their foreign fighters from Syria and reduce the threat of re-emergence of terrorist groups in the Middle East.

TURKEY AS A THIRD COUNTRY MOST AFFECTED

As a neighboring country with Syria, Turkey has largely been affected by the crisis in the Middle East. Many foreign fighters traveled to Syria through Turkey and some of them were captured at the Syrian-Turkish border. Turkey spent enormous financial and human resources to fight FTF flows and ISIS networks. An official from the Ministry of Foreign Affairs of Turkey stated during an interview that Turkey has struggled under this heavy burden. "Our security forces have been carrying out anti-DAESH operations. One should not forget that Turkey's efforts in the fight against DAESH had a greater impact than the combined endeavors of the international community as a whole. We are actually the only coalition member that put its troops in harm's way and fought DAESH on the ground, clearing 8200 km^2 from DAESH and PKK-YPG," the Turkish official stated.[52]

Turkey also captured hundreds of fighters and deported many of them to their home countries. Turkey's position is clear: foreign fighters and their family members should go home. The Turkish government has reminded states that repatriation remains a major responsibility of UN Member States. The Turkish official from the Turkish MFA, whom I met in Vienna, said during an interview that states should comply with UN resolutions and fulfill their international responsibilities. "Certain security, political and financial reasons have been mentioned to explain the rationale behind the nonrepatriation policy. However, those reasons tend to ignore long-term security threats posed by the FTFs that are not rehabilitated. States should assume their responsibility and repatriate their citizens," the Turkish official stated.

Turkey has struggled to transfer foreign fighters in its custody to their home countries. After capturing ISIS fighters and their family members, the identification process started. FTFs are most commonly held in so-called Removal Centers until they are deported. Turkey refers to the process as administrative detention. However, Turkey faces difficulties in handing over them, as countries are not keen to accept them back. "The number of persons kept in custody can change on a daily basis. We plan to send them to their countries of origin or any other country where they want to go, provided that they have legal documents for that destination. We coordinate the whole process with the Embassies of the relevant countries," the Turkish official stated. However, the Turkish government faces obstacles to negotiating and receiving the approval of countries to repatriate their nationals. Some countries are reluctant to do so and deny travel documents. Home countries also request DNA tests for children. "Turkish authorities welcome requests for DNA tests to facilitate the process. Yet again, the results of DNA tests carried out by Turkey are not accepted by certain countries, which insist on conducting their own tests. Turkey also accommodates this request despite its extremely lengthy process. All these measures affirm Turkey's constructive approach in the repatriation of FTFs and their families, despite the obstacles created by certain countries," stated the Turkish official who preferred to remain anonymous.

Turkey has not provided the exact number of fighters that are currently being held in Turkish prisons. Still, it is clear that women and children also are being held in Turkish custody. Although certain countries accept repatriation, the process can be complicated by different circumstances. For example, certain countries embrace policies that would result in the separation of mothers and children. Turkey refused this request after long negotiations, as separating children and mothers undermines deradicalization efforts in the long run. Turkey has been forced to bear a significant burden as a transit country through which the majority of ISIS fighters entered Syria. According to the MFA of Turkey, around 96,000 ISIS-linked individuals are banned from entering Turkey. Since 2011, Turkey has captured over 8,000 men and women and deported them to their home countries.[53]

Turkey maintains the position that repatriation is the most appropriate solution. All ISIS fighters, both those held in northeast Syria and in Turkish prisons, should be repatriated, brought to justice and rehabilitated in their countries of origin. The Turkish government expects countries of origin to cooperate and expedite the process of repatriation of foreign fighters and their family members that are also kept in custody in Turkey. Turkey rejects all other proposals stating that stripping their citizenship violates fundamental human rights law and does not tackle FTFs-related challenges. Establishing an ad hoc international tribunal would not serve this purpose and can be ineffective, and Turkey considers granting SDF the right to try foreign fighters unacceptable.

In October 2019, Turkey conducted a military operation, code-named Operation Peace Spring (*Barış Pınarı Harekâtı*). The Turkish Armed forces launched airstrikes on border towns in northeast Syria to expel the Kurdish forces. After Turkey's assault, at least 750 foreign fighters escaped from the camp Ain Issa, located near Raqqa. The camp held about 12,000 people, predominantly internally displaced persons. About 1,000 inhabitants were ISIS fighters' family members. Kurdish forces later declared that, following the Turkish assault, about 800 ISIS affiliates fled the camp. International media platforms, such as the Guardian and the Independent, also reported the escape of 750–800 women from the camp, which were linked to ISIS.[54] The Turkish government denies that ISIS affiliates escaped due to the Turkish assault. The official from the MFA of Turkey stated during an interview that Operation Peace Spring did not cover the area of the Ain Issa camp or its adjacent areas.

"Thus, allegations that the camp was destroyed by the operation or that people escaped is not true. During OPS, the Turkish Armed Forces (TAF) and the Syrian National Army (SNA) took control over only one detention facility which was located in Tel Abyad. It had been deliberately vacated by the PKK/YPG terrorist organization prior to the arrival of TAF and SNA forces. The Turkish authorities are not in a position to accurately determine the exact number of DAESH individuals released by PKK/YPG from the said detention facility," the Turkish official stated.[55]

Since no other independent body was present and witnessed the assault, the claim of over 800 ISIS escapees might be exaggerated. However, some circumstances prove that ISIS affiliates have escaped the Ain Issa camp during or after the Turkish assault. First, UN agencies and other reliable sources confirm that ISIS family members have recently only been held in the two camps of Roj and Al-Hawl; all sources have stopped mentioning Ain Issa. Secondly, the case of Litha Smith, an Irish woman who escaped the Ain Issa camp, demonstrates that there were escapees. She escaped from the camp with other women, reached the Syrian-Turkish border, and was captured by Turkish law enforcement agencies. After spending time in a Turkish prison with her newborn, she was handed over to Ireland. The Irish government arrested her at Dublin airport and charged her with terrorism.

At the same time, Turkey captured hundreds of ISIS affiliates during Operation Peace Spring. The Ministry of Foreign Affairs of Turkey stated during an interview that these people were captured in the area covered by the operation. "Hundreds of DAESH affiliates (mostly women and children) were captured in the OPS area by TAF during and after the operation. These FTFs and their family members were kept in areas, freed from terror within Syria, and their repatriation process to their countries of origin is underway in cooperation with these countries," the representative of the MFA of Turkey stated.[56]

Although Turkey has not disclosed how many ISIS fighters and associates are still in its custody, it is clear that Turkey is holding internal negotiations with states to hand over their citizens in Turkish jails. Turkey is displeased with the fact that the Kurdish forces have been designated to hold former fighters and their associates. Turkey has its own understanding of the situation with limited trust in the SDF, believing that the Kurdish forces are doing business with ISIS affiliates. During a side event in the premises of the Vienna conference in February 2020, the Turkish official declared that the Kurdish forces free ISIS fighters in exchange for payment.

ESTABLISHING AN AD HOC TRIBUNAL FOR ISIS FIGHTERS

If states continue to refuse the repatriation of their citizens, the only remaining viable solution will be the creation of an ad hoc tribunal. The only state that can momentarily be considered as a host country, is Iraq. It also has been cooperating with the international community as close as possible. Though, the pitfalls of their judicial system still hinder fair trials and must be considered as a serious problem. The fact that the majority of men and women are sentenced to death is also a crucial reason for not transferring foreign fighters to Iraqi prisons. The alternative for creating an ad hoc tribunal has nevertheless gained momentum in Europe in 2019. Several European states have initiated expert meetings and ministerial discussions to pave the way for such a special tribunal where foreign fighters can stand trial. Since the threat of terrorism is on the rise, an ad hoc tribunal for terrorists is increasingly plausible, but the scheme has its pitfalls.

On 3 June 2019, Sweden hosted a meeting of senior experts at an official level, with participants from eleven EU countries, including Sweden, Germany, France, the UK, and the Netherlands, and representatives of the EU and the UN. The Swedish government was the first country to take the lead in launching the discussion of the creation of a tribunal. The Ministry of Home Affairs of Sweden regarded this step to be an important progression for finding the right measure to ensure justice regarding foreign fighters. While there is growing interest in exploring alternatives to hold ISIS fighters accountable for their crimes, Sweden envisions a tribunal to sentence foreign fighters for having committed crimes in Syria and Iraq. "Establishing a tribunal or some other legal mechanism is no simple matter, and the path to a possible process would take time and would require cooperation between many parties. This was the case for previous tribunals and would naturally be the same in this case, too. But because something is hard is no reason for failing to investigate the possibilities," said Minister for Home Affairs Mikael Damberg.[57]

Perhaps the establishment of an ad hoc tribunal is the only solution to address the situation in light of the unwillingness of states to repatriate their citizens. However, it is an initiative that would cease repatriation to home countries and remove states' responsibility. As Impunity Watch underlines, "the proposal for an ISIS-only tribunal represents an effort by European states to outsource their responsibility for dangerous or highly vulnerable individuals to a region recovering from decades of conflict with plenty of its own challenges to address."[58] The main problem is that establishing an ad hoc tribunal is a long and laborious process. It demands not only unity among states, but also significant financial resources. As Fionnuala Ní Aoláin, the

UN Special Rapporteur on the promotion and protection of human rights and fundamental freedoms while countering terrorism, stressed in the interview, there is no clarity among states on if they are prepared to spend such resources. "Perhaps a permanent ad hoc tribunal, which would address the concerns in the region and could be done fairly and equitably, is the only solution, but that would require states to be prepared to spend a great deal of money to produce that outcome and it's not clear that they're willing to do that," said Ms. Ní Aoláin.[59]

The international ad hoc tribunals such as of Nuremberg and Tokyo were created to address crimes committed of an international character by individuals, later to be known as war crimes, crimes against humanity, and genocide. Other major tribunals in history were established in postconflict situations to bring justice for victims, such as the ICTY and ICTR, which were created to respond to atrocities committed during the conflict in the former Yugoslavia and the mass killings in Rwanda respectively. Both of them were created by the UN Security Council. A tribunal to try ISIS fighters may similarly also be established by the UN Security Council. However, taking into account the lack of unity among states on the initiative and the fact that the UN has never discussed the question, it may prove difficult to bring the issue to the Security Council.

Generally speaking, ad hoc tribunals play an important role by bringing those suspected of committing crimes before the courts and ensuring justice for victims. If domestic trials are impossible to hold or not guaranteed, an international tribunal should serve the need to establish the truth for victims. Impunity is unacceptable; thus, ISIS fighters should be brought to justice either domestically or internationally. The international community should therefore thoroughly investigate all the different options and come to a decision. However, all states should be prepared to carry that burden and responsibility.

The proposal of Sweden to establish an international tribunal was met with criticism by civil society groups. Seven Syrian and European rights and law groups, including the Open Society Justice Initiative, expressed their reservations about the proposal to establish an international tribunal exclusively focusing on ISIS's crimes.[60] They urged caution in the initiative and to reflect on past experiences in Iraq, the broader region, and the world. Civil society experts warned that the effort would encounter numerous challenging questions, including the tribunal's jurisdiction, the scope of prosecutions, the extent of international and domestic elements, structure and financing, and oversight.

SWITZERLAND AS A DIALOGUE-BUILDING ACTOR

The scale of radicalization in Switzerland is comparatively low and Switzerland has the least number of foreign fighters compared to other European countries.[61] Since 2001 to date, only ninety-two individuals from Switzerland have traveled to conflict zones such as Syria, Afghanistan, Somalia, the Philippines, and Pakistan. Out of the total ninety-two cases that occurred in the last two decades, seventy-seven of them joined terrorist groups in Syria and Iraq.[62] In 2014, the case of two siblings—second-generation immigrants from Kosovo who traveled to Syria—made headlines in the Swiss media.[63] The brother and sister, who were only 15 and 16 years old at the time of their travel, left Switzerland to join ISIS and lived in Syria until their mother arrived to bring them back. They were fortunate to have managed a safe return to Switzerland after one year in the conflict zone. Radio Television Suisse (RTS) journalists interviewed Selina, another Swiss woman who previously lived in Lausanne and currently lives in the camp in Syria. She wishes to return to Switzerland with her daughter and awaits repatriation by the Swiss government. She told the RTS journalists that she and her daughter have been treated like animals there.[64]

According to the official numbers, of the ninety-two individuals who traveled to different conflict zones, only sixty-one of them can be considered to be alive. Some were killed in the conflict zones, some have returned to Switzerland and others may have moved to other places. About thirty people who traveled from Switzerland to the conflict zones, such as Afghanistan, Syria, and Somalia have died. Switzerland confirms at least twenty-five deaths.[65] With regard to the Middle East, currently, about twenty Swiss citizens (men, women, and children) are in Syria and some have been detained by the Kurdish forces. The Federal Council made a decision that the Swiss government should take all necessary measures at its disposal to prevent an uncontrolled return of foreign fighters to Swiss soil. It also raised its concern that "there is a risk that these people will be released without control."[66]

According to a recent study, the Swiss foreign fighters are mainly "second-generation immigrants, persons living in urban areas who tend to have a low level of education and who are poorly integrated into the employment market."[67] The research conducted by Zurich University of Applied Sciences found that 32.3 percent of the travelers originated from the former Yugoslavia, 20.8 percent from North African countries, 15.4 percent from Middle Eastern countries, and a small group from sub-Saharan Africa (4.6 percent).[68] Nearly 100 percent of Swiss foreign fighters are therefore immigrants or children of immigrants who faced difficulties with their integration into the Swiss society.

On 8 March 2019, the Federal Council of Switzerland set objectives and strategies in addressing Swiss citizens who traveled to conflict zones. The Federal Council stressed that the primary objective is the security of Switzerland and the protection of its population, which comes before individual interests. In accordance with the decision of the Federal Council, Switzerland would not seek active repatriation of terrorist fighters, but would prefer prosecution and if applicable punishment in the state where crimes were committed in accordance with international standards. Switzerland could also, in a subsidiary manner, support the creation of an international special court on the ground with adequate means. Nevertheless, a Swiss citizen has the constitutional right to reenter the country under article 24, al.2 of the Federal Constitution. Accordingly, the return of any Swiss citizen cannot be prohibited, but the Federal Council advises against active adult repatriation.

However, Switzerland has not declined the option of repatriating minors, but challenges arise when it comes to implementation, including the lack of consular access and the involvement of a non-state actor detaining the fighters and their families. The Swiss government considers the repatriation of children on a case-by-case basis. "Nevertheless, for minors, repatriation can be examined, in the best interests of the child. The repatriation of minors can only be done with the expressed agreement of competent child protection services (cantonal and communal authorities), as well as the parents if they have the right of custody."[69] Eventually, in December 2021, Switzerland repatriated two sisters, aged fifteen and nine, from Northeast Syria.

Switzerland has a clear position that male fighters should be brought to justice for their committed crimes in conflict zones. If criminal proceedings are impossible in the conflict zone, the Swiss government takes its responsibility seriously for holding its nationals accountable regarding their actions once they are returned. In its session, the Federal Council reiterated that foreign fighters with Swiss nationality should not remain unpunished. In terms of bringing foreign fighters to justice, the Federal Act 122 prescribes punishment for supporting and joining two terrorist groups: Al-Qaeda (art. 1a) and the group Islamic State (art. 1b). The legislation also states in Article 2 paragraphs 1 and 2 that any person supporting the group in "human resources or material terms, organizes propaganda campaigns [. . .] recruits for them or promotes their activities [. . .] shall be liable to a custodial sentence not exceeding five years or to a monetary penalty."[70] There are two matters to consider concerning these punitive measures. One is the crime of joining a terrorist organization abroad and the other is the evidentiary challenge of addressing crimes committed in the conflict zone. Prosecution for crimes committed in the conflict zone is challenging—not only for Switzerland but for all states. Therefore, Switzerland wishes foreign fighters to be punished, not only for joining ISIS but also for the atrocities they committed in the conflict zones. Thus, the main question is about building credible evidence and bringing them to justice based on that evidence. According to press reports, Switzerland participated in negotiations organized by Sweden to discuss the option of an ad hoc tribunal to try ISIS fighters, but the meeting hosting six European countries did not reach a consensus.[71]

Although Switzerland has the least number of foreign fighters, the country has taken a leading role in facilitating international dialogue regarding the issue of foreign fighters. Switzerland acknowledged early on "the need for a multilateral approach in dealing with jihadist foreign fighters."[72] It played an important role in building dialogue and norms around the issue by mobilizing actors and resources. In 2013, Switzerland set the issue of foreign fighters as a priority for the 2014 Swiss Chairmanship of the Organization for Security and Co-operation in Europe (OSCE). While holding the chairmanship of the OSCE, Switzerland prioritized three goals: tackling terrorism financing and kidnapping for ransom, counterterrorism in accordance with human rights, and responding to the phenomenon of foreign fighters. Switzerland also engaged actively in interstate discussions to facilitate dialogue on options to address returning fighters. The country also supported the 2014 UN Security Council resolution 2178 on the issue of foreign terrorist fighters and was actively involved in various initiatives by the Global Counterterrorism Forum.

GERMANY'S CLEAR MESSAGE ABOUT JUSTICE

Germany is one of the most affected countries in Europe, having over one hundred self-returnees from Iraq and Syria. Officially, 1,060 German citizens went to Syria or Iraq and joined ISIS and other terrorist groups. In total, more than 300 German citizens returned from the conflict zone. Germany is dealing with voluntarily returned fighters and also struggling to decide to repatriate women and children. On 30 November 2021, Germany repatriated twenty-two women and children from Northeast Syria and the country is taking a holistic approach by creating deradicalization and reintegration programs. There are hundreds of German women and children currently held in camps in Northeast Syria. And the German government is facing public pressure for their repatriation, even in court hearings. There are cases where Germany's Higher Administration Court (OVG) in Berlin-Brandenburg ruled that children and their mothers must be brought back from northern Syria. Thus, Germany started the repatriation of children and their mothers slowly at the end of 2021. On 30 November 2021, Germany repatriated eight women and twenty-three children from the Roj camp in Northeast Syria. Germany's Foreign Minister Heiko Maas said that children are not responsible for the situation and will be protected, while women should be held responsible for their actions.

What is important is that Germany has created an important precedent by bringing ISIS fighters to court for their crimes committed in the Middle East. Germany convicted several fighters and their wives for their involvement in the genocide against the Yazidi community in Iraq. The twenty-nine-year-old German man and his wife were charged with crimes against humanity and genocide for the death of a Yazidi girl in Iraq. In the summer of 2015, the German fighter, together with his wife, "purchased" and enslaved a five-year-old Yazidi girl named Reda and her mother. They held Reda and her mother as captives and forced them to practice Islam and work as slaves. They beat them daily and violently abused them. One day the little girl wet her bed and was chained outdoors to the bars of the window as a punishment. Reda ultimately died after being left hanging to the bars of the window in hot weather and her mother was not allowed to help her. The German fighter was sentenced to life in prison and his wife was sentenced to ten years of prison. The court ordered them to pay 50,000 euros, as compensation to the girl's mother, who was a co-plaintiff in the case and was present when the verdict was read. She has been living in Germany under the witness protection program.

This is the first genocide conviction of an ISIS fighter, which systematically persecuted the Yazidi ethnic group in Iraq. As I discussed in Chapter 3, ISIS killed thousands of Yazidi men, and kidnapped, raped, and forced thousands of Yazidi women and girls into slavery. As Amal Clooney said, this is a historic moment that the Yazidis have been waiting for. This court verdict is very important and a clear message to other countries. Even though the crime was committed in Iraq, the trial was held on the principle of universal jurisdiction, which means that crimes like this must be prosecuted wherever and whenever they occur. Several court hearings are not enough in the light of war crimes and crimes against humanity committed by ISIS fighters. Thus, every state should start making real efforts to bring male fighters to justice for their war crimes, genocide, and crimes against humanity.

TAJIKISTAN'S FULL AMNESTY AND REPATRIATION EFFORTS

It is estimated that about 1,900 Tajik citizens traveled to Syria and Iraq since the unfolding of the conflict. Tajikistan experienced a five-year-long civil war between government forces and a coalition of democratic, Islamic, and various smaller ethnic groups known as the United Tajik Opposition. Since then, the threat of religious radicalization remains high in the country. The Tajik government has been very sensitive to religious radicalization and strives to restrain any kind of religious activity. There have been campaigns, such as the shaving of men's beards by force and a crackdown on Islamic parties and movements.

What is remarkable is that the Tajik government adopted a soft policy toward foreign fighters in Syria and Iraq. In 2014, Tajikistan announced the implementation of full amnesty for those who return from Syria voluntarily. As a result of this approach, 111 individuals were granted amnesty upon their return to Tajikistan.[73] Since they met the conditions for amnesty, they were pardoned by the government, and no charges were made. There were three preconditions for full amnesty. First, a foreign fighter or their associates should find the means to return to the country voluntarily. Second, returnees should realize their mistake and confess to them. Third, only those who did not participate in combat operations or committed crimes can fall under amnesty. Consequently, not all returnees were pardoned. According to Rustam Azizi, Deputy Director of Center on Study of Islam under the President of Tajikistan, the Tajik authorities had evidence associated with some returnees. "More than 200 returnees asked for amnesty but only 111 were granted because the remaining had committed crimes and were combatants in Syria. They were arrested and charged with terrorism offenses and fighting abroad. Among 111 cases that were granted amnesty, only one person returned to Syria afterwards. Despite one case, all of them were successfully rehabilitated and reintegrated," stated Rustam Azizi.[74]

On 12 February 2019, Tajikistan officially announced that negotiations were underway to bring back all Tajik women and children living in the two camps in northeast Syria. Sirodjiddin Mukhriddin, Minister of Foreign Affairs, declared that Tajikistan would not allow Tajik children to remain in Syria or Iraq.[75] Tajikistan identified all Tajik women and children in the Roj and Al-Hawl camps. The embassies of Tajikistan in Kuwait and Syria worked hard to identify them, visit and conduct interviews. Thus the 575 Tajik women and children living in camps were prepared for repatriation. "Thanks to the efforts of our ambassadors in Syria and Kuwait, the negotiations with the SDF and other parties were successful. We were ready to repatriate our women and children, but the Turkish Special Operation interrupted and overthrew what we had achieved. A huge amount of work was completed, but the Turkish airstrikes affected the operation. Our government is trying to resume negotiations and restart everything," Rustam Azizi stated in an interview.

In 2019, Tajikistan successfully brought back eighty-four children from Iraqi prisons. In total, there were 108 Tajik children in Iraqi prisons living with their mothers who were serving their terms. These women were sentenced by Iraq for joining ISIS and for their affiliation with ISIS. Tajikistan cannot demand Iraq to allow these women to return home; they should remain in prisons and serve their terms. However, governments can save their children from imprisonment. Tajikistan sought to bring home all 108 children, but by the end, only eighty-four children had been repatriated, as mothers of the remaining children decided not to allow them to go home. The main reason for this decision was that mothers could not find relatives whom they could trust and grant guardianship to.

Returned children are currently living in orphanages and boarding schools. The Tajik government analyzed the profiles of families to know who can take them under their care. However, the Tajik government failed to find legal guardianship for children as many of the families do not meet the requirements for adoption. Some families do not show sufficient desire and motivation to take up responsibility. Children are, in the meantime, under the guardianship of the Ministry of Education and Ministry of Social Protection. Psychologists who worked with returnee children advised the government to disperse them so as to not remind one another about their days in the conflict zone. Thus, only siblings remain together while other children have been dispersed among various boarding schools across the country. Children are heavily affected by the war and are in need of long-term psychological support and rehabilitation. Young girls in particular will need special attention and care to recover from their inflicted harm.

Experts highlight that Tajikistan benefited from its experiences in postconflict trauma after the civil war in formulating its policy. "We saw a civil war and our experience working with post-trauma syndromes helped us in working with returnees," Rustam Azizi stated. He also highlighted that the negotiations with local actors in Syria were not easy. "If some states think that it is only diplomatic work, they are wrong. It is very dirty and dangerous work. You must deal with Kurdish forces, then you have to talk to Shia militia, etc. You need to understand the realities of the Middle East and to have highly skilled diplomats who have old networks in the region," Rustam Azizi stated. He also highlighted the financial aspect of the deal. Both the SDF and Iraqi government demanded payment in compensation for each person. Tajikistan paid a certain amount for each child for their days spent in Iraqi prisons. There have been allegations that the Kurdish forces also demand compensation for each repatriated individual, but I was unable to acquire official confirmation from the SDF. After two years, Tajikistan eventually repatriated hundreds of women and children from northeast Syria. On 25 July 2021, 104 Tajik children and 42 women were repatriated from Al-Hawl and Roj camps. The Tajik authorities made an official statement saying that Tajik women and children were saved from hopelessness and returned to a peaceful life in their native country.

CONCLUSIONS

The current situation with ISIS fighters and their associates will have a huge impact on global security if states fail to manage the current crisis effectively. It is an unprecedented and difficult dilemma for the whole world. None of the states can be assured that there is no risk for national security if they come back. However, while remaining together in the Middle East, they are in a favorable environment for further radicalization. The current state policies have shortages and pitfalls. None of them seem to be effective. The Iraqi prisons are full and profound deficits of its judicial system make the task unfeasible. The next viable solution could be establishing an ad hoc tribunal to try ISIS fighters. Major tribunals in history were established in postconflict situations to bring justice to victims. The first international criminal tribunals were established in the 1990s to respond to atrocities committed during the conflict in the former Yugoslavia and the mass killings in Rwanda, both of which were created by the UN Security Council. A tribunal to try ISIS fighters similarly can be established by the UN Security Council. However, taking into account the lack of unity among states on the initiative and the fact that the UN has never discussed the question, it seems difficult to bring the issue on the agenda of the Security Council. Establishing and maintaining a tribunal demands tremendous financial resources and so far, none of the countries have shown their commitment to invest.

Abandoning ISIS fighters and stripping their citizenship signifies neither fighting against terrorism nor bringing foreign fighters to justice for their crimes. Abandonment contributes to further radicalization and moreover diminishes the possibility of tracking their actions. Fighters move into illegality and an underground existence, making it difficult to detect and monitor terrorist plots. It is important to remember the destiny of Bin Laden who was left stateless and continued to operate terrorist schemes underground. Foreign fighters stripped of their citizenship will acquire a new goal: to enact revenge and prove their existence.

States considered many options so far, while many of them proved to be inefficient, and the international community has been very slow in finding appropriate solutions. The only appropriate legal solution is repatriation and bringing the fighters to justice in their home countries. The COVID pandemic has affected further developments, otherwise, the United Nations could have put strong pressure on states to enforce repatriation efforts, especially women and children. In October 2021, the UN has launched the Global Framework on United Nations Support to Repatriate and Rehabilitate Third Nationals from Syria and Iraq. The Global Framework has two objectives: (1) to respond to and assist the needs of children and adults requiring protection; and (2) to support requesting Member States to promote security and address accountability through prosecution, rehabilitation, and reintegration processes. What is important, under this initiative, is the creation of a Multi-Partner Trust Fund. So now states can receive funding for their repatriation and rehabilitation. To enable rapid, coherent, and coordinated repatriation and rehabilitation, the pooled fund is governed by a Steering Committee at the UN. So, any UN member state can receive full assistance for the repatriation and rehabilitation of ISIS-associated women and children through this initiative.

NOTES

1. Amnesty International UK, "Global Executions Fell by Nearly One Third Last Year—New Report," Press Release, April 10, 2019, https://www.amnesty.org.uk/press-releases/global-executions-fell-nearly-third-last-year-new-report.
2. Human Rights Watch, "Everyone Must Confess: Abuses Against Children Suspected of ISIS Affiliation in Iraq," March 6, 2019. https://www.hrw.org/sites/default/files/report_pdf/iraq0319_web_1.pdf.
3. Jo Becker, "ISIS Trials Don't Deliver Justice—Including for Children," *Human Rights Watch*, January 31, 2020. https://www.hrw.org/news/2020/01/31/iraqs-isis-trials-dont-deliver-justice-including-children.
4. Human Rights Watch, "Everyone Must Confess."
5. Pilar Cebrán, "They Left to Join ISIS. Now Europe is Leaving Their Citizens to Die in Iraq," *Foreign Policy*, September 15, 2019. https://foreignpolicy.com/2019/09/15/they-left-to-join-isis-now-europe-is-leaving-their-citizens-to-die-in-iraq/.
6. Office of the United Nations High Commissioner for Human Rights, "Iraq: UN Report on ISIL Trials Recognizes Efforts and Raises Concerns," January 28, 2020.
7. Human Rights Watch, "Iraq: Change Approach to Foreign Women, Children in ISIS-Linked Trial," June 21, 2018.
8. UN Special Rapporteur, interview by the author.
9. Jacob Schulz, "France Makes a Play to Try Foreign Fighters in Iraq," *Lawfare*, June 7, 2020. https://www.lawfareblog.com/france-makes-play-try-foreign-fighters-iraq.
10. Pilar Cebrián, "They Left to Join ISIS. Now Europe is Leaving Their Citizens," Foreign Policy, September 15 2019, https://foreignpolicy.com/2019/09/15/they-left-to-join-isis-now-europe-is-leaving-their-citizens-to-die-in-iraq/.
11. Oscar Schneider, "Iraq Wants 2 million Euros for Each Foreign Fighter Tried on its Territory," *Brussels Times.* October 1, 2019, https://www.brusselstimes.com/all-news/belgium-all-news/71090/iraq-wants-2-million-euros-for-each-foreign-fighter-tried-on-its-territory/.
12. Simona Foltyn, "Inside the Iraqi courts sentencing foreign ISIS fighters to death," *The Guardian,* June 2, 2019, https://www.theguardian.com/world/2019/jun/02/inside-the-iraqi-courts-sentencing-foreign-isis-fighters-to-death.

13. Elian Peltier, "France Repatriates Several Orphan Children Who Were Stranded in Syria," *New York Times,* March 15, 2019, https://www.nytimes.com/2019/03/15/world/europe/france-isis-repatriates-children.html.

14. Counter-Extremism Project, "France: Extremism & Counter-Extremism," (2019), https://www.counterextremism.com/sites/default/files/country_pdf/FR-01062020.pdf.

15. Peltier, "France Repatriates Orphan Children."

16. H.J. Mai, "Why European Countries Are Reluctant to Repatriate Citizens Who Are ISIS Fighters," *NPR,* December 10, 2019, https://www.npr.org/2019/12/10/783369673/europe-remains-reluctant-to-repatriate-its-isis-fighters-here-s-why.

17. New Wires, "Syrian Kurds transfer 12 orphans from jihadist families to France for repatriation," *France 24,* June 10, 2019, https://www.france24.com/en/20190610-france-orphans-jihadist-families-syria-kurds-transfer.

18. "UN expert to France: Bring home citizens facing hanging in Iraq," *Aljazeera,* 13 August 2019, https://www.aljazeera.com/news/2019/08/expert-france-bring-home-citizens-facing-hanging-iraq-190813012621682.html.

19. Aljazeera, "UN expert to France."

20. John Irish, "France's Le Drian to go to Iraq to Discuss Trials for Jihadists from Syria," *Reuters,* October 16, 2019, https://www.reuters.com/article/us-mideast-iran-france/frances-le-drian-to-go-to-iraq-to-discuss-trials-for-jihadists-from-syria-idUSKBN1WV0RG.

21. "'Ce serait un immense déshonneur pour notre pays': l'apel de 45 avocats contre les condamnations à mort de neuf Français en Irak," *Franceinfo,* June 3, 2019. https://www.francetvinfo.fr/monde/proche-orient/francais-condamnes-a-mort-en-irak/tribune-ce-serait-un-immense-deshonneur-pour-notre-pays-l-appel-de-44-avocats-contre-les-condamnations-a-mort-de-neuf-francais-en-irak_3469333.html.

22. Adam Nossiter, "Paris Trial Shows Faltering Evolution of a Jihadist Cell," *New York Times,* April 13, 2018, https://www.nytimes.com/2018/04/13/world/europe/paris-trial-lunel-ihadist-cell.html.

23. Adam Nossiter, "How ISIS Changed France," *New York Times,* October 31, 2019, https://www.nytimes.com/2019/10/31/world/europe/al-baghdadi-isis-france.html.

24. Counter-Extremism Project, "France: Extremism & Counter-Extremism."

25. Joana Cook and Gina Vale, "From Daesh to 'Diaspora': Tracing the Women and Minors of Islamic State," Georgetown Institute for Women, Peace, and Security, (2018), 28 -30, https://giwps.georgetown.edu/resource/from-daesh-to-diaspora/.

26. Peltier, "France Repatriates Orphan Children."

27. Ben Hubbard and Constant Méheut, "Western Countries Leave Children of ISIS in Syrian Camps," *New York Times*, May 31, 2020, https://www.nytimes.com/2020/05/31/world/middleeast/isis-children-syria-camps.html.

28. Sudip Kar-Gupta, "Top French Court Rejects Syria-based French Jihadis' Repatriation Demands," *Reuters,* April 23, 2019, https://www.reuters.com/article/us-syria-security-france-nationals/top-french-court-rejects-syria-based-french-jihadis-repatriation-demands-idUSKCN1RZ1B2.

29. Marc Daou, "France Taken to Court for Refusing to Repatriate the Children of Jihadists," *France24,* May 7, 2019, https://www.france24.com/en/20190507-france-taken-court-over-repatriating-children-jihadists.

30.AFP, "French Families Sue Government Over Children of Jihadists Stuck in Syria," *The Local,* September 16, 2019. https://www.thelocal.fr/20190916/french-families-sue-government-over-children-stuck-in-syria.

31. GLOBALCIT, "Global Database on Modes of Loss of Citizenship version 1.0. Robert Schuman Centre for Advanced Studies," European University Institute, (2017), available at: http://globalcit.eu/loss-of-citizenship.

32. Dr. Bérénice Boutin, "Administrative Measures Against Foreign Fighters: In Search of Limits and Safeguards," International Center for Counter-Terrorism—The Hague, December 2016. https://icct.nl/wp-content/uploads/2016/12/ICCT-Boutin-Administrative-Measures-December2016-1.pdf.

33. UK Parliament, "Counter Terrorism and Security Act 2015." Accessed October 23, 2020. http://www.legislation.gov.uk/ukpga/2015/6/contents.

34. European Parliamentary Research Service, "The Return of Foreign Fighters to EU Soil: Ex-Post Evaluation," 55. https://www.europarl.europa.eu/RegData/etudes/STUD/2018/621811/EPRS_STU(2018)621811_EN.pdf.

35. UK Parliament, "Counter-Terrorism and Border Security Act 2019." Accessed October 23, 2020. http://www.legislation.gov.uk/ukpga/2019/3/contents.

36. UK Home Office, *Factsheet: Syrian Travellers.* Home Office News, February 15, 2019, https://homeofficemedia.blog.gov.uk/2019/02/15/fact-sheet-returnees-from-th-conflict-zone-in-syria/.

37. UK Parliament, "Immigration Act 2014." accessed October 22, 2020, http://www.legislation.gov.uk/ukpga/2014/22/contents.

38. Richard Hall, "There's No Way Back for British ISIS Prisoners Languishing in a Syrian Jail," *The Independent*, December 18, 2019, https://www.independent.co.uk/news/world/middle-east/isis-british-fighters-syria-baghdadi-aseel-muthana-ishak-mostefaoui-a9251391.html.

39. "Shamima Begum: IS bride 'Would Face Death Penalty in Bangladesh," *BBC News,* May 3, 2019, https://www.bbc.com/news/world-asia-48154781.

40. "Shamima Begum loses first stage of appeal over citizenship," *BBC News,* February 7, 2019, https://www.bbc.com/news/uk-51413040.

41. Boutin, "Administrative Measures Against Foreign Fighters."

42. Parliament of the Netherlands, "Vreemdelingenwet 2000 [Aliens Act 2000]," accessed June 7, 2020, https://wetten.overheid.nl/BWBR0011823/2015-07-20.

43. Rod McGuirk, "Australia's Citizenship Stripping Policy Again Sparks Controversy," *The Diplomat*, January 3, 2019. https://thediplomat.com/2019/01/australias-citizenship-stripping-policy-again-sparks-controversy/; and Rod McGuirck, "Australia Insists Man Who Lost Citizenship Isn't Stateless," *Associated Press*, January 2, 2019, https://apnews.com/03c56ff6ca02478ea0276a4dceff6d3d.

44. "Six Combattants Etrangers Partis en Syrie Perdent Leur Nationalité Belge," *Flandreinfo Belge* - L'Actu de Flandre, January 2, 2020, https://www.vrt.be/vrtnws/fr/2020/01/02/six-combattants-etrangers-partis-en-syrie-perdent-leur-nationali/.

45. Bérénice Boutin, Grégory Chauzal, Jessica Dorsay, Marjolein Jegerings, Christophe Pualussen, et al., "The Foreign Fighters Phenomenon in the European Union," International Centre for Counter-Terrorism—The Hague, April 2016, DOI: 10.19165/2016.

46. Charlie Savage, "American-Born Woman Who Joined ISIS Is Not a Citizen, Judge Rules," *New York Times*, November 14, 2019, https://www.nytimes.com/2019/11/14/us/hoda-muthana-isis-citizenship.html.

47. Meghan Benton and Natalia Banulescu-Bogdan, "Foreign Fighters: Will Revoking Citizenship Mitigate the Threat?" Migration Policy Institute, April 3, 2019. https://www.migrationpolicy.org/article/foreign-fighters-will-revoking-citizenship-mitigate-threat.

48. UN Human Rights Council , "Arbitrary Deprivation of Nationality: Report of the UN Secretary-General, Annual Report of UN High Commissioner and the Secretary-General," A/HRC/10/34, 26 January 2009, https://digitallibrary.un.org/record/647823?ln=en.

49. Trump vs Macron on ISIS Fighters, Wall Street Journal, The Editorial Board, 05 December 2019, https://www.wsj.com/articles/trump-vs-macron-on-isis-fighters-11575590830.

50. Chris Harnisch, "Foreign Terrorist Fighters: Addressing Current Challenges," *US Mission to the OSCE* February 11, February 11, 2020. https://osce.usmission.gov/foreign-terrorist-fighters-addressing-current-challenges/.

51. Press Release of the United States Department of Justice from 01 October 2020, available at The United States Has Repatriated twenty-seven Americans from Syria and Iraq Including Ten Charged with Terrorism-Related Offenses for Their Support to ISIS | OPA | Department of Justice.

52. Interview with the Turkish official.

53. The information was provided by the Ministry of Foreign Affairs of Turkey to the author.

54. Bethan McKernan, "At Least 750 ISIS Affiliates Escape Syria Camp After Turkey Shelling," *The Guardian,* October 13, 2019, https://www.theguardian.com/world/2019/oct/13/kurds-say-785-isis-affiliates-have-escaped-camp-after-turkish-shelling.

55. The interview with the official from MFA of Turkey.

56. The interview with the Turkish official.

57. Government Offices of Sweden, "Sweden Hosted Expert Meeting on Tribunal," Press Release, Sweden Ministry of Justice, June 3, 2019, accessed at: https://www.government.se/press-releases/2019/06/sweden-hosted-expert-meeting-on-tribunal/.

58. Impunity Watch, "ISIS-Only Tribunal: Selective, Politicised Justice Will Do More Harm Than Good," Policy Brief, October 31, 2019. https://www.impunitywatch.nl/docs/PolicyBrief_Iraq_ISIS_Tribunal_2019_eng.pdf.

59. Fionnuala Ni Aolain, interview.

60. Open Society Justice Initiative, "NGOs Challenge Sweden's Proposal for an ISIS-Only War Crimes Tribunal," Open Society Justice Initiative, June 3, 2019, accessed at:https://www.justiceinitiative.org/newsroom/ngos-challenge-swedens-proposal-for-an-isis-only-war-crimes-tribunal.

61. Daniel Glaus and Lorenzo Vidino, "Swiss Foreign Fighters Active in Syria," Combatting Terror Center (CTC) *Sentinel* 7, no. 7 (2014): 8–11.

62. Swiss Confederation, "Chiffres des voyageurs du djihad—Février 2019," Département fédéral de la défense, de la protection de la population et des sports DDPS, (2019), accessed at : https://www.vbs.admin.ch/fr/themes/recherche-renseignements/voyageurs-djihad.detail.document.html/vbs-internet/fr/documents/servicederenseignement/djihad/2019/Zahlen-Dschihadreisende-Februar-2019-f.pdf.html.

63. Kurt Pelda and Thomas Knellwolf, "Mother Risked Her Life to Save her Children," *Tages Anzeiger*, December 1, 2018, https://www.tagesanzeiger.ch/schweiz/standard/die-odysseeder-isgeschwister/story/26224134.

64. RTS, "Une Lausannoise, ex-djihadise en Syrie, souhaite revenir en Suisse," *Radio Television Suisse (RTS),* February 9, 2019, https://www.rts.ch/info/suisse/10205792-une-lausannoise-ex-djihadiste-en-syrie-souhaite-revenir-en-suisse.html.

65. Swiss Confederation, "Chiffres des voyageurs du djihad."

66. Swiss Confederation, "Voyageurs à motivation terroriste: stratégie et objectifs du Conseil federal," Federal Council of Switzerland, March 8, 2019, accessed at: https://www.admin.ch/gov/fr/accueil/documentation/communiques.msg-id-74258.html.

67. Miryam Eser Davolio et al., "Updated review and developments in jihadist radicalisation in Switzerland—updated version of an exploratory study on prevention and intervention," *Institute of Diversity and Social Integration*, Zurich Universities of Applied Sciences and Arts, June 2019, https://doi.org/10.3929/ethz-b-000351454.

68. Davolio et al., "Updated review and developments."

69. Swiss Confederation, "Voyageurs à motivation terroriste."

70. Swiss Confederation, "122 Loi fédérale interdisant les groupes « Al-Qaïda » et « Etat islamique » et les organisations apparentées," Federal Assembly of the Swiss Confederation, December 12, 2014, accessed at: https://www.droit-bilingue.ch/rs/lex/2014/29/20142993-unique-de-fr.html & https://www.admin.ch/opc/fr/classified-compilation/20142993/index.html English translation (not official): https://www.admin.ch/opc/en/classified-compilation/20142993/index.html.

71. RTS, "Faut-il créer un tribunal international pour juger les djihadistes?" *Radio Television Suisse (RTS),* June 4, 2019. https://www.rts.ch/info/monde/10482439-faut-il-creer-un-tribunal-international-pour-juger-les-djihadistes-.html.

72. Fabien Merz, "Switzerland and Jihadist Foreign Fighters," ETH Zurich, *CSS Analyses in Security Policy* 199, (2016), https://css.ethz.ch/content/dam/ethz/special-interest/gess/cis/center-for-securities-studies/pdfs/CSSAnalyse199-EN.pdf.

73. Anushervon Aripov, "'There Were Deaths Every Day': People Are Returning to Tajikistan From ISIS in Syria and Iraq," *Настоящее Время [Current Time],* February 9, 2018, https://www.currenttime.tv/a/29029380.html.

74. Rustam Azizi, interview by the author on 11 April 2020.

75. Farangiz Najibullah and Mumin Ahmadi, "You Can't Remain Behind. Widows and Children of IS fighters From Central Asia," Радио Азаттык *[Radio Azattyk],* February 21, 2019, https://rus.azattyq.org/a/why-tajikistan-is-fighting-to-bring-its-islamic-state-widows-back-home/29782290.html.

Chapter 8

States Responsibility

Repatriation Cases as a Model to Study

Despite the UN's efforts, repatriation from Syria and Iraq has been slow and only a handful of countries have repatriated their citizens, mainly women and children. European countries have stood firm in their position against repatriation based on two arguments: national security and public opinion that rejects their return. Several European countries have been challenged by families who demanded to bring back their children, sisters, or brothers that have been held by the Kurdish forces in Northeast Syria. Three countries in particular—France, Belgium, and the Netherlands—were skeptical over the lawsuits from their citizens. The Belgian woman who gave birth in Syria and is currently living in Roj camp, filed her case before the Belgian court demanding repatriation. She was married twice to ISIS fighters and both of her husbands died on the battlefield. The Tribunal of First Instance of Brussels ordered that Belgium should repatriate her with her two children. However, the decision was reversed on appeal. The judgment also stipulated that Belgium should ensure that all its nationals, detained in camps in Syria, should not only receive consular assistance through its embassies located in the three neighboring countries, but also through its honorary consulate in Latakia. Collaboration with NGOs that had access to the camp was also ordered and the Court found that Belgium had the ability to repatriate its nationals currently detained in the camps in Syria. However, the Belgian government achieved the annulment of that decision through appeal.

In the Netherlands, the court considered a lawsuit filed by twenty-three women. All of them are citizens of the Netherlands and are currently being held in Roj and Al-Hawl camps. They demanded that the court order their repatriation. In November 2019, the District Court in Amsterdam met their demands, but The Hague Court of Appeal and the Supreme Court, both reversed this decision. The main argument offset forward by the two courts was that "the Dutch State has no jurisdiction in Syria for the purposes of the extraterritorial application of the CRC, International Covenant on Civil and Political Rights, and the ECHR. The Court of Appeal and the Supreme Court made it clear that, whilst the Dutch State could indirectly exercise a degree of influence over the claimants, it had no jurisdiction over them."[1] None of the lawsuits have been successful, neither in France nor in Belgium or the Netherlands. European countries refer to the absence of consulates in northeast Syria and the unacceptability of negotiations with the non-state actor that exercises its power there. While no country in the world has consular services in Northeast Syria, repatriation operations have been facilitated by UNICEF, UNOCT, and the United States. These kinds of reasons are just the pretext, but their main concerns are different. European countries consider fighters and their family members to be a threat to national security and they refer to public opinion.

Some Western countries have softened their positions toward minors. So far France, Austria, Denmark, Germany, Netherlands, and Belgium have repatriated small children, but mainly orphans, and some EU countries brought back very few women. European experts also consider children to be victims, especially small ones. Anne Speckhard, Adjunct Associate Professor of Psychiatry at Georgetown University Medical School, said during the discussion that I organized for the Bulan Institute, that mostly, reasonable people would agree that children should not be detained in those camps. "Children are innocent, they haven't committed any crimes. The kids are for the most part under seven and we can say that maybe seven- to eight-year-olds can be ideologically indoctrinated, maybe shown how to use a gun. But it's unlikely that a three-year-old is a real danger" said Professor Speckhard.[2] But she highlighted that the main issue would revolve around family reunification laws. "But the argument in the EU against taking the children back is that the EU has family reunification laws. So, the mothers and the fathers could petition to also be repatriated if their children are repatriated. So, that's a real issue," she said. Indeed, EU countries are mainly repatriating orphans out of fear that if they separately repatriate so their parents might file a case to be reunited with their children.

In light of reluctance of Western countries, the repatriation cases of USA, Kosovo, Tajikistan, Kazakhstan, Kyrgyzstan, and Uzbekistan have been drawing much attention from states, diplomats, UN experts, and researchers. These cases should be observed and studied as a model; more research should be done to study their experiences and share good practices and challenges. The experiences of these states are unique, while most of them had no previous experience of repatriation and rehabilitation, and learned while doing.

KOSOVAR FIGHTERS ARE AT HOME

In April 2019, Kosovo repatriated 110 citizens, including four men, thirty-two women, and seventy-four children. At the airport of Pristina, the four men were immediately arrested. Women and children were transported under police escort to the asylum center just outside Pristina, which was prepared to receive them. They spent three days in the asylum center where each person was assessed for immediate medical and psychological needs. Women and children were then returned to their families and hometowns, but female returnees were placed under house arrest, whilst investigations into possible criminal activity were conducted.[3] Returnees also received psychiatric, psychotherapeutic, and religious counseling sessions in the community, with trauma symptomatology addressed as a priority for all.[4]

Approximately 400 Kosovars are thought to have traveled to Syria since 2012, with the vast majority leaving prior to 2016.[5] Eighty-one Kosovar children have been born in the region following 2016.[6] The Kosovar government has supported the idea of repatriation since the outset and consistently expressed its position that FTFs should be repatriated and prosecuted for terrorism offenses where applicable. Former Prime Minister Ramush Haradinaj stated, "Kosovo will take full responsibility for its citizens. However, everybody who returns will be subject to the law."[7] In Kosovo, joining terrorist and military groups during foreign conflicts is punishable by law with a sentence of up to 15 years in prison. As above mentioned, the four male fighters were immediately arrested at the airport and were charged with the offense of joining terrorist groups abroad. After investigations, about twenty female returnees were found guilty and indicted for participating in a terrorist or foreign paramilitary group.[8] Qendresa Sfishta, a woman repatriated by the Kosovar government, was given a two-year suspended sentence for participating in a terrorist group in January 2020 following a guilty plea. She admitted to providing logistical support to her husband in 2015, for which she received money from a terrorist organization.[9] Other women remain under house arrest and have no right to travel, including within Kosovo.

CENTRAL ASIA: TAKING LEAD AND BEING A MODEL TO FOLLOW

The Central Asian region has taken the lead to repatriate its citizens from Syria. Uzbekistan and Kazakhstan carried out large-scale repatriation operations bringing back more than 1,500 people in total, while Tajikistan and Kyrgyzstan each brought back about eighty children from Iraqi prisons. The region can be regarded as the third largest region of foreign fighters headed to Syria and Iraq.[10] Many sources indicate that around 5,000 people from the region traveled to Syria and Iraq between 2011 and 2016.[11] Even though the outflow of people to the conflict zones began in 2011, Central Asian governments were initially unaware of the scale of mobilization of foreign fighters to Syria, and it was also unclear which country had the largest number of departees heading to the conflict zone. At the same time, Central Asians made up "20 percent of all foreign fighters originating from Central Asia while this region accounts for less than 5 percent of global Muslims."[12]

Religious radicalization is present in Central Asia, with Wahhabi-Salafism being widespread. The region has also experienced terrorist attacks resulting in casualties. Central Asian states experienced eighteen deadly attacks between 2009 and 2018, but most of them "targeted government officials, including police, rather than civilians."[13] However, there were attacks against foreigners. In the summer of 2018, four tourists from Europe were killed in Tajikistan. They were apprehended while cycling, before they were stabbed to death. Even though there was no direct link with ISIS, the crime still made international headlines when the Islamic State terrorists claimed credit. The suicide bombing of the Chinese Embassy in Kyrgyzstan in 2016 was carried out by individuals "inspired by IS propaganda, though we do not know how much the group was involved in planning the attack, if at all."[14] There had been cases where Central Asians had been involved in terrorist attacks abroad. For example, the U.S. stated that the 2013 Boston Marathon bombers were ethnic Chechens who grew up in Kyrgyzstan, while in 2017 the Uzbek immigrant killed eight people in New York with a rented truck. The international media attention attracted Central Asians who reached high ranks within ISIS. Gulmurod Halimov, who was the head of Tajikistan's paramilitary police, or OMON, was appointed as minister of war of ISIS in May 2015. He had been active on social media, playing a key role in the recruitment of fighters and his photo was in the international media for several years. His destiny is unknown and he might have been killed in Syria.

The Central Asian countries have been authoritarian regimes with long-serving presidents. They usually made headlines in international media with their poor human rights records. They always had low evaluations when it came to freedom rankings, including freedom of speech, freedom of assembly, and ranked highly in corruption indexes. As Gavin Helf stated, for those who follow Central Asia, the story about repatriation is a good news story coming out of Central Asia. "For experts, who have been studying this part of the world for several decades, we don't have a lot of great stories coming out of Central Asia. Usually, you know, in Central Asia, we get something like 'Freedom House says that the oppression of media is down by 10 percent this year,' which is not that great a story," said Gavin Helf during the discussion organized by the Bulan Institute where I work. For Gavin Helf, the experiences of repatriation in Central Asia are a model to study and follow and something that should be commended. However, sending a flight and bringing citizens back is only the start of a huge pile of work that still has to be done. "But repatriation is in a way the easy part. Everyone likes the pictures of people coming off the plane and being greeted back home into the loving embrace of the motherland. I think the harder piece, that we have been working on over the last year and a half at USIP, has been the reintegration part and trying to figure out what you do after that photoshoot," said Gavin.[15]

There is a tendency among diplomats and experts to say that the U.S. had put pressure on Central Asian states to carry out their repatriation. However, it is safe to conclude that political will and mentality played a key role in the decision-making process. As Keneshbek Sainazarov, Central Asia Director at the Search for Common Grounds, said, the Central Asia leaders had the major important thing- political will. "There was no pressure from outside. The decision was made by the leaders of these four nations unilaterally and the international entities and institutions have come to support everything with all of the resources they have. And especially, I would highlight the role of three particular institutions. The UN system, including UNICEF, and in all these countries they are really championing, especially when it comes to children's rights, and they are playing a very critical role. The second is the neighboring countries including Russia. And the third one is the role of U.S. government, which has even arranged most of the flights of these individuals back home. So, it was truly an international effort to make this happen and work," Keneshbek Sainazarov told me during the interview.[16]

The main challenges Kazakhstan, Kyrgyzstan, Uzbekistan, and Tajikistan faced, were to stand against the stigmatization of returnees and to prepare the public opinion on them. So, the main success that should be mentioned was the framing of the repatriation operations. Kazakhstan, Uzbekistan, and Tajikistan have built similar narratives that focused on the Motherland, women, and children. The first message was "we never abandon our women and children." The second narrative was about "deceived people who were victims of recruitment." The third narrative was "everyone has a right to return to their own Homeland even if one committed crimes." Even though the public opinion was against repatriation, the government managed to avoid an emotional clash in society. During the past five years, local media demonized these people, but the governments managed to convey the above-mentioned three narratives, prior to the repatriation of the people. As Rustam Azizi, an expert on religious extremism in Tajikistan, explained to me, the media changed their position accordingly to those narratives. "For five years media outlets were saying that these people are dangerous and threat to national security, they're terrorist, etc. And now media started to show the human face of the problem. Journalists focused on human stories and how they suffered there, and they showed faces of small children. So the media strategy was not to blame them, not to talk about their crimes, but to show the human faces" said Rustam Azizi.[17] Indeed, all four countries realized that a good media strategy was also important. Since these countries have strong presidential power, the political will of the country leaders was important. In each phase of the repatriation operations, the Presidents of these countries urged the population to show compassion for these people.

However, there is still stigmatization in society and critique that governments, instead of solving long-existing problems such as poverty and unemployment, brought back these people and provided them with social benefits. On social media, I have read many comments like "I also should have gone to Syria to receive such attention and support." I asked the Deputy Minister of Kazakhstan during the Vienna conference in 2020 how they deal with such reactions in society. He told me that "they had to choose less evil." The Kazakh government is trying to provide support to rehabilitate and deradicalize, but there is still a credibility problem. As Gavin Helf said, state officials also recognize that credibility problem.

> We have really seen a problem with stigma and stigmatization of the returnees in the larger community. As one government official from the region mentioned to me, "we've got a credibility problem because the state media, for the last five to six years, has been demonizing the people who went to Iraq and Syria from Central Asia as Salafi Wahhabi zombies, as mentally defective, as inferior people." As another of the regional officials told me, "We really didn't expect any of them to come back alive." That left them with a credibility gap, "we've been describing people in this way, now suddenly, we're turning around and saying no, you know it turns out, in reality, they are just lost little sheep that we are going to return to the loving embrace of the motherland and look at these wonderful pictures of people getting off the plane and kissing the ground."

One of the useful lessons to learn from Central Asian experiences is that many civil society organizations were widely integrated into the development, design, and implementation of the reintegration, rehabilitation, and resocialization processes. Usually, the Central Asian governments, especially in Uzbekistan, Kazakhstan, and Tajikistan, have been known for the crackdown of free media and civil society. The Karimov regime in Uzbekistan was a brutal dictatorship that did not give any space for NGOs to work. The Uzbek authorities even shut down the offices of international human rights organizations, such as Human Rights Watch, Internews, and RFERL. An almost similar situation could be witnessed in Kazakhstan, where judicial harassment and attacks against civil society were widespread. Bearing in mind such a hostile environment for NGOs, it is remarkable how Central

Asian governments cooperated with them in the repatriation and reintegration of returnees. The governments understood that it is a hard problem to tackle on its own. Engaging with civil society and community leaders was important because they have credibility, expertise, and skills to meet the needs of returnees. Usually, civil society and community leaders have the trust of the people and access to the affected individuals and communities.

A crucial role has been played by the women-led organizations in Kazakhstan and Uzbekistan. Women leaders such as Olga Ryl, Gulnaz Rasdykova, Lola Shakimova, Oliya Ilmuradova, Nazifa Kamolova, Malika Dodoeva, Nazifa Kamalova, Vasiliya Alimova, Gulnaz Isaeva, Aliza Soltonbekova and Liliya Gainutdinova have been working hard with the returnees from the first day onwards. They met the returnees upon their arrival at the airport and have been accompanying them since then, helping them deal with psychological, legal, social, and other problems. The women-led organizations have been playing a crucial role to integrate women and facilitate the community acceptance of female returnees. They embraced reintegration efforts, which include vocational and psychological training programs led by women and mothers, working with local communities in providing sociopsychological work as group therapy and psychological counseling to women during the process of reintegration.

The Central Asian countries have been learning from each other and projects have been implemented by UNOCT, Search for Common Ground, the Bulan Institute, USIP, Nordic Centre and Hedayah to examine their models of rehabilitation and reintegration and share their experiences. The specialists of each country, including psychologists, social workers, and NGOs, communicate with each other. There have been interstate learning visits and information exchanges between four countries. In general, we have been observing similarities and differences between the approaches of the four countries. Kazakhstan's rehabilitation program is institutionalized and state-controlled, and focused on three pillars: an ideological, psychological, and social pillar. The most important feature is the religious work that has been done by theologians. They talk to returnees to explain to them that Salafi-Wahhabism is not real Islam and they try to dispatch them from radical ideologies and encourage them to learn Islam in depth. Uzbekistan's approach relies on the support of communities and families. Tajikistan had many voluntary returnees as it has announced an amnesty in 2014 and its approach is more straightforward "confess, change your behavior, find a job and work." The similarity between the countries is that each country has involved civil society organizations that have experience with migrants, prisoners, and postconflict trauma.

OPERATION MEHR: HANDS-OFF APPROACH TO WOMEN AND CHILDREN

Uzbekistan repatriated more than 500 people from Syria, only women and children in 2020 and 2021. Operation Mehr, meaning kindness, was implemented in four stages by sending three flights to the Middle East. The Ministry of Foreign Affairs of Uzbekistan issued a statement to explain the operation. The statement said that it is a message to its Uzbek citizens abroad: "It is important to inform our compatriots who are in difficult life situations in foreign countries for various reasons that they are all under the protection of the Republic of Uzbekistan, and that the state will take all necessary measures to protect their rights and interests," said the ministry.[18] The Uzbek government excluded male fighters from the repatriation operation and none were taken back. The policy of Uzbekistan was hands-off as it does not charge women and none were punished for joining ISIS. Uzbekistan framed Mehr as humanitarian and the government built a narrative on human mistake and forgiveness. These individuals have been referred to as "adashganlar," meaning one who was misled or deceived. Local Uzbek media, which is under strict control of the government, has shared the voices of women returnees who spoke about how they were deceived and duped by their husbands or other people.

Experts stress that Uzbekistan had prior experience in the rehabilitation of persons with the post-traumatic syndrome. The rehabilitation program of Uzbekistan was "largely modeled on initiatives developed since the early 2000s for former members of groups such as the Islamic Movement of Uzbekistan and Hizb ut-Tahrir al-Islami (HTI)."[19] Keneshbek Sainazarov, Central Asia Director for Search for Common Grounds, said that Uzbekistan's rehabilitation program "puts a lot of emphasis on the community level, meaning traditional leaders in the community and community institutions, so that it creates an enabling welcoming environment for these individuals to come and interact."[20] All returnees are brought back to their local villages or towns and supported by local NGOs, religious leaders, and social services. The overarching principle is that individuals should return to their normal lives in their own community and remain dispersed to minimize interaction with one another. Uzbekistan also imposed restrictions on the movements of returnees.

Uzbekistan involved civil society organizations in the rehabilitation and reintegration processes of returnees. The role of women-led civil society organizations has been significant. I met Oliya Ilmuradova in 2020, director of an NGO named Barqaror Hayot based in Uzbekistan, during the Vienna conference on foreign fighters organized by the OSCE and UNOCT. She presented how her organization worked with returnees. Since then, we have been in touch and had several meetings to discuss how returnees are feeling at home. She knows every returnee personally and has been assisting them with their legal, social, and economic problems. The rehabilitation program in Uzbekistan mainly relies on the family members of returnees and their communities to help them to reintegrate.

More than two years have passed since the repatriation of the first group of women and children and some women have already started working. According to Oliya Ilmuradova, women have few choices in the job market and their main option is to create a small business. "There are four women who are running their own small business and quite successful," said Oliya Ilmuradova.[21] The female returnees in Uzbekistan received short professional courses to work in beauty salons, to operate a greenhouse, to maintain cattle, and other agricultural courses. However, not all women are ready to reintegrate, work and earn money. Some women have strong free meal-ticket mentalities and always expect that the government or someone else will provide them with financial resources.

The public opinion in Uzbekistan about repatriation was divided. However, there were no protests or open condemnations from populations. Uzbek journalists published articles and shared their opinions about female returnees. Even though returnee women have no right to give interviews without permission, the NGOs helped the journalists to meet with the returnees. The article that was published on the website Nuz.uz, says that not all women are sincere in their comments about the homeland which saved them from their death. "There are some women who did not step away from the radical ideology. Imitating remorse, regret about life in the caliphate, they do not even realize how they are bad in it" says the article.[22] Further, it comments that in conversation with the female returnees one can understand how the female returnees are still deeply radicalized. In general, the majority of women who returned from Syria believe that the secular states are evil and they oppress Muslims by depriving them of justice and well-being.

Uzbekistan has not repatriated male fighters and the Uzbek official, whom I met in Vienna, explained this approach as seeking justice for their crimes. "Uzbekistan has a clear position that all male fighters should be tried. We expect that there will be coordinated action with international community to try all ISIS fighters in the Middle East," he told me. Regarding other state policies, Uzbekistan has no cases of deprivation of citizenship, even though Uzbekistan adopted the legal norm, regarding the stripping of citizenship for serious crimes, in 2015. Article 33 of the Law on Citizenship does not explicitly target foreign fighters, but it states that citizenship can be revoked when resulting in significant damage to public and state interests by working for a foreign state, or by committing crimes against peace and security. Despite this, Uzbekistan did not revoke the citizenship of foreign fighters who traveled to Syria and Iraq.

Initially, Uzbek President Mirziyoev promised that the Uzbek government will provide the repatriated women and children with medical and psychological assistance, as well as social and financial support. Since last year, women have been receiving financial support and some of them even received accommodation from the government. However, the abundance of social support has its own shortages. As one of the social workers in Uzbekistan told me, a majority of the women have no willingness to work. "They have not been adapted to be independent as relied only on their husbands. Even some of them think that women should not work and must stay at home. This is our main challenge as the government cannot finance them for their whole life," she told me. In the rehabilitation program of Uzbekistan, the families and communities should be playing an active role. However, not all families are ready to accept and support them. There have been cases where the family accepted but then refused, due to conflicts between them. So, the rehabilitation process is indeed a very difficult task and it will last for a minimum of five or seven years.

OPERATION ZHUSAN: STATE-LED AND INSTITUTIONALIZED REHABILITATION

Kazakhstan saw a wave of foreign fighters leaving for Syria and Iraq from 2011 until 2017. According to official information provided by Kazakhstan's diplomat, 850 Kazakh citizens, including women and children, traveled to Syria during this period.[23] However, in reality, this number might be much higher for two reasons. Firstly, the official numbers from Central Asian states usually do not reflect reality, as these states do not have the manpower or technological capacity to the track movements of large numbers of people traveling to Syria via Turkey or Moscow. Secondly, according to information provided by Kazakh authorities during an interview, about 700 citizens have been placed on a blacklist of people who joined terrorist groups abroad, and other hundreds of Kazakh citizens have been killed in Syria. If we add these numbers to the number of repatriated people, it is clear that the total number of Kazakhs who traveled to Syria is in fact much higher.

The echoes of religious radicalization in Kazakhstan first appeared in 2011. On 21 October 2011, the terrorist group Djund-al-Caliphate published a video statement where they threatened that brutal attacks will follow if the Kazakh government did not change the legal norms that control religious activities. Ten days later, two explosions occurred in Atyrau, with Djund-al-Caliphate claiming responsibility. A third terrorist attack by the same group followed on 12 November of the same year. These attacks demonstrated the presence of deep religious radicalization in Kazakhstan, and that some religious fanatics were ready to carry out terrorist attacks and were prepared for further extremist actions. In the midst of these attacks, the outflow of people from Kazakhstan to Syria and Iraq had already started. Departees flew to Turkey, either through Kyrgyzstan or directly. Later, the scale of such traveling became clear when foreign fighters became active on social media. They created YouTube videos, became active on Facebook and on Russian-speaking platforms, such as Odnoklassniki and Mail.ru. The Kazakh government soon realized there were hundreds, if not thousands, of Kazakh citizens traveling to Syria, and began to take action in 2016 to tackle the phenomenon of foreign fighters.

At first, Kazakhstan did not consider repatriation as an option, as it did not anticipate that it would have to decide whether or not to repatriate its own citizens from Syria, once ISIS was defeated. The main concern of the Kazakh government at the time was that these people may return with the intention to carry out terrorist attacks in Kazakhstan. Thus, in 2017, Kazakhstan amended its criminal code and added a new provision stipulating the stripping of citizenship for participation in terrorist acts, creation of terrorist groups, and being a member of them, including terrorist groups outside of the country. The Minister of Justice of Kazakhstan, Marat Beketayev, explained that the new norm only targets those who traveled abroad and committed severe crimes. "This norm does not apply to citizens who are in the territory of Kazakhstan, but it aims to protect the country from people who are abroad and have committed crimes," said Mr. Beketayev.[24] As an example, he cited those people who have participated in terrorist and combat operations in Syria. "This is a protective measure to prevent them from returning to Kazakhstan and spreading that ideology. By stripping citizenship, we are depriving them of the right to return to their home country. But if that person is already in the territory of Kazakhstan, stripping citizenship does not make sense. Given the gravity of the crimes committed, that person should instead be sentenced for up to 20 years in prison," he said.[25]

In general, Kazakhstan places severe punishment on its people for terrorism and any support for or participation in terrorist organizations. Terrorist attacks carried out in Kazakhstan in 2016 led to the adoption of strict legal norms for any kind of terrorist activity. In December 2016, the Senate of the Kazakh Parliament adopted amendments to its criminal code, increasing the lower and upper threshold of the permitted terms of imprisonment for such crimes. Subsequently, those who participate in any kind of terrorist and extremist activities could be sentenced to up to twenty years, and also be subjected to the confiscation of their property.

In 2019 and 2020, Kazakhstan carried out the repatriation operations in five phases. The operation Zhusan brought back 722 people in total. Thirty-two male returnees were immediately arrested and charged with terrorism-related crimes. The provisions in the criminal code of Kazakhstan permit sentences of up to 20 years of imprisonment upon conviction. The court hearings took place at Prison No. 166/10 in Nur-Sultan in October 2019 and all thirty-two men were sentenced to prison ranging from eight to thirteen years. They were charged with terrorist crimes, with prosecutors providing evidence that included gruesome photographs and videos taken in Syria. In one such photograph submitted as evidence, a thirty-three-year-old Kazakh man, who was captured in Syria, stood against a background of severed human heads with his foot on one of them. The same defendant was also shown in terrorism propaganda videos.[26] As stated, Kazakh fighters played an important role in combatant operations under ISIS. During the court hearings, it was revealed that Nurlan Kamalov, forty-one, served as a commander and Amīr, with a big house, an office, and a personal chauffeur. Another returnee, Amanjol, thirty-three, was a trained sniper and served in ISIS's Amiyat security agency. The court heard shocking confessions from the returned fighters. One of them said that he dreamed of ending up at the American prison at Guantanamo Bay in Cuba where, according to him, "the punishment is milder." All of the returned Kazakh men served in the ranks of ISIS to whatever extent they could as active combatants and, as such, committed war crimes.[27]

Kazakh Djamagaat in Syria and Iraq

In 2013, a large group of Kazakh people, who joined ISIS, posted a video on YouTube titled "Family of 150 Kazakh Muslims Relocated to the Land of Sham." About 150 Kazakhs, including children, appeared in the video, announcing that they were all from Kazakhstan and were now in Syria to participate in jihad. From their appearance, it was clear that they were indeed Kazakhs, as they spoke Kazakh and Russian. One man spoke in Kazakh, "We performed hijra and relocated to the land of Sham to commit jihad. Allah indicated to us that jihad is the highest peak of Islam." Four Kazakh men stated in Kazakh that they went to Syria for jihad with the will of Allah. One of them, named Saif-ad-din-al-Kazakh, said, "Jihad is a duty of every Muslim, we have to fight against enemies." His reference to enemies pertains to people of other beliefs, whom such extremists call infidels. He urged other Kazakhs to come to the so-called caliphate, which he called "paradise," and to join them in Allah's jihad.[28] This video exposed hundreds of Central Asians to be present in Syria, and the public at home was shocked to see children standing alongside their fathers and posing in the video. What horrified many was how dozens of Kazakh children were playing, running around, exercising, with young girls in niqabs and some boys reading the Quran and even holding arms. The video was a wake-up call for Central Asian countries, proving that there were Central Asians who had joined ISIS and that, shockingly, it was a family jihad. Foreign fighters had gone to Syria with their family members, including small children, and the family jihad was different and more dangerous.

The next video that dumbfounded Central Asian society concerned Kazakh children who had been trained by ISIS. Children, aged ten to thirteen, were posing with weapons and spoke in Kazakh about jihad. In one of the propaganda videos produced by ISIS, a Kazakh boy is asked, "Who will you become in the future?," to which he answers, "The one who cuts the throat of infidels." This kind of ISIS video was shocking, as people realized that not only men but women and children were also traveling to Syria to join ISIS. Another example came from a man who called himself Artem. He was very active in posting photos from Syria and some of his posts clearly threatened his home country and other states in the region: "Our Jihad will reach Kazakhstan, Kyrgyzstan, and the whole Central Asia," he stated. Artem, who was from Kazakhstan, posted photos with men and children from Kazakhstan and Kyrgyzstan.[29] Later, these ISIS-related videos were removed from YouTube and local media was asked not to disseminate further.

While hundreds of Kazakh children went to Syria with their parents, hundreds more were subsequently born in Syria and Iraq. ISIS wanted to see more children and women within their ranks, and child soldiers were trained and indoctrinated from an early age. According to Yulia Denisenko, an independent expert on countering extremism and deradicalization in Kazakhstan, ISIS used children for several purposes, including ideological and military goals. Yulia Denisenko said in an interview:

> First, ISIS used children as an ideological tool to convey a message to the enemy and threatening that the next generation was coming. ISIS used children as human bombs on the front lines. They taught children that the most honorable future for them was to become suicide bombers. They used young children of four to five years of age for propaganda, while children of twelve to fifteen years were trained and participated in combat operations. We need to understand that instead of mathematics, these children counted cartridges, instead of physical education there was military training, instead of drawing—Arabic calligraphy, instead of literature—memorizing doctrinal provisions and rules of terrorist groups. Children were very profitable warriors for ISIS since they cannot evaluate the consequences of their actions.[30]

The peak of the outflow was in 2013 when 40 percent of all known Kazakh foreign fighters left the country to join terrorist groups. The number of foreign fighters from Kazakhstan might be higher compared to other neighboring countries, simply because the country has a higher population compared to some other Central Asian states. Those who traveled to Syria and spent several years there informed me during interviews that the Kazakh community in Syria was quite large. At the beginning, there were three Kazakh Djamagaats under ISIS—Ontustik, Batys, and Ortalyk. They gave these names to djamagaats according to geographical places in Kazakhstan from which people came. Later these three small djamagaats were united to one big Kazakh Djamagaat. Maria, a woman from Russia who had been living in the Al-Hawl camp at the time of the writing of this book, stated in her interview that there were thousands of women who were part of the Kazakh community, whom they collectively called Kazakh Djamagaat. "I saw many Kazakh women and children. I do not know how to describe their numbers, maybe hundreds or thousands of them. I did not count, but when I walked in the streets, I could see them every two meters. Not in every city of course, but in some cities, there was a big Kazakh Djamagaat," said Maria.[31]

Another Kazakh woman whom I interviewed said that many Kazakh women just disappeared in Syria, but might still be alive. "Thousands of Kazakh women traveled to Syria. Where are they now? Their husbands were killed, but they might be alive. Arab men do not want to let them go home. For example, I know that in Mosul, where I lived, there were hundreds of other Kazakh women too. Why they did not return? Where are they? Arabs sold some of them to Shi'ites in Iran but many of them are still in captivity. Arabs hide them and keep them as their concubines. They treat them with violence and indignity. We were lucky having reached camps and later being repatriated," she said.[32] According to these accounts, the Kazakh community in Syria was quite large. Even in the absence of accurate official numbers, it can be assumed that more than 2,000 people from Kazakhstan joined ISIS. The numbers were high enough for the community to attract its own name—the Kazakh Djamagaat. This community had other Russian-speaking members from Kyrgyzstan, Russia, Caucasus, and Tajikistan, but the majority were Kazakhs. Many returnees whom I interviewed spoke about the Kazakh community, which they described as large, with many women and children. Furthermore, Kazakh fighters reached high-ranking positions in ISIS and were active combatants. The existence of the community and its activities in support of ISIS was revealed during court hearings against returned Kazakh fighters, where clear evidence was presented about the Kazakh Jamagaat and how Kazakh men actively recruited many other people from their home country.

Kazakh Djamagaat in Syria lived in different cities of Iraq and Syria. They were part of different terrorist groups, but mainly under ISIS and Al Nusra Front. The largest portion of the Kazakh community lived in Al-Shaddadah in Syria for several years. The city first was attacked and captured by al-Nusra front, then later it was taken by ISIS. More than three years Al-Shadadi remained one of the strongholds of ISIS where the biggest Kazakh Djamagaat lived. They describe the years spent in Al-Shahhadah as the most prosperous and peaceful. "People left their houses with full of furniture and food by escaping ISIS. Then, we lived in their houses. Amirs were responsible managing families and distributing houses to them. When we lived in Al-Shaddadah we had everything. We lived in a big and comfortable house. In Kazakhstan, we did not have own accommodation, so I was very happy that we are finally possessing it. My son had everything there. We never were afraid of something there until the Kurdish forces surrounded us," said the Kazakh woman who was repatriated from Roj. She said that while living in Al-Shaddadah she never regretted and believed that they will continue living peacefully. "I was so naïve. I thought that finally we have a big house and we are living peacefully among Muslims," she said. They saw bombing rarely, and never worried about this. "Every family had to dig trench to hide from bombings. So my husband prepared for us one too. I was pregnant and now recall how hugging my son was hiding in trench. I was praying and asking God to save us. The most difficult moments started when the coalition forces started bombing us. One day, they dropped fifty-six bombs, so then I understood that we are going to die there," she told me. After having lived for two years in Shahhadeh they had to escape bombings and moved to Ravi, Iraq.

Kazakh Djamagaat had eighteen leaders, whom they called Amir. Each Amir was responsible for different aspects of their community: Amir on border guarding issues, Amir on food supply, Amir on security and army, and even they had Amir on the issues of widows. On 31 December 2017, the house where all eighteen Kazakh Amirs gathered to have a meeting was bombed and all of them died. One of the returnees, Nuraiym, lost her husband and four children and one grandchild in Syria. "My husband was in that meeting and he was killed in this bombing. Amirs were discussing relocation of the whole community as the Kurds were very close to us. My husband told me before going to that meeting that I need to prepare children for relocation. He left and in ten minutes we heard the huge explosion nearby. I looked through the window, and I saw that the house of our Amir was on fire." This was a house of Amir Aby Faiza, who was a main leader of Kazakh community under ISIS. Abu Faiza was popular among Kazakhs under ISIS as he united three small djmaghaats and united Kazakhs under one. He became a main Amir of all Kazakhs there. We don't know his real name, but he was from Chimkent city. Nuraiym lost her husband who was one of the Kazakh Amirs under ISIS, and also her five children and granddaughter in Syria. "At night our house was bombed, all of them were left under ruins. Only me and my granddaughter survived. I was heavily wounded, as my arms, jaw and skull were broken. In the field hospital, my jaw and mouth were wound with simple wire and did it so professionally that even our Almaty doctors were surprised. They told me it is unnecessary to do anything as it worked perfectly," she says.[33] She is currently living in Kazakhstan with her granddaughter who had survived the bombing in Syria together with her.

Kazakh women who were essential part of the Kazakh Djamagaat said that their life in the Middle East after leaving Al-Shaddadeh became unbearable. "My one and half year in Al Shaddadi was the most peaceful period in the Middle East. Then, we had to flee all time by relocating from one town to another of Syria and Iraq to escape bombings. Wherever we were I had a backpack ready to flee. All of us were instructed by Amirs to have always ready a backpack per person with food, water and medicals when it is necessary to flee. We changed dozens of towns and each time the Kurdish forces were following us. Even at night we had to escape bombings or the assault of the Kurdish forces and every single day became a nightmare. Sometimes we lived in ruins and were left without food. My children were starving and gave them herbs and bran to keep them alive," told me another Kazakh woman. Many Kazakh families reached Baghouse, which was last stronghold of ISIS. They were surrounded to the Kurdish forces in the Baghouse battle and were taken to Al-Hawl and Roj camps.

Preparation Process and Five Phases of the Operation

From 2019 to 2021, Kazakhstan officially repatriated 722 citizens, including hundreds of children, about 200 women, and 33 men. This does not mean that no other Kazakh citizens remain abroad in the ranks of terrorist groups. According to the official information provided by the Kazakh government, there are hundreds of people still on a so-called blacklist. "According to our law enforcement agencies, there are approximately 700 people on the list of people who have joined terrorist groups abroad. We have information that some of them were killed, but we don't possess clear evidence of their death. At the same time, some of them still continue their destructive activities. Therefore, we always need to be careful and ready for any actions from their side," said the Kazakh official who wanted to stay anonymous during the interview.[34]

The UN Security Council adopted two resolutions dealing with returning foreign fighters, according to which member countries have to fulfill certain obligations. Kazakhstan has tried to fulfill its obligations under the international community but seems concerned that other states are not following the same path. The Ministry of Foreign Affairs of Kazakhstan reiterated the states' obligations, thereby aiming to reconvey the message to other countries. Mr. Yerzhan Ashikbaev mentioned the same during the conference in Vienna in 2020: "Our country takes its international obligations seriously.

Since we see that there is a humanitarian crisis in the camps in Syria, countries should unite to end this problem. We should not discuss humanitarian corridors to win time, but to take serious and concrete decisions. We hear many statements of appreciation from other countries, but each state needs to take concrete actions. To leave their own citizens to survive in camps in the desert contradicts any norm of moral and international law," said Ashikbaev.[35]

Kazakhstan has led repatriation efforts, having sent four chartered aircraft in four different phases to Syria and Iraq during Operation Zhusan. There was a fifth phase of the operation that did not involve air transportation. This kind of large-scale repatriation operation was the first of its kind in modern history. According to the statistics, 24 percent of the returnees had spent more than six years in Syria, 42 percent of them were there for four to six years, 24 percent for two to four years, and only 6 percent had spent one to two years in the conflict zone.[36] These numbers demonstrate that the majority of returnees spent a significant amount of time in Syria and as a consequence, were undeniably psychologically and physically heavily affected. Operation Zhusan was named after bitter wormwood, the smell of this herb is associated with homesickness and longing for the homeland among Kazakh people. There is a legend about a mother who was reunited with her son through the smell of Zhusan. In the story, the son had quarreled with his parents and left them, traveling to another country. His parents wanted him to return, but he was steadfast. They were tired of pleading and eventually his mother sent him a wormwood twig instead. The son received the herb and once he inhaled its fragrance, he realized how much he truly missed his homeland and his parents. Thanks to Zhusan, he returned to them. Kazakh people know this legend well, thus the government decided to name the operation Zhusan.

Kazakhstan's operations demanded thorough preparation and huge diplomatic efforts. Kazakhstan was in a privileged position since it had been the mediator of negotiations between Syria, Turkey, Iran, and Russia. Kazakhstan hosted several rounds of peace talks in Astana, possessed first-hand information on the development of the conflict, and had built good diplomatic relations with all parties. Deputy Minister of Foreign Affairs, Mr. Yerzhan Ashikbaev, stated in the conference in Vienna in 2020 that there was very little time for preparation. "We knew that we had to act immediately. Since we had been involved in the peace talks on Syria, we had many details on the conflict and possible future scenarios. As a country that possessed such information, the main driving principle was—the sooner, the better. We needed to act urgently as the situation was changing rapidly."

Operation Zhusan involved difficult preparations, demanding thorough and meticulous steps to be taken. The first task was to identify Kazakh citizens in Syria and Iraq: how many men, women and children were present and how many were in the camps and in the prisons. The most difficult part was the negotiation with both state and non-state actors in Syria and Iraq. Kazakhstan had the privilege of the availability of channels and diplomatic relations. The Kazakh official told me that the operation was not as simple as sending charter flights to bring citizens back. "We cannot disclose details and schemes of the negotiations publicly. However, we are providing them to partner states who are interested to learn from our experience. For example, Kyrgyzstan requested it and we gave them all the information accordingly. The main task of the negotiations was to receive guarantees from the main parties, including the Syrian Democratic Forces. The negotiations were very complicated and hard. Each step was difficult. We needed to verify, to make them match like small puzzles," the Kazakh high-level official told me during the interview. Finally, on 8th January 2019, the first returnee flight landed at the Aktau airport with forty-three people on the board. twelve women and twenty-two children had arrived safely in their homeland. "When they arrived, what we saw was heartbreaking. You needed to see in what psychological and emotional conditions they arrived. Children were wounded with amputated legs. All of them were exhausted, underweight, sick, and wounded with shrapnel," said the Kazakh official.

The Kazakh authorities had serious concerns regarding public opinion and how to manage and eliminate the stigma associated with being a former foreign fighter in society. Therefore, Kazakhstan framed Operation Zhusan as a humanitarian mission and, in doing so, created several important narratives. First, Kazakhstan declared that Operation Zhusan was centered on saving the lives of Kazakh citizens. Second, Kazakhstan claimed that those who had traveled to Syria had been misled and deceived. On day one of the first phases of the operation, President Nursultan Nazarbaev made a statement, mentioning that the operation had been sanctioned by him. "These citizens were deceived and misled, and they have been held as hostages by terrorists. Our main goal is to ensure the security and integrity of our country. We will continue the work to repatriate our citizens from the conflict zones where they have been held against their will."[37]

Each phase of Operation Zhusan was followed by a press conference at the Ministry of Foreign Affairs where results of the operation were presented. These press briefings reiterated that the humanitarian operations were aimed at saving the country's citizens, who had been led to a crisis-hit country under false claims and subsequently caught up in an armed conflict. The Kazakh officials noted the importance of providing innocent children with an opportunity to live, be able to develop in peace and security and be recognized as fully-fledged citizens of Kazakhstan.[38] Kazakhstan built a sound media strategy to further convey these messages to the population. A pool of leading media outlets was selected to work with them, and in turn, these media outlets were granted access to returnees for interviews.

The Kazakh government started the preparation phase of Operation Zhusan immediately after the fall of ISIS. The aforementioned diplomatic negotiations took place alongside a thorough identification process of each returnee, which was done with the help of parents and other relatives of those who were thought to be in Syria and Iraq. Parents and siblings brought photos and showed details of their conversations with their loved ones on WhatsApp or Telegram. The special services started the verification process with the information they possessed. Governmental bodies in Kazakhstan worked with international organizations such as the Red Cross, UNICEF to share information and discuss logistics.

The last step of the verification process involved sending a dedicated mission of officials and special services to Syria and Iraq to meet with the people identified. The mission visited camps and prisons and met with every citizen of Kazakhstan that had been made known to them. During the first meeting at the camps in Syria, officials explained to every person, whom they intended to extract, that returning had to be done willingly and, in cases where there was clear evidence of any wrongdoing, returnees would be held responsible for their actions. Consequently, some wanted to return and have signed the necessary official documents, but others did not. There is no exact number accounting for those who declined the option to return. However, according to one official number provided by the Deputy Minister of Foreign Affairs during an interview, 114 Kazakh citizens currently remain in Syria, including women and children.[39] Why they ultimately decided to stay is a difficult question. Some of them may have been confident that Kazakh authorities had clear evidence about their criminal and terrorist activities and, thus, did not want to return in order to escape prosecution. Some may have still believed in the ISIS ideology and hoped that the caliphate would re-evolve. Some women may have felt ashamed of being a part of ISIS and simply could not face the associated stigma that would likely arise, following their return.

According to Yerzhan Ashikbaev, there were several challenges during the verification process. One such challenge was that citizens of other countries pretended to be citizens of Kazakhstan in order to be evacuated. They knew that their country might not come to repatriate them or that they would have to wait for a very long time. "We understand that they just wanted to be extracted from Syria. Unfortunately, we were not in the position to repatriate citizens of other countries due to security and legal challenges. Our only goal was to save our own citizens."[40] Similarly, a further challenge was to identify orphaned children born of Kazakh citizens, so DNA tests were carried out to confirm their identities.

The Kazakh government gave its citizens a second chance. When the Kazakh military-chartered aircraft landed in northeast Syria to repatriate them, the other women in the camps looked at them with envy and tears in their eyes. Everybody wanted to be in their shoes. One of the returnees told me that she was very proud at that moment. "I know I betrayed my country. I rejected the existence of my homeland and sought to live in another place. But Kazakhstan saved us by sending a flight. I boarded the plane and started crying. The social workers thought that I was sick or something. They asked why I was crying. I could not explain why. I will spend the rest of my life here and I want my children to live in Kazakhstan. I will raise my children as patriots of my country and will do my best to become a responsible citizen," she said.

MEETING RETURNEES: QUARANTINE TIME AND MEDICAL CHECK-UPS

The Kazakh government prepared a rehabilitation center to host returnees in Aktau, which is a small city in northern Kazakhstan. Aktau was chosen for two reasons—the presence of the airport and a venue convenient enough where one could accommodate a large group of returnees. The health and rehabilitation center, known as "Flamingo," which was built in a Soviet era near the Caspian Sea, was chosen to host women and children. Flamingo was dedicated to fostering children's well-being and as such, was prepared to receive them comfortably. The five buildings that made up the center were adapted to receive returnees, with one building designated for administration and kitchens, three buildings converted into living quarters for the women and children, and one building designed to accommodate personnel. Medical personnel, social workers, security personnel, theologians and other officials arrived in advance to get ready to work with the returnees.

The first floor of the main building contained medical facilities, teaching rooms, a playing room for children, and a dining room where meals were served. The women were to serve the meals and clean up themselves. "Returnees had very rich meals five times per day because the children were underweight due to malnutrition, so we tried to give them a lot of vitamins including meat, fish and fruits every day. They were fed better than us," one of the social workers told me.[41] According to Yulia Denisenko, an independent expert in Kazakhstan, in rehabilitation programs restoring physical health should come first. "These women and children spent several years in the war zone, then lived in camps. They should be given time to restore the normal functioning of the gastrointestinal tract. Because they starved, their bodies were malnourished. Therefore, any country that will build rehabilitation programs should remember that you need to address other things after having provided medical assistance and food," said Yulia Denisenko in an interview.

For the first month of their stay at the rehabilitation center, all returnees were placed in quarantine. Returnees neither went beyond the Centre's grounds nor met with their parents or relatives. Women and children were isolated while they received medical checks and any necessary urgent care. The first step was to give them a shower and change their clothes, which were burned and replaced by the attending social workers. "All the women were dressed in black niqabs covering their faces. When they arrived, we approached them and said, 'You've arrived home, you are safe, so now you can show your faces,'" said Gulnaz Razdykova, a psychologist and director of the Center of Study and Development of Interfaith Relations in Kazakhstan who worked with returnees, during an interview.[42] "From the beginning, we wanted them to get rid of the black clothes that they wore in Syria and we prepared clothes in bright colors. Black clothes could be depressing, reminding them of their worst experiences in Syria, so they got dressed in rose, green, red, and other bright colors," said Olga Ryl, director of the NGO Pravo in Kazakhstan.[43]

Medical exams were completed during quarantine by approximately twenty different medical specialists. According to Gulnaz Razdykova, the medical exams included fluorography and blood tests. In total, eighteen different medical tests were undertaken to detect infections and bacteria. "We needed to identify all of the infections and diseases they might have. Some women and children had typhoid fever, whooping cough, and problems with the kidneys. Those who had wounds and amputations were examined by doctors and had x-ray examinations. During the first three days, they slept a lot because they were exhausted. In the beginning, we had to deal with lice and fleas too," said Gulnaz.[44] A common problem among women and children was anemia and other illnesses associated with it.

The majority of returnees were children, heavily affected by their experiences. Some of them had been taken to Syria by their parents against their will, while others were born there. When they arrived in Kazakhstan, they were in horrible condition. Four of them had become disabled after being wounded from bombings, with amputations on their legs or arms. The first thing that social workers did was to wash them and cut their hair. Most of them kept silent throughout because they were reserved, inhibited, traumatized, and frightened of people. They had never seen normal life, and those who had been born in Kazakhstan were too young to remember it. They had never seen toys and books. All of the returned children, even those who were eleven or twelve years old, did not know the alphabet and had never been to school. "In the initial few days, we started teaching them simple everyday routines. They had never cleaned their teeth, so we had to explain to them. We had to teach them how to go to the toilet, use the sink, wear pajamas at night, wash their face and hands and how to go to bed," said Gulnaz Razdykova.

The most urgent medical assistance was provided to the wounded and starving. Many women and children had been wounded during bombings and had splinters in their heads, backs, or legs. One woman, who got wounded during an air attack, had a splinter very close to her heart, which was successfully operated on in Astana. Doctors advised that some splinters be left untouched due to the possibility of additional complications. Two children who were disabled underwent surgery and were subsequently able to use wheelchairs. A two-year-old baby was urgently operated upon due to a heart defect. As many women gave birth in Syria at home without any medical assistance, they required medical treatments to address unresolved physical issues. The children had never received any vaccinations, so doctors created vaccine cards for them and started providing them with any vaccines that were required. Kazakhstan requires that every child be vaccinated by law, however, it took some time and explanation to convince the mothers to agree to it. Most of them were resistant, stating that their children did not need them.

The fact that the rehabilitation center was located near the Caspian Sea created favorable conditions to work with the returnees. Gulnaz Razdykova, one of the leading PRR practitioner and psychologist in Kazakhstan, stated that she organized meditation sessions and relaxing therapies for women and children by the sea. Some boys shouted "Euphrates, Euphrates!" seeing the Caspian Sea. In Syria, some boys swam in the Euphrates River so they associated the Caspian Sea with it. Children had their first swim in the Caspian Sea, slept in the sand, and played with seashells. They played volleyball and football on the beach. The women did not swim in typical swimsuits but in long dresses. At first, their children were surprised at their mothers swimming. Some boys were asking their mothers not to overstep the line laid out by the religious dogma they had been socialized into. Soon, the children simply accepted the fact that their mothers were swimming and enjoying themselves.

The next intervention stage, undertaken simultaneously, was an individual legal assessment of each case. The Kazakh government started investigations into each of the women on the subject of their alleged participation in terrorist propaganda and subsequently any further crimes committed in the territories of Syria and Iraq. As a result, thirteen women were arrested because special services had clear evidence that they had recruited other women into ISIS and had produced propaganda materials.[45] Returnees had no identity documents since those had immediately been confiscated by terrorist groups following their arrival in Syria. The next goal, therefore, was to restore the women's identity documents and resolve legal issues so that children born in Syria could be documented.

One further and very important part of the rehabilitation operation was to mobilize social workers, psychologists, and theologians to work with returnees. The Kazakh government sought civil society organizations with experience of working with post-traumatic stress disorder and the rehabilitation of trauma survivors. The government involved organizations such as Akniet and Pravo to work along three lines: religious education, psychological therapy, and resocialization. Akniet and Pravo mobilized dozens of theologians, psychologists, and social workers and provided specialist training on how to work with the returnees. These rehabilitation workers did not approach the returnees during the first three days at the center, in order to give them enough time and space to rest and receive urgent medical assistance. Individual and group rehabilitation sessions started up step by step. The theologians and psychologists who attended them highlighted that some returnees had been strongly radicalized. Tulegen Taldybaev, a theologian who worked with women returnees, said that during the early stages of rehabilitation, some of the more radicalized women appeared to pose a risk to society. "About twenty women were very radicalized and needed to be isolated from the society," he shared. "These women stayed at the rehabilitation center for four months and intensive work was done with them."[46]

Rehabilitation and Religious Enlightening

The rehabilitation program in Kazakhstan started from psychological assistance and theological lessons. Psychologists and social workers who worked with the returnees highlighted that they presented tunnel vision thinking and appeared unable to think critically about what they had been taught under ISIS. "We were working hard to broaden their thinking, to give them some further education. This meant some pedagogical-social work needed to be done. We were involving teachers, psychologists, psychotherapists, and trauma-therapists since all of them had post-traumatic stress. Receiving all this new knowledge and developing discrepancies between what they were hearing and their religious beliefs led, to internal conflicts within the women," said Olga Ryl, the head of the NGO Pravo in Kazakhstan. As an example, a fourteen-year-old girl, who had never studied at school, believed that the Earth was flat and she did not want to accept that it was round. She was taught in Syria at a madrasa that the earth was flat and could not believe that it revolves around the sun. She and other children saw a globe for the first time, as well as toys, books, and classrooms.

The first group of returnees under Operation Zhusan, who arrived in January 2019, was very small. They were considered the lucky ones who were brought back very early and had not suffered a great deal. The twelve women with children in the first group appeared calmer, cleaner, and less exhausted. However, the picture painted of the following groups was very different. All of the returnees in those groups were exhausted, sick, and suffering from malnutrition. Olga Ryl described how, after the returnees had landed and as she and her colleagues were walking towards them, the group appeared to resemble a big black avalanche coming down. "It reminded me of a black avalanche approaching full of dust because all of them were dressed in black, very dirty and dusty. It was May of 2019. They had lived in the desert in camps in very hot weather conditions. The children were so dirty and black from the sun, it seemed like a very dirty avalanche was slowly approaching," said Olga Ryl, director of the NGO Pravo.

Other social workers told me how the thing that struck them the most, at the moment of the returnees' arrival, was their sheer number. They had never seen such a big group of returnees from conflict zones. "I had worked with prisoners, victims of violence, and members of extremist groups before. But I had never been confronted with such a big group of radicalized or traumatized people. We received the first group, which was small. The subsequent groups were huge, and when they arrived, I was a bit shocked to see them," said Gulnaz Razdykova.

During their stay at the rehabilitation center, theologians played an important role. The most crucial component of the rehabilitation and reintegration process was the ideological part. To that end, Kazakhstan mobilized theologians across the country to work with returnees to convince them that their radical ideology was not true Islam. Sixty percent of the theologians who were selected to carry out this work were affiliated with a rehabilitation center known as Akniet, which specialized in the deradicalization of inmates and members of extremist groups. Akniet Center has been operational since 2014 and has regional offices in six cities in Kazakhstan. "Our government invited us to work with the returnees, and our forty specialists have been involved ever since. We knew what kind of contingent we would have and how they had been radicalized. We knew how to work with them. There was no shortage of specialists. Sixty percent were our own theologians and 40 percent were invited from other regions," said Alim Shaumetov, director of Akniet Center.[47] According to Alimov, theologians had an important role to explain to returnees their religious misconceptions and false assumptions about Islam.

Theologians organized individual conversations with returnees and group sessions. Some women behaved aggressively, displayed highly radicalized characteristics, and appeared deeply committed and convinced by the idea of the caliphate. These women did not want to recognize the secular existence of states and the possibility of peaceful coexistence alongside other religions. They believed that jihad and the existence of the caliphate were the only ways to live according to Islam and the killing of non-Muslims was a normative aspect of those beliefs. The women whom theologians identified as the most radicalized, twenty in total, were assigned to the rehabilitation center "Shans" where they stayed for an additional four months. "These women were isolated from the society for four months. They stayed in the rehabilitation center, with theologians and psychologists working with them intensively," said Tulegen Taldybaev, a theologian who worked with returnees.[48]

Specialists who worked with the returnees highlighted that these women lacked a broader religious education, even with respect to differences within the Islamic faith. Some of them had never read the Quran for themselves and they were not aware of the existence of Hanafi Madhhab. According to Alim Shaumetov, the attending theologians asked the women if they knew of the Hanafi school of Islam, which has been practiced in Central Asia since the twelfth century. "The women did not know what Hanafi Madhhab is, which is why we started to explain how our ancestors have been practicing this school of Islam, meaning that we live in tolerance and peace and respect other religions. They had never heard about the Islam we really believe in and practice. We explained it to them and gave them literature to read. Some of them got really interested and asked lots of questions," said Alim Shaumetov.[49] He informed me that after many sessions with theologians, some women stepped away from their radical ideas and admitted their mistakes of ignoring true Islamic concepts and not attempting to learn the authoritative opinions of Islamic scholars.

During the period that the returnees spent in Syria, members of ISIS and other terrorist groups continually planted radical ideas into the minds of the women and children. During sessions with psychologists and theologians, the women described how Amirs of ISIS in Syria organized group lessons and discussions three to four times per week to cement these ideas. The women and children were effectively brainwashed about the idea of a utopian life in the caliphate, the need to fight for it, and how to create the dream life within it. Even though 80 percent of the women repatriated from Syria claimed they stayed at home cooking and taking care of the children, they had a special role in the ranks of ISIS and other terrorist groups fighting in Syria. ISIS was calculated in its efforts to instill its message into the mind of every person so that each individual under the caliphate felt they had a special mission. It was a requirement for every child to learn Arabic and be able to read the Quran by heart. Therefore, the children knew Arabic and could read surahs of the Quran, but none of them knew the Kazakh alphabet. Spending between four and seven years in Syria under the caliphate gave plenty of time for the women and children to be radicalized by the leaders in the community.

When the initial treatment period in the rehabilitation center was completed, returnees met with their parents and relatives. This step illustrated that the next stage of reintegration should be undertaken with the support of their family members. Some of the women started living with their parents or sisters and, as such, the returnees dispersed to different regions of Kazakhstan to join their loved ones. However, the social workers continued to remain involved in their lives. Some women attended short professional courses in order to find a job, to support their reintegration and to foster their independence.

Diverse Group of Female Returnees

ISIS had its own agenda when it came to the women they recruited. They needed women for more than cooking and taking care of husbands and children alone. Women in Syria were constantly brainwashed and trained. ISIS trained women to become suicide bombers and combatants. Kazakhstan did not possess evidence about whether the women returnees participated specifically in combat operations or had been trained to do so. However, thirteen of the women brought back were arrested and charged with terrorist offenses. One of the arrested women claimed that a photo where she could be seen holding a weapon was taken by her husband accidentally. She claimed that she took ahold of the weapon just for a photo because her husband had asked her to, but she stated she was never taught how to shoot or hold it. However, it is clear that many women were involved in recruitment and propaganda for ISIS.

Women who went to Syria had different backgrounds and different destinies. As such, each case should be considered and analyzed individually. They had their own motivations to flee their country and to go to the conflict zone. The major reason that I usually heard from approximately 70 percent of the Kazakh women, was that they followed their husbands. Terrorist groups demanded foreign fighters to call on their wives and children to follow them. Some Kazakh men traveled to Syria with their family members, some of them reached the conflict zone alone and then invited their wives and children to join. If a man was single, he had to marry in Syria or find someone through the Internet and recruit her. The terrorist groups' goal was to have more women and children in Syria to expand the community under the caliphate, which is why their recruiters were particularly skilled and had the money to do what was necessary to entice them.

Kazakh women who went to Syria can be divided into several groups according to their backgrounds. The psychologists and theologians in Kazakhstan who worked with them helped me to analyze their profiles and identify these groups. One of the common features among those who traveled to Syria from Kazakhstan was a history of family conflict and interpersonal problems. According to Erlan Karin, who analyzed about 200 profiles of foreign fighters and their associates, these people were lonely and felt out of harmony with their parents and other family members, communication with whom had typically broken down.[50] Erlan Karin, current State Secretary of Kazakhstan and Political Scientist, said,

> During the last two decades, values have changed, and as well as social relations changed. During the Soviet period, youngsters were not alone being a part of the system of social relationships. If they encounter problems could have been immediately assisted and accompanied. After the collapse of the USSR, Kazakhstan became independent and market economy brought into our lives new norms and values. Everyone should survive and earn money. Success criteria has also been changed. Now being successful means having a big car and nice apartment. The role of family institution has weakened and relations between generations have been complicated. As a result, people feel abandoned having broken relations with loved ones.

The observations of Erlan Karin have serious grounds. Indeed, many women who went to Syria had family conflicts, divorces, and childhood trauma. My analysis of the profiles of those I interviewed, showed that women who went to Syria had experienced problems either in their adult lives or had different childhood traumas. Their parents were typically divorced or they found themselves in constant conflict with other family members. Usually, they had struggled at school and either did not graduate or did not advance beyond their basic mandatory education. Being forced to marry extremely young was also very common for them. Most of the female returnees had gotten married at sixteen, seventeen, and eighteen years old and had no chance to study or enjoy their youth. They were totally economically dependent on their husbands, while staying home with no prospect of work.

Those who had experienced trauma during childhood seemed to lack loving attention, understanding, and compassion from the people who had been in their lives prior to leaving for Syria. According to psychologist Lola Shakimova, people who seek attention and love can be drawn towards a group or community that might fill the void. "Recruiters first study what kind of problems that person has. Depending on the personal problems of that person, they use psychological influence such as offering moral support, giving additional attention, offering financial assistance, and showing compassion. In our society, some people lack simple positive human relations and the recruiters benefitted from that vacuum," said Lola Shakimova.[51]

As for those who had followed their husbands to Syria, the women were morally and financially dependent upon their husbands. Usually, they were religious and believed in Sharia, which says that women should obey their husbands. A majority of women told me that they had no choice but to follow their husbands, who were usually the first to decide to go to Syria. Often, the women did not actually know about the eventual plan to reach Syria and were not fully informed of this intention prior to leaving. There were very sad stories about husbands selling all of the family's property, leaving the women with little option but to agree to join them. Some of the husbands went as far as threatening their wives that they would take away the children and leave them with nothing if they did not comply. According to Olga Ryl, there were very rich families who had possessed properties, and the wives had been unaware that their husbands had sold everything to prepare for the trip to Syria.

On the other hand, the women who followed their husbands also did not want to think about what was happening or take responsibility. They usually did not work and stayed at home. For them, a family income was important, but it did not matter what the source was. Their husbands convinced them that they would earn a minimum of 50 U.S. dollars every day and they believed them. They thought that their standard of living would be better in Syria than in Kazakhstan. It is important to add that not all women were naïve in this sense. Some knew more about the situation there and wanted to go simply because they had been radicalized and believed in the idea of jihad and the caliphate.

The third group of women was those who were divorced or unmarried. Feeling alone and unhappy, these young girls and young women had hoped to marry someone after finding them through the Internet. "These women sought to receive the love, attention, and affection they had lacked in their lives previously. They went to Syria in hope to get married and to be happy. Unfortunately, they had to remarry again when their husbands died," said Olga Ryl. This group also included women who were divorced, had been disappointed with marriage, and sought better husbands.

In summary, each female returnee's case is unique and it would be inappropriate to generalize the experience of female foreign fighters as if they were a homogeneous group. Currently, the Kazakh government is working hard to resocialize female returnees and help them reintegrate into society. An important goal for these women is to achieve employment through gaining new skills, which they can use to find work. Some of the women have already started working as hairdressers, tailors, and manicurists, but employment rates are only approximately 10 percent. Many of the women have young children and they feel they should stay home to take care of them. A significant problem of accommodation was somewhat alleviated by the Kazakh government that provided free accommodation to some of the returnees. Currently, seventeen women are living at the rehabilitation center because they do not have another place to go as their parents and other relatives have refused to welcome and shelter them.

Long-Term Goal: Will They Become Normal?

The Kazakh repatriates have spent almost three years in their homeland. What has changed so far? Specialists highlight that rehabilitation and reintegration is a long process that will take at least four or five years. Presently, thirty-one women from all four phases of Operation Zhusan can be considered deradicalized. Some of them have started working with the rehabilitation program as volunteers. The government aims to involve them as ambassadors to talk with other returnees and volunteers who can convey the message to the population to prevent religious extremism. I met two of those volunteers: Sabinella and Aida. Both women returned to Kazakhstan with their children. Recently, they have been traveling a lot with a delegation of the Kazakh government. I saw them speaking at the United Nations, both in Geneva and New York. They also spoke at the European Parliament in Brussels and at the recent OSCE conference in Vienna. During these conferences, diplomats and experts from Europe were quite shocked to see women returnees who had lived under ISIS and were able to tell their stories as well as thank their government for bringing them back. It was indeed weird but powerful to see former ISIS associates sitting alongside with diplomats and telling their stories.

Kazakhstan's repatriation and rehabilitation programs have been sparking high interest. Specialists say that a majority of the first year was devoted to resolving urgent issues, such as medical assistance, working on deep psychological traumas, restoration of identity documents, schooling for the children, finding accommodation, and rebuilding relationships with family members. The second year was spent for reintegration and resocialization of women and children. The theologians have also continued working with the returnees and intend to do so as the rehabilitation process continues for several years. "Our goal at the rehabilitation center is to help them explore true Islam, which should lead to the rejection of the radical ideology. We need to teach them that Islam is a religion of peace and mutual coexistence. Our traditional Islamic values are peaceful and forbid violence. We have to work hard and deradicalize them so they return to normal lives as ordinary citizens. Otherwise, why did we repatriate them? We cannot fail," said Alim Shaumetov.[52]

The women and children who returned from Syria and Iraq still face many challenges when it comes to their reintegration. According to Olga Ryl, during their first year back in Kazakhstan, the women and children only received assistance for their everyday problems. They should receive welfare allowances, but the government is still resolving legal issues before they can be allocated. Many of the children needed extra tutoring on school subjects, including key skills in reading and mathematics. The specialists highlight the continued efforts needed to build harmonious relationships between the mothers and their children. Many children remain very nervous and struggle to regulate their emotions. One of the women told me that avoiding conflict with the children is a daily preoccupation for her. "I am very nervous, but my children are more nervous than me. They cry and throw things. I don't know how to deal with this. I want to run away somewhere and spend some time alone hiding. I am so tired," one of the Kazakh returnees said during an interview.

The women returnees continue to struggle in their parenting roles. The specialists highlight their experience of being married several times and the pressure they faced to have children with each of these different husbands. They never experienced a consistent, loving, and financially stable family life. Their husbands were often away fighting and only periodically spent time with them and their children. Some women had already experienced parental separation themselves, either through a divorce or when growing up in orphanages. Notably, the realities of the conditions in which they lived and fled in Syria prevented the women from being able to attend to the full range of needs of their children. They might have been able to feed them, but they could not provide their children with a high standard of stimulation, proper medical care from birth, or a balanced and well-rounded education. The consequences of this are yet to be addressed and the social workers continue to support the women in these areas.

Tulegen Taldybaev, a theologian who worked with returnees to deradicalize them for several months, shared his impressions after the completion of his mission. "I finished my work with the returnees and I want to say that they are good citizens. They have a deep interest in learning and a thirst for knowledge. They are not different. They are one of us. They differ from us only by the fact that they experienced the war, violence and fear. If you ask them to tell you about the best day in their life, they cannot recall one. But if you ask about the worst days, they will tell you dozens of heartbreaking and horrible stories. This is the only difference. They are our citizens and I hope everything will be good in their lives here in the homeland," said Tulegen Taldybaev.[53]

The women had little opportunity in their lives previously, especially for education. However, they possess the full capacity to learn and study. When social workers and theologians organized a quiz for the women returnees at the rehabilitation center, Tulegen recalls that 83 percent of them gave the correct answers to the questions. "After the quiz, we had dinner together and everyone shared their emotions and concerns. I would like to say that these women are very smart and learn fast. They deserve respect and compassion. What I wanted to highlight is they are very sensitive and take everything to heart. That's why they need our support and the support of society," said Tulegen. Social workers and theologians urged the wider society to help returnees adapt and integrate. "They feel very constrained and very stressed in dealing with their emotions. We need to help them, not let them to be lost. If they feel our support, they will integrate. Sixty-seven percent of returnees are children. We want them to become good citizens of our country," said Tulegen.

Restrictions have been imposed on the returnee women concerning their current lives and they may face more in the future. Each has a supervising officer from special services and law enforcement agencies. It is understandable that their movement and actions be monitored further. They do not give interviews without permission from their supervising officers and their actions on social media are carefully observed. They cannot join religious groups on social media, nor visit group lectures in their communities or in local mosques. The most important restriction is that returnees have no right to travel. They cannot go outside of Kazakhstan anymore. It is forbidden for the rest of their lives. They do not even have the right to travel to neighboring Kyrgyzstan. In one case, a returnee wanted to visit her mother who is living in Kyrgyzstan. She wanted to avoid public attention and isolate herself there for a while, but the Kazakh authorities did not allow her to do so.

Some returnee women are actively participating in raising awareness and countering violent extremism. Kazakhstan is trying to use the voices of the women returnees to eliminate stigma and prevent future travel to conflict zones. Aida Sarina is one of these active volunteers. She delivers speeches and participates in televised debates regularly. She spoke at the UN in New York and Geneva at high-level conferences on countering violent extremism. "Addressing the UN is a great chance to speak out about the war in Syria and the fraud caliphate that the terrorists built there," she said in Geneva. Aida urges other people not to be seduced by the propaganda of radical terrorist groups and wants her story to be a wake-up call for others.

"When I saw the rescuers from Kazakhstan with my own eyes, I realized we had not been abandoned," Sarina said, recalling the day when the mission from the Kazakh government arrived to take them home. "Next to me were women from France, Germany, and other countries. I remember them looking enviously at us. They asked to find out if Kazakhstan could also take them, pleading to at least take their children from Syria," said Aida. Aida Sarina and several other women declared that they are determined to fight against terrorism. "Yes, I am a victim of terrorism, but now I want to become a fighter against terrorism, to contribute and be a part of this great purpose. I want to be the voice of all female victims of terrorism," she said.

Another volunteer who is also actively delivering speeches and is often traveling is Sabinella. I met her in Vienna at the conference on foreign fighters organized by the OSCE. She was wearing very beautiful hijabs. During the two days, I saw her in two different hijabs: rose and light green. She looked very different from how she looked when she arrived from Syria. I had seen her sitting at the rehabilitation center in the official video produced by the Kazakh authorities. Back then, she looked very tired and exhausted. In Vienna, we drank coffee together with another lady from Uzbekistan who was also a returnee from Syria. The Uzbek lady had also delivered a speech at the Vienna conference thanking her government for repatriation. As I sat with them, I observed how they discussed their previous lives in Syria, asked each other about their children, and sometimes laughed as if their memories were something from a horrible dream that they had just the night before.

Kazakhstan took a big risk by repatriating its citizens from the conflict zones. The whole world is observing the rehabilitation and reintegration programs to find out what fails and what works. Even though Kazakhstan is a rich country compared to others in the Central Asian region, it needs manpower and financial support from the international community. There are some projects with UN agencies and OSCE, but most of these involve hearing about Kazakhstan's experience. What Kazakhstan needs is concrete input in the form of consultation and technical support. Since Operation Zhusan was the first-ever large-scale repatriation in the world, Kazakhstan cannot fail. After the bloody conflict that took place at the beginning of 2022, there is some skepticism on Kazakhstan`s will to continue rehabilitation and reintegration processes. If Kazakhstan will continue achieving the rehabilitation and reintegration goals, it would grant the international community an evaluated model on how to address this ongoing crisis with former fighters.

KYRGYZSTAN'S "MEERIM" OPERATION: CHILDREN FROM IRAQI PRISONS

About thirty Kyrgyz women were convicted in Iraq and sentenced to death in Iraq. They were living with their children for more than two years in small cells in the Iraqi prison. Some women have three children, some have two. The most horrific day in their lives was when they had to give up their children for repatriation. Everyone cried when they had to say goodbye to their children. They knew that they might be seeing their children for the last time. In 2021, Kyrgyzstan repatriated seventy-nine children from Iraqi prions by separating them from their mothers. They lived in inhumane conditions in the Iraqi prison with their mothers who should serve their terms. The Kyrgyz delegation spent one month in Iraq to deal with all the legal issues to prepare the children for their repatriation. Only a few Kyrgyz women did not give consent for their children's repatriation, as they had no close relatives to be legal guardians.

On March 16, 2021, Kyrgyzstan repatriated seventy-nine children from Iraq during Operation Meerim, translated as Grace, thus becoming the fourth country in Central Asia that has brought back its citizens from Syria and Iraq. Operation Meerim was orchestrated in response to public pressure following several organized protests held by family members and their supporters near the White House and Ministry of Foreign Affairs in Bishkek. Ruslan

Kazakbaev, Minister of Foreign Affairs, told journalists that Operation Meerim followed long negotiations. "The Kyrgyz government started the negotiations with the Iraqi government, UNICEF, and The Red Cross in 2019, but the operation was delayed due to several reasons. However, this time it was successful, thanks to the political will of the new authorities in Kyrgyzstan," he said.

Children were repatriated in cases when two conditions were met. Firstly, the imprisoned mothers of Kyrgyz children in Iraq were required to give their consent for their children to be repatriated. The second condition was that close relatives in Kyrgyzstan must be ready for the adoption of the children. The Kyrgyz working group spent one month in Iraq meeting with officials, paying a fine for every child for their illegal residence in Iraq, participating in court hearings defending the rights of children, and arranging temporary legal guardianship. A significant element of the domestic preparations before Operation Meerim was the work undertaken with relatives and communities to prepare them to accept returnee children. Kyrgyz authorities spent almost one-year identifying appropriate relatives, assessing their socioeconomic conditions, and preparing them to adopt the children. Consequently, all returned children were adopted and now live with their legal guardians, who are mainly their grandparents or close relatives.

Children who returned to Kyrgyzstan were first accommodated in a children's residential home in the Chuy region which was originally equipped for disabled children. The children were reportedly amazed at the sight of snow as well as the extent of their newfound freedom. A remarkable sight was how the children were running around the territory of the residence and playing with snow. Some of them had spent four years in the Iraqi prison and had never had the opportunity to move freely and run. The very first stage of rehabilitation was medical quarantine. Medical personnel were ready to work with the children and all of them passed the medical examination. Dozens of analyses were made to check for infections, but nothing serious was found. The children, aged between two and eighteen, were generally in good health, but initially appeared small or young for their age as a result of malnutrition. Social workers taking care of the children have described how much they have changed in appearance during their first two months in their home country. They have reportedly grown and continue to get stronger and are eating and sleeping well.

Whilst the returnee children speak several languages between them, they cannot read or write. "Our children speak Turkish, Arab, Uzbek, and Kyrgyz. Some of them know some English and French. They never went to school, so now we are starting an assessment of every child's preparedness for education. We need to identify which grade they should go into, as their learning level does not currently match their chronological age. Additional tutoring will be organized for many of them," stated Aliza Soltonbekova, the Deputy Minister of Ministry of Labour and Social Protection of Kyrgyzstan.[54] The Kyrgyz authorities handed over the children to their grandparents or other close relatives after five months. During these five months, children went through a rehabilitation process and the government prepared all legal documentation processes. Now, children have been living in different regions of the country. Kyrgyz authorities are hiding their past in secret in order to avoid stigmatization. In some cases, even school administrations are not aware that these children were returned from the Middle East. Compared to Tajikistan, Kyrgyzstan was successful in finding legal guardianship for children, while Tajik children repatriated from Iraq are still living in state institutions.

CONCLUSIONS

Repatriation of children and their mothers is a law-compliant solution in this current situation. Even though only several countries have repatriated their citizens, such successful cases give hope that the returned children will become responsible citizens of their countries. As we can see in the cases of Kazakhstan, Kyrgyzstan, Tajikistan and Uzbekistan, early repatriation makes the rehabilitation of small children much easier. The more they spent time in camps, the more they get indoctrinated. A family jihad is having huge consequences, as thousands of children and women are left in the desert. Thousands of children were born under ISIS whose citizenship is also arguable. Women married three of five times, as ISIS had a policy that women should be married and give birth to as many children as possible. Countries need to undertake DNA tests to identify kinship to their potential relatives in home countries.

Rehabilitation and reintegration processes are very complex and no guarantee that they will be successful. Children's trauma may sleep for many years but return in dozens of years later. However, abandoning them in the desert will have a more catastrophic impact on international peace. They may come back to the international arena as the most brutal terrorists in the future. It is crucial for states to take responsibility for their citizens, especially to save the minds of children. Psychologists who work with returnees in Central Asia observe that children are most adapted to rehabilitation programs rather than adults. The main issue is also countries cannot separate them from their mothers. While European countries have a firm position against repatriation, several European countries have had scrutiny over the lawsuits from their citizens, who demanded to bring back their children, sisters, or brothers that have been held by the Kurdish forces in Northeast Syria. Europe prefers to repatriate only children, but leave their mothers in the camps. However, separating children from their mothers will deepen their trauma and also violates international human rights laws. The main challenge in rehabilitation processes is to deal with postconflict trauma and other psychological disorders of returnees. They presented tunnel thinking and appeared unable to think critically. Returnees are also deeply brainwashed by the radical ideology and have a black-white mindset. The experiences of Central Asian countries demonstrate that rehabilitation and reintegration is difficult but possible.

NOTES

1. Alessandra Spadarro, *Repatriation of Family Members of Foreign Fighters: Individual Right or State Prerogative?*, (Cambridge University Press for the British Institute of International and Comparative Law, 2020).

2. Anne Speckhard on the EU Policy Toward Foreign Fighters, Bulan Institute, Expert Talks, 25 February 2021.

3. Kujtim Bytyqi and Sam Mullins, "Returnee Foreign Fighters from Syria and Iraq: The Kosovan Experience," *Combatting Terrorism Center (CTC) Sentinel 12*, no. 7, (August 2019).

4. Sara Manisera, "After ISIS: How Kosovo is Rehabilitating Women and Children Repatriated from Syria," *The National*, July 25, 2019, https://www.thenational.ae/world/mena/after-isis-how-kosovo-is-rehabilitating-women-and-children-repatriated-from-syria-1.890533.

5. BIRN, "Kosovo Govt Allocates €250,000 to Fight against ISIS," *Balkan Insight*, January 10, 2020, https://balkaninsight.com/2020/01/10/outgoing-government-allocates-e250000-to-the-fight-against-isis/.

6. Maximilian Ruf and Annelies Jansen, "Study Visit: Returned Women and Children—Studying an Ongoing Experience on the Ground," Radicalisation Awareness Network (RAN) Centre of Excellence, December 2019, https://ec.europa.eu/home-affairs/sites/homeaffairs/files/what-we-do/networks/radicalisation_awareness_network/ran-papers/docs/ran_study_visit_kosovo_11_10122019_en.pdf.

7. Valerie Hopkins and Serbeze Haxhiaj, "ISIS Fighters Struggle on Return to Balkan States," *Financial Times*, May 20, 2019, https://www.ft.com/content/24835626-762a-11e9-be7d-6d846537acab.

8. Ezel Sahinkaya, Rikar Hussein, and Edlira Bllaca, "Why is Kosovo Taking Home Islamic State Members?" *Voice of America,* January 15, 2020, https://www.voanews.com/extremism-watch/why-kosovo-taking-home-islamic-state-members.

9. BIRN, "Kosovo Govt Allocates."

10. Thomas F. Lynch III, Michael Bouffard, Kelsey King, and Graham Vickowski, "The Return of Foreign Fighters to Central Asia: Implications for U.S. Counterterrorism Policy, Institute for National Strategic Studies," *Strategic Perspectives 21*, (October 2016).

11. Elena Zhurikhina, "Foreign Fighters from Central Asia: Between Renunciation and Repatriation," *Prague Institute of International Relations*, 03 October 2019,

available at https://www.ispionline.it/en/pubblicazione/foreign-fighters-central-asia-between-renunciation-and-repatriation-24072.

12. F. Lynch III et al., "The Return of Foreign Fighters to Central Asia."

13. Edward Lemon et al., "Jihadists From Ex-Soviet Central Asia: Where Are They? Why Did They Radicalize? What Next? Russia Matters/U.S.-Russia Initiative to Prevent Nuclear Terrorism," Belfer Center for Science and International Affairs, Research Paper, (December 2018).

14. Edward Lemon et al., "Jihadists From Ex-Soviet Central Asia."

15. Gavin Helf's presentation at the Bulan Institute's panel discussion on returning foreign fighters organized on 15 March 2021.

16. Keneshbek Sainazarov, interview by the author on 6 May 2020.

17. Rustam Azizi, interview by the author.

18. Maksim Yeniseyev, "Uzbekistan begins rehabilitation of repatriated 'victims of deception' from Syria," *Asia-news.com*, 11 June 2019, accessed at: https://central.asia-news.com/en_GB/articles/cnmi_ca/features/2019/06/11/feature-01.

19. Soliev Nodirbek, "Syria: Uzbekistan's Approach to IS Detainees," RSIS Commentary, October 2019, https://www.rsis.edu.sg/wp-content/uploads/2019/10/CO19199.pdf.

20. Keneshbek Sainazarov, interview.

21. Oliya Ilmuradova, interview by the author in March 2021.

22. Nuz.uz, "Returned from the Hell," 31 Oct 2020, accessed at: Возвращенные из ада... - Новости Узбекистана сегодня: nuz.uz.

23. An interview with Kazakh diplomat was conducted by the author during the OSCE conference in Vienna in February 2020. The official wanted to remain anonymous.

24. Today.kz, "Ministry of Justice of Republic of Kazakhstan: Those who are in the territory of the country won't be revoked citizenship for terrorism." The article in Russian: Живущих в стране казахстанцев могут не лишать гражданства за терроризм—МЮ РК, 24 May 2017, translated by the author, accessed at: http://today.kz/news/kazahstan/2017-05-24/742936-zhivuschih-v-strane-kazahstantsev-mogut-ne-lishat-grazhdanstva-za-terrorizm---myu-rk/.

25.Ministry of Justice, interview.

26. Aydar Ashimov, "Kazakhs on trial for joining IS in Syria committed 'horrific' crimes," *Caravanserai*, 21 November 2019, accessed at: https://central.asia-news.com/en_GB/articles/cnmi_ca/features/2019/11/21/feature-01.

27. Aydar Ashimov, "Kazakhs on trial for joining IS in Syria committed 'horrific' crimes."

28.Asem Tokaeva, "One more video of Kazakh jihadists in Syria has been published," *Azattyq*, 20 July 2014, accessed at: https://rus.azattyq.org/a/video-jihadistov-iz-kazakhstana-v-sirii-i-irake/25463575.html.

29. Informburo Kz, "Photos of allegedly Kyrgyz children in ISIS appeared on Internet," translated by the author, accessed at: https://informburo.kz/novosti/v-seti-poyavilis-fotografii-centralnoaziatskih-detey-igil-6734.html.

30. Yulia Denisenko, interview by the author on 15 May 2020.

31. An interview was conducted by the author via Telegram on 15 March 2020 while Maria was living in the Roj camp.

32. Interviews with returnees in Kazakhstan were conducted by the author via Skype and WhatsApp.

33. Nuraiym Bakytzhanova: My husband, five children and grandchild died in Syria, Kazislam.kz, 15 June 2021, https://kazislam.kz/nurajim-bakitzhanova-u-menya-v-sirii-pogibli-muzh-pyatero-detej-i-vnuchka/.

34. Interview was conducted with the Kazakh official in Vienna in 2020, who wanted to stay anonymous.

35. Yerzhan Ashikbaev's answer to the questions during the side event at the Vienna conference on 11–12 Febuary 2020.

36. From the presentation by Gulnaz Razdykova at the Vienna conference on foreign fighters, organized by the OSCE,11–12 February 2020.

37. "These are innocent people, Nazarbaev about the evacuation of people from Syria," *IA Total Kazakhstan,* 9 January 2019, accessed at: https://total.kz/ru/news/obshchestvosobitiya/etonevinnieludinazarbaevobevakuatsiikazahstantsevizsiriidate_2019_01_09_16_01_09.

38. Kazakhstan MFA, "MFA of Kazakhstan gave information on Zhusan-2 operation," translated by the author. Accessed at: http://www.mfa.gov.kz/en/london/content-view/syrtky-ister-ministrliginde-zusan-2-operaciasyny-ntizesi-turaly-ajtyp-berdi.

39. Ashikbaev, interview.

40.Ashikbaev, interview.

41. Interviews with social workers, psychologists, and theologians in Kazakhstan, conducted by the author in person and via Skype and WhatsApp.

42. Gulnaz Razdykova, interview by the author on 20 March 2020.

43. Olga Ryl, interview by the author via Skype on 22 March 2020.

44. Razdykova, interview.

45. Information provided to the author by the Ministry of Foreign Affairs of Kazakhstan.

46. Tulegen Taldybaev, interview by the author on 03 April 2020 via Skype.

47. Alim Shaumetov, interview by the author on 25 March 2020 via Skype.

48. Taldybaev, interview.

49. Shaumetov,interview.

50. Karin, interview.

51. Shakimova, interview.

52. Interview with Alim Shaumetov was conducted by the author.

53. Taldybaev, interview.

54. The interview with Aliza Soltonbekova was conducted by the author.

Conclusion

While states were slow and reluctant in finding a solution to manage the situation with postconflict ISIS fighters and their associates trapped in Northeast Syria, ISIS attacked the prison of Ghuwayran in Hasakah on 20th January 2022. ISIS is still alive and we are witnessing the acceleration of the reconstitution of ISIS not only as a covert network but as a mighty armed group. While ISIS used jail breaks as a strategic tool, there always has been a risk that the Syrian Democratic Forces may lose control over camps and terrorists can escape. The SDF had been warning that ISIS is reviving and if it comes, they do not have arms and manpower to stand against them. Eventually, what we had feared since the defeat of ISIS happened: ISIS attacked the biggest Ghuwayran prison near Hasakah to free its 5,000 fighters. The US-led coalition forces came to support the Kurdish forces and regain control over the prison. After the ten-days-fight, the Kurdish forces managed to retake control over the prison. However, hundreds of fighters managed to escape and there is no clear information on casualties and escaped fighters. It is alarming that ISIS is gaining foot again and more attacks will follow to free its fighters from Kurdish custody.

States have an opportunity to pay the smaller price now by repatriating, prosecuting, rehabilitating their citizens who are in Kurdish custody. But it seems states prefer to pay a higher price later. Abandonment will be a direct way to further radicalization and networking that will result in the rise of more dangerous terrorist group than ISIS and Al Qaeda. Moreover, they are in the custody of an illegitimate power, namely the SDF which is a non-state actor. There is a legal vacuum which states need to fill in, but states preferred stripping citizenship and sentencing some fighters in absentia by walking away from the problem. People who joined ISIS are not adversaries sent from outside, but they are all citizens of more than sixty countries worldwide. States needed to assume their responsibility for own citizens, but they are failing.

Foreign fighters are the products of our societies. They are neither zombies that arrived from other planets, nor adversaries that came from outside. They turned to radical paths living alongside us, and rejected their societies where they were struggling with socioeconomic and political problems, or because they believed to be discriminated. The background condition for radicalization might vary and be very simple: unemployment, poverty, feeling of injustice, discrimination, conflicts in the families, childhood trauma, or horizontal inequalities. In the non-enigma cycles radicalization process, which was proposed in this book, two cycles are significant. First, their grievances matter, as grievances of people and resentment are fertile ground that produces further developments that lead to radicalization. Feelings of people are important. Feeling of injustice or feeling of being discriminated develops a loss of significance. Then, people started seeking significance, support and belonging in religious ideas.

The main message that states must receive, digest and take measures: jihadism primarily is a product of bad governance. States need to fulfill their direct obligations toward their citizens on safeguarding human rights, eradicating corruption, building equal economic opportunities and opening civic spaces. Democracy is in decline, and authoritarian regimes are in rise. Greater and greater share of the global population is living under autocrat leadership and more and more dictators started to redefine norms and set new boundaries of acceptable behavior. While states are becoming predatory with flourishing corruption and antiwelfare inefficient policies, terrorist groups will continue exploit grievances of people in weak states. In countries where corruption is flourishing and the small political elite is becoming rich by exploiting public goods, there is economic deprivation, frustration and desperation. People living in these kinds of societies decide to find justice elsewhere, but not in their home countries. The major problem is poor governance and a failure of states that equip jihadists with new narratives about "evil" governance. Becoming evil means failure to build efficient state institutions and failing to eradicate pervasive corruption that enriches only small elites. The vicious cycle of corruption and nepotism has never stopped in developing countries. People are being disappointed after long decades and losing hope that their life will advance in their home countries. The main source of terrorism is injustice, more specifically perceived injustice, which can be economic, social, cultural or political. The feeling of injustice is directly related to human rights. In countries where human rights are respected, terrorism has less chance. There is difference between grievances of people in developing and European countries. In Europe, immigrant Muslims feel discriminated and marginalized, while in developing countries people are frustrated with corruption, unemployment, poverty and unequal opportunities.

Second, in the radicalization process of jihadists the ideological pillar turned out to be tremendously powerful. The Salafi-Wahhabi ideology is a powerful soft power which poisons minds of people. We need to understand that jihadism is not about military confrontation, but more about battle of ideas for minds of people. The radical ideology is a soft power, which can be countered only by education, alternative narratives, and by building just society. Militarization of counterterrorism strategies is a failure. Military interventions, bombing or sending a drone are counterproductive, as it does not eradicate root causes. As discussed in chapter 2, it is about mindset so we need to talk to people and understand their motivations. It is about listening people, to understand their feeling, talking to them. We need to stop seeing them as an ideological enemies or psychologically deviant people. We say that jihadists have a rejectionist mindset, but at the same time states also took a rejectionist mindset. We, researchers, policy makers and state officials, also have taken a rejectionist mindset. We reject that terrorists are products of our societies and our policies. The main problem is that states need to assume that jihadists have socioeconomic and political grievances which they later put into the religious framework to make them more appealing. At the same time, it is evident that Muslim communities need more education, story-telling and counternarratives to propagate true Islam. Muslim states and communities should build new policies to raise awareness about Islam as a religion in order to win discourses of jihadists.

Another side of the reality is, as my empirical evidence has shown, that those who joined jihadist groups lacked education and critical thinking. They lack education and simply don't bother to think. They perceive the radical ideology as a ready-made recipe for their life. They don't want to think, they give up or don't bother making efforts to build better lives for themselves and their loved ones. They had given up their fight, instead they chose very convenient way to rely on Allah's will. They prefer blindly follow the radical ideology as a set of rules, values and guidance for the whole life. Lack of education and critical thinking is key factor in such behavior. The absence of these two things make people believe that the jihadist ideology granted them a direct deal with a God to ascent heaven as reward for doing Jihad against infidels. Thus, education is a key instrument to fight terrorism. States need to ensure that youth get education and is able to think critically. Girls need to go to universities, instead of getting married at the age of sixteen, seventeen, or eighteen. Early marriage makes them vulnerable, backward and dependent. Muslim countries need to build new policies to empower women and girls to make them well educated and independent. Otherwise, women are fragile, dependent, totally incapable to take decisions and cannot defend themselves and their children. Marriage is a refuge that gives them a chance to survive. Majority of women who went to Syria had no critical thinking, had no education and were incapable to earn money. A majority of the women I interviewed, were forced to marry at the very early age of fifteen, sixteen, and seventeen and were not given a chance to study.

The most striking finding of my research is that men and women who joined ISIS lacked knowledge about Islam. Religion had no place in their lives, but they became familiarized with the Salafi-Wahhabism in a short time just before traveling to the Middle East. Once they were in contact with recruiters, they started gaining knowledge about radical Islamic ideology on YouTube and other websites. A majority of them had never been religious before and did not study Islam. Thus, to counter jihadism Muslim countries need to prioritize building new strategies on how to propagate true Islam. They need to invest on Islam scholars who can disseminate narratives to defeat the radical mutated concepts. The original sources need to be translated widely into different languages and mainstreamed. While the radical jihadist groups have enormous resources for propaganda, true Islam has limited resources to be widely discussed and mainstreamed. This needs to be fixed with the support of authoritative Islamic scholars and preachers. While Islamic fundamentalism "has become a well-financed, multifaceted global movement that operates like a juggernaut in much of the developing world, and even among immigrant Muslim communities in the West,"[1] there is a vacuum in promoting true Islam. Muslim scholars and imams need to be mobilized to mainstream discourses about peaceful tenants of Islam so Muslims can learn Islam from original sources.

The world has faced a new kind of terrorism- family jihad, which is a new phenomenon that has many implications for terrorism and international peace. Having a global appeal to build an Islamic state without any borders and uniting Muslims of the world is a dangerous state-building project that challenges not only current international system, but peace in every corner of the world. Thus, it is tremendously important that states realize that fighting religious extremism, namely jihadism has reached another level. Subsequently, states need to reconsider their policies and approaches. ISIS is not dead. Even though it has lost its territories, it is continuing to take a new shape and concur the minds of people. The urgent dilemma is how to manage the current situation with former ISIS fighters and their family members. Women held in Al Hawl and Roj call their sons "lions cubs" and claim "Our lions are growing; they will restore our dignity." Our worries need to go out to the thousands of small children growing up in these two camps. We still have a chance to save their minds. The more days spent in the camps, the more they will get radicalized. The states should not lose the momentum to take control over their citizens in these camps. Repatriation of ISIS associates remain as only law-complaint solution at the moment. The experiences of Kazakhstan, Uzbekistan, Kosovo, USA, Tajikistan and Kyrgyzstan have shown that repatriation, rehabilitation and reintegration is difficult, but possible. Especially, states need to act at the best interests of children. We need to save minds of children. Every day spent in Al Hawl and Roj camps leaving the detrimental impact on their minds, mental and physical health. The more days they spent there, the more they get radicalized. Al Hawl and Roj can give to the world hundreds of Usama ben Ladens if children won't be repatriated.

No country in the world can claim to be immune against terrorism. Terrorism does not recognize any borders. Thus, we need to be mindful of concerns of states about national security. After being repatriated, some returnees can turn into terrorists. Those who were repatriated compose a nonhomogenous group and some of them are still radical. However, many returnees are at least trying to return to normal life and their efforts should be supported. Terrorists and jihadists always chose violence to achieve their goals, but states should take a nonviolent approach by building inclusive societies and upholding human rights. States should pay smaller price now, otherwise they will pay a huge price later. States need to show compassion, inclusivity and responsibility, and to prove that jihadists lie when they say that states are evil. Not to be evil, states always act in a human way and fulfill their obligations. Furthermore, states have shared responsibility for international peace and also responsibility for their citizens. In this context, repatriation, prosecution at home and rehabilitation is the only adequate solution to manage the current situation with returning fighters.

Where the global jihad stands now? After Taliban`s takeover of Afghanistan jihadis groups got inspired, because Taliban proved that terrorists can take over the country and govern it. Jihadists won't sleep but will continue winning minds of people. The first supporters of them are bad governments, which fail to eradicate corruption and to build efficient public institutions. Global jihad will focus on weaker and poorer states, where people's grievances are huge and people live with the burning sense of injustice. Bad governance creates open space for jihadism. As the non-enigma cycles radicalization has shown grievances and resentment of people are the fertile ground from which radicalization starts. Thus, states need to become less exclusive, less corrupt, and less oppressive. Opting for purely military approach to fight jihadism is a total failure. Jihadism can be fought only by building appropriate policies and right narratives, and each state need to address local grievances of people. My empirical evidence has shown that the majority of those who joined ISIS had the burning sense of injustice. If there is injustice within the country, people may think that jihadist's state project is better. They may continue feeling that their suffering at home is a part of the wider pattern of persecutions of Muslims. They will turn their grievances into group grievances, which gives them a power and feeling of the significance.

NOTES

1. Abdurrahman Wahid, Right Islam vs. Wrong Islam: Muslims and NON-Muslims Must Unite to Defeat the Wahhabi Ideology, in The Theory and Practice of Islamic Terrorism, an Anthology, Edited by Marvin Perry and Howard Negrin, Palgrave Macmillan, 2008, pp. 113–117.

Bibliography

AFP. "French Families Sue Government over Children of Jihadists Stuck in Syria." The Local France, September 16, 2019. https://www.thelocal.fr/20190916/french-families-sue-government-over-children-stuck-in-syria/.

Agara, Tunde. "Gendering Terrorism: Women, Gender, Terrorism and Suicide Bombers." *International Journal of Humanities and Social Science* 5, no. 6 (2015).

Ajil, Ahmed. "Politico-Ideological Violence: Zooming in on Grievances." *European Journal of Criminology*, 2020, 147737081989622. https://doi.org/10.1177/1477370819896223.

Al Jazeera. "UN Expert to France: Bring Home Citizens Facing Hanging in Iraq." ISIL/ISIS News | Al Jazeera. Al Jazeera, August 13, 2019. https://www.aljazeera.com/news/2019/8/13/un-expert-to-france-bring-home-citizens-facing-hanging-in-iraq.

Amnesty International UK. "China Remains World's Top Executioner - Followed by Iran, Saudi Arabia, Vietnam and Iraq." Amnesty International UK, April 10, 2019. https://www.amnesty.org.uk/press-releases/global-executions-fell-nearly-third-last-year-new-report.

Amnesty International. "Gruesome Evidence of Ethnic Cleansing in Northern Iraq as Islamic State Moves to Wipe out Minorities." Amnesty International, August 17, 2021. https://www.amnesty.org/en/latest/news/2014/09/gruesome-evidence-ethnic-cleansing-northern-iraq-islamic-state-moves-wipe-out-minorities/.

Amnesty International. "Syria: Rule of Fear: Isis Abuses in Detention in Northern Syria." Amnesty International, June 2, 2021. https://www.amnesty.org/en/documents/MDE24/063/2013/en/.

Anonymous Kazakh diplomat, and Cholpon Orozobekova. Interview during the OSCE conference in Vienna. Personal, February 2020.

Anonymous Turkey MFA Official, and Cholpon Orozobekova. Interview. Personal, n.d.

Antunez Moreno, Juan Carlos. "DAESH EUROPEAN FOREIGN FIGHTERS: IDEOLOGY, MOTIVATION AND PROFILING." GESI, 2016. https://www.researchgate.net/publication/318393476_DAESH_EUROPEAN_FOREIGN_FIGHTERS_IDEOLOGY_MOTIVATION_AND_PROFILING_1.

Aoláin, Fionnuala Ní. "Time to Bring Women and Children Home from Iraq and Syria." Just Security, December 11, 2019. https://www.justsecurity.org/64402/time-to-bring-women-and-children-home-from-iraq-and-syria/.

Aqjaiyq TV. "Вернувшиеся Из Сирии - Долгая Дорога Домой. ЭКСКЛЮЗИВ, 'Returnees from Syria: A Long Journey to Home.'" YouTube. YouTube, 2019. https://www.youtube.com/watch?v=M7q_LRQsNKY&t=197s.

Aripov, Anushervon. "'There Were Deaths Every Day': People Are Returning to Tajikistan From ISIS in Syria and Iraq." Настоящее Время [Current Time], February 9, 2018. https://www.currenttime.tv/a/29029380.html.

Arraf, Jane. "Visiting Imprisoned Isis Fighters." NPR. NPR, December 8, 2019. https://www.npr.org/2019/12/08/786039731/visiting-imprisoned-isis-fighters.

Ashikbaev, Yerzhan, and Cholpon Orozobekova. Interview. Personal, February 11, 2020.

Ashimov, Aydar. "Kazakhs on Trial for Joining Is in Syria Committed 'Horrific' Crimes." Caravanserai. Caravanserai, November 21, 2019. https://central.asia-news.com/en_GB/articles/cnmi_ca/features/2019/11/21/feature-01.

Atwan Abdel Bari. *Islamic State: The Digital Caliphate*. UNIV OF CALIFORNIA Press, 2019.

Azizi, Rustam, and Cholpon Orozobekova. Interview. Personal, n.d.

BBC News. "Shamima Begum: Is Bride 'Would Face Death Penalty in Bangladesh.'" BBC News. BBC, May 3, 2019. https://www.bbc.com/news/world-asia-48154781.

Becker, Jo. "Iraq's ISIS Trials Don't Deliver Justice—Including for Children." Human Rights Watch, January 31, 2020. https://www.hrw.org/news/2020/01/31/iraqs-isis-trials-dont-deliver-justice-including-children.

Benjamin, Daniel, and Steven Simon. *The Age of Sacred Terror: Radical Islam's War against America*. New York: Random House Trade Paperbacks, 2003.

Benton, Meghan, and Natalia Banulescu-Bogdan. "Foreign Fighters: Will Revoking Citizenship Mitigate the Threat?" Migration Policy Institute, April 3, 2019. https://www.migrationpolicy.org/article/foreign-fighters-will-revoking-citizenship-mitigate-threat.

Berko, Anat, and Edna Erez. "Gender, Palestinian Women, and Terrorism: Women's Liberation or Oppression?" *Studies in Conflict & Terrorism* 30, no. 6 (2007): 493–519. https://doi.org/10.1080/10576100701329550.

Bin Ali, Mohamed. "Co15251: Forging Muslim and Non-Muslim Relationship: Contesting the Doctrine of Al-Wala' Wal Bara.'" Nanyang Technological University Think Tank and Graduate School. RSIS Commentary, 2015. https://www.rsis.edu.sg/rsis-publication/srp/co15251-forging-muslim-and-non-muslim-relationship-contesting-the-doctrine-of-al-wala-wal-bara/.

Birn. "Kosovo Govt Allocates €250,000 to Fight against Isis." Balkan Insight, January 10, 2020. https://balkaninsight.com/2020/01/10/outgoing-government-allocates-e250000-to-the-fight-against-isis/.

Booth, Ken, and Tim Dunne. *Worlds in Collision: Terror and the Future of Global Order*. Houndmills, Basingstoke: Palgrave Macmillan, 2002.

Borum, Randy. "Understanding the Terrorist Mindset." *FBI Law Enforcement Bulletin* 72, no. 7 (2003): 7–10.

Boukhars, Anouar. "Islam, Jihadism, and Depoliticization in France and Germany." *International Political Science Review* 30, no. 3 (2009): 297–317. https://doi.org/10.1177/0192512109105642.

Boutin, Bérénice, Grégory Chauzal, Jessica Dorsay, Marjolein Jegerings, and Christophe Pualussen. "The Foreign Fighters Phenomenon in the EU - Profiles, Threats & Policies." ICCT International Centre for Counter-Terrorism—The Hague, April 2016. https://icct.nl/publication/report-the-foreign-fighters-phenomenon-in-the-eu-profiles-threats-policies/.

Boutin, Bérénice. "Administrative Measures against Foreign Fighters." International Center for Counter-Terrorism—The Hague, December 2016. https://icct.nl/app/uploads/2016/12/ICCT-Boutin-Administrative-Measures-December2016-1.pdf.

Buzan, Barry. "Will the 'Global War on Terrorism' Be the New Cold War?" *International Affairs* 82, no. 6 (2006): 1101–18. https://doi.org/10.1111/j.1468-2346.2006.00590.x.

Bytyqi, Kujtim, and Sam Mullins. "Returnee Foreign Fighters from Syria and Iraq: The Kosovan Experience." *Combatting Terrorism Center (CTC) Sentinel* 12, no. 7 (August 2019).

Callamard, Agnes. "Extra-Territorial Jurisdiction of States over Children and Their Guardians in Camps, Prisons, or Elsewhere in the Northern Syrian Arab Republic: Legal Analysis." OHCHR, 2018. https://www.ohchr.org/Documents/Issues/Terrorism/UNSRsPublicJurisdictionAnalysis2020.pdf.

Cebrián, Pilar. "They Left to Join ISIS. Now Europe Is Leaving Their Citizens to Die in Iraq." Foreign Policy, September 15, 2019. https://foreignpolicy.com/2019/09/15/they-left-to-join-isis-now-europe-is-leaving-their-citizens-to-die-in-iraq/.

Charles, Mink. "It's About the Group, Not God: Social Causes and Cures for Terrorism." *Journal for Deradicalization* 16, no. 5 (n.d.).

Chatterjee, Debangana. "Gendering ISIS and Mapping the Role of Women." *Contemporary Review of the Middle East* 3, no. 2 (2016): 201–18. https://doi.org/10.1177/2347798916638214.

Cook, Joana, and Gina Vale. "From Daesh to 'Diaspora': Tracing the Women and Minors of . . . " International Center for the Study of Radicalization. King's College London, 2018. https://icsr.info/wp-content/uploads/2018/07/Women-in-ISIS-report_20180719_web.pdf.

Coolsaet, Rik, Sven Biscop, Alexander Mattelaer, Bernard Siman, Nanae Baldauff, and Eleonora Milazzo. "Facing the Fourth Foreign Fighters Wave. What Drives Europeans to Syria, and to Islamic State? Insights from the Belgian Case." Egmont Institute, March 1, 2016. https://www.egmontinstitute.be/facing-the-fourth-foreign-fighters-wave/.

Counter-Extremism Project. "France: Extremism and Terrorism." Counter-Extremism Project, 2019. https://www.counterextremism.com/countries/france.

Cragin, Kim, and Sara A. Daly. *Women as Terrorists: Mothers, Recruiters, and Martyrs*. Santa Barbara, CA: Praeger Security Internat., 2009.

Crawford, Julia. "Do We Need an International Tribunal for Islamic State?" JusticeInfo.net, August 26, 2019. https://www.justiceinfo.net/en/42224-do-we-need-an-international-tribunal-for-islamic-state.html.

Cunningham, Karla J. "Cross-Regional Trends in Female Terrorism." *Studies in Conflict & Terrorism* 26, no. 3 (2003): 171–95. https://doi.org/10.1080/10576100390211419.

Daou, Marc. "France Taken to Court for Refusing to Repatriate the Children of Jihadists." France 24. France 24, May 7, 2019. https://www.france24.com/en/20190507-france-taken-court-over-repatriating-children-jihadists.

Davis, Sean. "Responding to Foreign Terrorist Fighters: A Risk-Based Playbook for States and the International Community," 2014. https://www.globalcenter.org/wp-content/uploads/2014/11/Nov2014_Responding-to-FTFs_SD.pdf.

Davolio, Miryam Eser. "Updated Review and Developments in Jihadist Radicalisation in Switzerland—Updated Version of an Exploratory Study on Prevention and Intervention." Institute of Diversity and Social Integration. Center for Security Studies | ETH Zurich, June 2019. https://css.ethz.ch/en/Themes/European-Security/all-publications/details.html?id=%2Fu%2Fp%2Fd%2Fa%2Fupdated_review_and_developments_in_jihad.

de Leede, Seran. "Women in Jihad: A Historical Perspective - ICCT." ICCT Policy Brief. ICCT, 2018. https://icct.nl/app/uploads/2018/09/ICCT-deLeede-Women-in-Jihad-Sept2018.pdf.

Dworkin, Anthony. "Beyond Good and Evil: Why Europe Should Bring Isis Foreign Fighters Home." ECFR, October 25, 2019. https://ecfr.eu/publication/beyond_good_and_evil_why_europe_should_bring_isis_foreign_fighters_home/.

The Editorial Board. "Opinion | Trump vs. Macron on ISIS Fighters." The Wall Street Journal. Dow Jones & Company, December 5, 2019. https://www.wsj.com/articles/trump-vs-macron-on-isis-fighters-11575590830.

European Parliamentary Research Service. "The Return of Foreign Fighters to EU Soil: Ex-Post Evaluation." European Parliamentary Research Service, n.d. https://www.europarl.europa.eu/RegData/etudes/STUD/2018/621811/EPRS_STU(2018)621811_EN.pdf.

European University Institute. "Global Database on Modes of Loss of Citizenship Version 1.0. Robert Schuman Centre for Advanced Studies." Global citizenship observatory (GLOBALCIT). European University Institute, 2017. https://globalcit.eu/loss-of-citizenship.

Federal Assembly of the Swiss Confederation. "122 Loi Fédérale Interdisant Les Groupes « Al-Qaïda » Et « Etat Islamique » Et Les Organisations Apparentées." 122 Loi fédérale du 12 décembre 2014 interdisant les groupes "Al-Qaïda" et "Etat islamique" et les organisations apparentées - 122 Bundesgesetz vom 12. Dezember 2014 über das Verbot der Gruppierungen "Al-Qaïda" und "Islamischer Staat" sowie verwandter Organisationen - RS bilingue. Swiss Confederation, December 12, 2014. https://www.droit-bilingue.ch/rs/lex/2014/29/20142993-unique-fr-de.html.

Flandreinfo Belge. "Six Combattants Étrangers Partis En Syrie Perdent Leur Nationalité Belge." Flandreinfo Belge - L'Actu de Flandre. Flandreinfo Belge, January 2, 2020. https://www.vrt.be/vrtnws/fr/2020/01/02/six-combattants-etrangers-partis-en-syrie-perdent-leur-nationali/.

Foltyn, Simona. "Inside the Iraqi Courts Sentencing Foreign Isis Fighters to Death." The Guardian. Guardian News and Media, June 2, 2019. https://www.theguardian

.com/world/2019/jun/02/inside-the-iraqi-courts-sentencing-foreign-isis-fighters-to-death.

France 24. "Head of UN Investigators Calls for an Is 'Nuremberg.'" France 24. France 24, July 29, 2019. https://www.france24.com/en/20190729-head-un-investigators-calls-nuremberg.

France 24. "Syrian Kurds Transfer 12 Orphans from Jihadist Families to France for Repatriation." France 24, June 10, 2019. https://www.france24.com/en/20190610-france-orphans-jihadist-families-syria-kurds-transfer.

Franceinfo. "Tribune. 'CE Serait Un Immense Déshonneur Pour Notre Pays': L'appel De 45 Avocats Contre Les Condamnations à Mort De Neuf Français En Irak." Franceinfo, June 3, 2019. https://www.francetvinfo.fr/monde/proche-orient/francais-condamnes-a-mort-en-irak/tribune-ce-serait-un-immense-deshonneur-pour-notre-pays-l-appel-de-44-avocats-contre-les-condamnations-a-mort-de-neuf-francais-en-irak_3469333.html.

Fukuyama, Francis. *Identity: The Demand for Dignity and the Politics of Resentment.* New York: Picador, 2019.

Genocide Network Secretariat. "The Prosecution at National Level of Sexual and Gender . . . ," 2017. https://www.eurojust.europa.eu/sites/default/files/Partners/Genocide/2017-07_Prosecution-at-national-level-of-sexual-and-gender-based-violence_EN.pdf.

Gillard, Emanuela-Chiara. "There's No Place like Home: States' Obligations in Relation to Transfers of Persons." *International Review of the Red Cross* 90, no. 871 (2008): 703–50. https://doi.org/10.1017/s1560775508000096.

Glaus, Daniel, and Lorenzo Vidino. "Swiss Foreign Fighters Active in Syria." Combatting Terror Center (CTC) Sentinel 7, no. 7, 2014. https://ctc.usma.edu/swiss-foreign-fighters-active-in-syria/.

"Global Jihadism after the Syria War / by Tore Refslund Hamming.," 2019. https://doi.org/10.29171/azu_acku_pamphlet_bp182_h366_2019.

Government Offices of Sweden. "Sweden Hosted Expert Meeting on Tribunal." Government Offices of Sweden, June 3, 2019. https://www.government.se/press-releases/2019/06/sweden-hosted-expert-meeting-on-tribunal/.

Guterres, Antonio. "Uniting the World against Terrorism Secretary-General." United Nations. United Nations, June 26, 2018. https://www.un.org/sg/en/content/sg/articles/2018-06-26/uniting-world-against-terrorism.

Hafez, Mohammed M. "Jihadafter Iraq: Lessons from the Arab Afghans." *Studies in Conflict & Terrorism* 32, no. 2 (2009): 73–94. https://doi.org/10.1080/10576100802639600.

Hall, Richard. "'Take Us to Court' Say British ISIS Prisoners Languishing in a Syrian Jail." The Independent. Independent Digital News and Media, December 18, 2019. https://www.independent.co.uk/news/world/middle-east/isis-british-fighters-syria-baghdadi-aseel-muthana-ishak-mostefaoui-a9251391.html.

Hall, Richard. "This Camp Is Holding Thousands of Isis Wives and Their Children in Syria. It's Close to Breaking Point." The Independent. Independent Digital News and Media, December 9, 2019. https://www.independent.co.uk/news/world/middle-east/isis-wives-al-hol-camp-syria-islamic-state-terror-uk-a9236221.html.

Hall, Richard. "Will British ISIS Prisoners Be Sent to Their Deaths without a Fair Trial?" The Independent. Independent Digital News and Media, February 3, 2020. https://www.independent.co.uk/news/world/middle-east/isis-iraq-international-law-prisoner-deaths-trial-a9311556.html.

Halliday, Fred. *Islam and the Myth of Confrontation: Religion and Politics in the Middle East*. London: I. B. Tauris, 1995.

Harnisch, Chris. "Foreign Terrorist Fighters: Addressing Current Challenges . . . " US Mission to the OSCE, February 11, 2020. https://osce.usmission.gov/foreign-terrorist-fighters-addressing-current-challenges/.

Hashemi, Nader. "The Isis Crisis and the Broken Politics of the Middle East." Institute on Culture, Religion, and World Affairs, University of Denver, November 2016. https://www.bu.edu/cura/files/2016/12/hashemi-paper1.pdf.

Hegghammer, Thomas. "Global Jihadism after the Iraq War." *The Middle East Journal* 60, no. 1 (2006): 11–32. https://doi.org/10.3751/60.1.11.

Hegghammer, Thomas. "The Rise of Muslim Foreign Fighters: Islam and the Globalization of Jihad." *International Security* 35, no. 3 (2010): 53–94. https://doi.org/10.1162/isec_a_00023.

Helf, Gavin. "The Bulan Institute's Panel Discussion on Returning Foreign Fighters." Speech, March 15, 2021.

Hoffman, Adam, and Marta Furlan. "Challenges Posed by Returning Foreign Fighters," March 2020. https://extremism.gwu.edu/sites/g/files/zaxdzs2191/f/Challenges%20Posed%20by%20Returning%20Foreign%20Fighters.pdf.

Hopkins, Valerie, and Serbeze Haxhiaj. "ISIS Fighters Struggle on Return to Balkan States." Financial Times, May 20, 2019. https://www.ft.com/content/24835626-762a-11e9-be7d-6d846537acab.

Howard, Lawrence, and Marthe Crenshaw. "How Terrorists Think: What Psychology Can Contribute to Understanding Terrorism." Essay. In *Terrorism: Roots, Impact, Responses*. New York: Praeger, 1992.

Hubbard, Ben, and Constant Méheut. "Western Countries Leave Children of Isis in Syrian Camps." The New York Times. The New York Times, May 31, 2020. https://www.nytimes.com/2020/05/31/world/middleeast/isis-children-syria-camps.html.

Human Rights Committee. "Human Rights Committee General Comment No. 36 (2018) on Article 6 of the International Covenant on Civil and Political Rights, on the Right to Life," October 30, 2018. https://tbinternet.ohchr.org/Treaties/CCPR/Shared%20Documents/1_Global/CCPR_C_GC_36_8785_E.pdf.

Human Rights Watch. "Everyone Must Confess: Abuses Against Children Suspected of ISIS Affiliation in Iraq." Human Rights Watch, March 6, 2019. https://www.hrw.org/report/2019/03/06/everyone-must-confess/abuses-against-children-suspected-isis-affiliation-iraq.

Human Rights Watch. "Flawed Justice: Accountability for ISIS Crimes in Iraq." Human Rights Watch, December 15, 2017. https://www.hrw.org/report/2017/12/05/flawed-justice/accountability-isis-crimes-iraq.

Human Rights Watch. "Iraq: Change Approach to Foreign Women, Children in ISIS-Linked Trials." Human Rights Watch, June 21, 2018. https://www.hrw.org/news/2018/06/21/iraq-change-approach-foreign-women-children-isis-linked-trials.

IA Total Kazakhstan. "These Are Innocent People, Nazarbaev about the Evacuation of People from Syria." IA Total Kazakhstan, January 9, 2019. https://total.kz/ru/news/obshchestvosobitiya/etonevinnieludinazarbaevobevakuatsiikazahstantsevizsiriidate_2019_01_09_16_01_09.

Ilmuradova, Oliya, and Cholpon Orozobekova. Interview. Personal, March 2021.

Impunity Watch. "ISIS-Only Tribunal: Selective, Politicised Justice Will Do More Harm than Good." Impunity Watch, October 31, 2019. https://www.impunitywatch.org/post/isis-only-tribunal-selective-politicised-justice-will-do-more-harm-than-good.

Informburo Kz. "Photos of Allegedly Kyrgyz Children in ISIS Appeared on Internet." Informburo Kz, n.d. https://informburo.kz/novosti/v-seti-poyavilis-fotografii-centralnoaziatskih-detey-igil-6734.html.

International Criminal Court. "Rome Statute International Criminal." The Hague: International Criminal Court, 2011. https://www.icc-cpi.int/resource-library/Documents/RS-Eng.pdf.

International, Impartial and Independent Mechanism. "Terms of Reference of IIIM - IIIM." United Nations. United Nations. Accessed June 6, 2020. https://iiim.un.org/terms-of-reference-of-iiim/.

Ip, John. "Reconceptualising the Legal Response to Foreign Fighters." *International and Comparative Law Quarterly* 69, no. 1 (2019): 103–34. https://doi.org/10.1017/s0020589319000447.

Irish, John. "France's Le Drian to Go to Iraq to Discuss Trials for Jihadists from Syria." Reuters. Thomson Reuters, October 16, 2019. https://www.reuters.com/article/us-syria-security-france-iraq-idUSKBN1WV0RG.

Kamali, Mohammad Hashim. *Shari'ah Law: An Introduction*. Oxford: Oneworld Publ., 2012.

Kar-Gupta, Sudip. "Top French Court Rejects Syria-Based French Jihadis' Repatriation Demands." Reuters. Thomson Reuters, April 23, 2019. https://www.reuters.com/article/us-syria-security-france-nationals-idUSKCN1RZ1B2.

Kelvington, Michael R. "Global Salafi-Jihadism Ideology the 'Soft Power' of the Enemy," 2016. https://www.ict.org.il/images/Global%20Salafi-Jihadism-Enemy%20Soft%20Power.pdf.

Khelghat-Doost, Hamoon. "Women of the Islamic State: The Evolving Role of Women in Jihad." *Counter Terrorist Trends and Analyses* 8, no. 9 (2016): 21–26.

Khosrokhavar, Farhad. *Inside Jihadism: Understanding Jihadi Movements Worldwide*. London: Routledge, 2016.

Kraehenmann, Sandra. "Foreign Fighters under International Law.": Geneva Academy of International Humanitarian Law And Human Rights, October 2014. https://www.geneva-academy.ch/joomlatools-files/docman-files/Publications/Academy%20Briefings/Foreign%20Fighters_2015_WEB.pdf.

Kretsch, Amanda. "The Misconception of Jihad in America." Undergraduate Library Research Awards, 2016. https://digitalcommons.lmu.edu/cgi/viewcontent.cgi?article=1109&context=ulra.

Lahoud, Nelly. *The Jihadis' Path to Self-Destruction*. New York: Columbia University Press, 2010.

Lahoud, Nelly. "The Neglected Sex: The Jihadis' Exclusion of Women from Jihad." *Terrorism and Political Violence* 26, no. 5 (2014): 780–802. https://doi.org/10.1080/09546553.2013.772511.

Le Conseil fédéral. Voyageurs à motivation terroriste: Stratégie et Objectifs du Conseil Fédéral. Swiss Confederation, March 8, 2019. https://www.admin.ch/gov/fr/accueil/documentation/communiques.msg-id-74258.html.

Lemon, Edward, Vera Mironova, William H. Tobey, Abolghasem Bayyenat, Marco Lyons, Graham Allison, and Jonah Glick-Unterman. "Jihadists from Ex-Soviet Central Asia: Where Are They? Why Did They Radicalize? What next?" Belfer Center for Science and International Affairs, December 2018. https://www.belfercenter.org/publication/jihadists-ex-soviet-central-asia-where-are-they-why-did-they-radicalize-what-next.

Lewis, Bernard. *The Crisis of Islam: Holy War and Unholy Terror*. New York: Random House Trade Paperbacks, 2004.

Lewis, James, and Mark Juergensmeyer. "Does Religion Cause Terrorism? ." Essay. In *The Cambridge Companion to Religion and Terrorism*. New York, NY: Cambridge University Press, 2017.

Lia, Brynjar. "Jihadism in the Arab World after 2011: Explaining Its Expansion." *Middle East Policy* 23, no. 4 (2016): 74–91. https://doi.org/10.1111/mepo.12234.

Lynch III, Thomas F, Michael Bouffard, Kelse King, and Graham Vickowski. "The Return of Foreign Fighters to Central Asia: Implications for U.S. Counterterrorism Policy." Institute for National Strategic Studies. Strategic Perspectives 21, October 29, 2016. https://inss.ndu.edu/Media/News/Article/990914/the-return-of-foreign-fighters-to-central-asia-implications-for-us-counterterro/.

Maher, Shiraz. *Salafi-Jihadism - the History of an Idea*. Penguin Books Ltd, 2016.

Mai, H.J. "Why European Countries Are Reluctant to Repatriate Citizens Who Are ISIS Fighters." NPR. NPR, December 10, 2019. https://www.npr.org/2019/12/10/783369673/europe-remains-reluctant-to-repatriate-its-isis-fighters-here-s-why.

Malet, David. "Why Foreign Fighters?" *Orbis* 54, no. 1 (2010): 97–114. https://doi.org/10.1016/j.orbis.2009.10.007.

Maneval, Théo. "Djihadistes Français Condamnés à Mort En Irak: Vers Une Solution Européenne?" Europe 1, June 4, 2019. https://www.europe1.fr/international/djihadistes-condamnes-a-mort-en-irak-vers-une-solution-europeenne-3902646.

Manisera, Sara. "After ISIS: How Kosovo Is Rehabilitating Women and Children Repatriated from Syria." The National. The National, July 5, 2021. https://www.thenationalnews.com/world/mena/after-isis-how-kosovo-is-rehabilitating-women-and-children-repatriated-from-syria-1.890533.

Martini, Alice. "Making Women Terrorists into 'Jihadi Brides': An Analysis of Media Narratives on Women Joining Isis." *Critical Studies on Terrorism* 11, no. 3 (2018): 458–77. https://doi.org/10.1080/17539153.2018.1448204.

McCauley, Clark R., and Sophia Moskalenko. *Friction: How Radicalization Happens to Them and US*. Oxford: Oxford University Press, 2017.

McGuirck, Rod. "Australia Insists Man Who Lost Citizenship Isn't Stateless." ABC News. ABC News Network, January 2, 2019. https://abcnews.go.com/International/wireStory/australia-insists-alleged-militant-left-stateless-60111237.

McGuirk, Rod. "Australia's Citizenship Stripping Policy Again Sparks Controversy." The Diplomat, January 3, 2019. https://thediplomat.com/2019/01/australias-citizenship-stripping-policy-again-sparks-controversy/.

McKernan, Bethan. "At Least 750 Isis Affiliates Escape Syria Camp after Turkish Shelling." The Guardian. Guardian News and Media, October 13, 2019. https://www.theguardian.com/world/2019/oct/13/kurds-say-785-isis-affiliates-have-escaped-camp-after-turkish-shelling.

Merz, Fabien. "Switzerland and Jihadist Foreign Fighters - Css.ethz.ch." ETH Zurich. CSS Analyses in Security Policy 199, 2016. https://css.ethz.ch/content/dam/ethz/special-interest/gess/cis/center-for-securities-studies/pdfs/CSSAnalyse199-EN.pdf.

MFA of Kazakhstan. "MFA of Kazakhstan Gave Information on Zhusan-2 Operation." MFA of Kazakhstan, n.d. http://www.mfa.gov.kz/en/london/content-view/syrtky-ister-ministrliginde-zusan-2-operaciasyny-ntizesi-turaly-ajtyp-berdi. Translated by the author.

Mohamedou, Mohammad-Mahmoud. *A Theory of Isis Political Violence, and the Transformation of the Global Order*. London: Pluto Press, 2018.

Moisi, Dominique. "The Clash of Emotions." Foreign Affairs, August 31, 2021. https://www.foreignaffairs.com/articles/2007-01-01/clash-emotions.

Murden, Simon. *Islam, the Middle East, and the New Global Hegemony*. Boulder, CO: Lynne Rienner Publishers, 2002.

Najibullah, Farangiz, and Mumin Ahmadi. "You Can't Remain Behind. Widows and Children of IS Fighters From Central Asia." Радио Азаттык [Radio Azattyk], February 21, 2019. https://rus.azattyq.org/a/why-tajikistan-is-fighting-to-bring-its-islamic-state-widows-back-home/29782290.html.

Neumann, Peter R. *Old and New Terrorism: Late Modernity, Globalization and the Transformation of Political Violence*. Cambridge: Polity Press, 2011.

Neumann, Peter R. *Radicalized: New Jihadists and the Threat to the West*. London: I.B. Tauris, 2016.

News24. "Iraq Sentenced 616 Foreigners for ISIS Links in 2018 | news24." News24, n.d. https://www.news24.com/news24/World/News/iraq-sentenced-616-foreigners-for-isis-links-in-2018-20181231.

Nodirbek, Soliev. "Syria: Uzbekistan's Approach to Is Detainees." Think Tank and Graduate School. RSIS Commentary, October 2019. https://www.rsis.edu.sg/rsis-publication/icpvtr/syria-uzbekistans-approach-to-is-detainees/.

Nossiter, Adam. "How ISIS Changed France." The New York Times. The New York Times, October 31, 2019. https://www.nytimes.com/2019/10/31/world/europe/al-baghdadi-isis-france.html.

Nossiter, Adam. "Paris Trial Shows Faltering Evolution of a Jihadist Cell." The New York Times. The New York Times, April 13, 2018. https://www.nytimes.com/2018/04/13/world/europe/paris-trial-lunel-ihadist-cell.html.

Nuz.nz. "Возвращенные Из Ада . . . 'Returned from the Hell.'" Новости Узбекистана сегодня: nuz.uz, November 12, 2020. https://nuz.uz/obschestvo/1176626-vozvrashhennye-iz-ada.html.

Office of the United Nations High Commissioner for Human Rights. "Iraq: UN Report on ISIL Trials Recognizes Efforts and Raises Concerns in Iraq." United Nations. United Nations, January 28, 2020. https://iraq.un.org/en/123056-iraq-un-report-isil-trials-recognizes-efforts-and-raises-concerns.

OHCHR. "Convention on the Prevention and Punishment of the Crime . . . ," 2019. https://www.un.org/en/genocideprevention/documents/atrocity-crimes/Doc.1_Convention%20on%20the%20Prevention%20and%20Punishment%20of%20the%20Crime%20of%20Genocide.pdf.

OHCHR. "Independent International Commission of Inquiry on the Syrian Arab Republic." OHCHR, 2019. https://www.ohchr.org/en/hrbodies/hrc/iicisyria/pages/independentinternationalcommission.aspx.

OHCHR. "Optional Protocol to the Convention on the Rights of the Child on the Involvement of Children in Armed Conflict." OHCHR, 2000. https://www.ohchr.org/EN/ProfessionalInterest/Pages/OPACCRC.aspx.

OHCHR. "Report on the Protection of Civilians in the Armed . . . ," January 5, 2016. https://www.ohchr.org/Documents/Countries/IQ/UNAMIReport1May31October2015.pdf.

OHCHR. "'I Lost My Dignity': Sexual and Gender Based Violence in . . . ," 2018. https://www.ohchr.org/Documents/HRBodies/HRCouncil/CoISyria/A-HRC-37-CRP-3.pdf.

OHCHR. "'They Came to Destroy': ISIS Crimes against the Yazidis - Human Rights Council Report (A/HRC/32/CRP.2) (Advance Version) - Syrian Arab Republic." ReliefWeb, 2016. https://reliefweb.int/report/syrian-arab-republic/they-came-destroy-isis-crimes-against-yazidis-human-rights-council.

"Open Letter from 126 Prominent Islamic Scholars to Al-Baghdadi and to the Fighters and Followers of the Self-Declared 'Islamic State.'" Open Letter to Baghdadi, 2014. http://www.lettertobaghdadi.com/.

Open Society Justice Initiative. "NGOs Express Caution on Sweden's ISIS Tribunal Proposal." NGOs Express Caution on Sweden's ISIS Tribunal Proposal - Open Society Justice Initiative. Open Society Justice Initiative, June 3, 2019. https://www.justiceinitiative.org/newsroom/ngos-challenge-swedens-proposal-for-an-isis-only-war-crimes-tribunal.

OSCE. "Guidelines for Addressing the Threats and Challenges of 'Foreign Terrorist Fighters' within a Human Rights Framework." OSCE: Office for Democratic Institutions and Human Rights, 2018. https://www.osce.org/files/f/documents/4/7/393503_2.pdf.

Parliament of the Netherlands. "Vreemdelingenwet 2000." wetten.nl - Regeling - Vreemdelingenwet 2000 - BWBR0011823. Parliament of the Netherlands. Accessed June 7, 2020. https://wetten.overheid.nl/BWBR0011823.

Paulussen, Christophe. "Towards a Right to Sustainable Security of Person in Times of Terrorism? Assessing Possibilities and Limitations through a Critical Evaluation of Citizenship Stripping and Non-Repatriation Policies." *Journal of Conflict and Security Law*, 2020. https://doi.org/10.1093/jcsl/kraa022.

Pektaş Şerafettin. *Militant Jihadism: Today and Tomorrow*. Leuven: Leuven University Press, 2019.

Pelda, Kurt, and Thomas Knellwolf. "Mutter Riskierte Ihr Leben, Um Is-Geschwister Zu Retten 'Mother Risked Her Life to Save Her Children.'" Tages. Tamedia AG, December 1, 2018. https://www.tagesanzeiger.ch/schweiz/standard/die-odysseeder-isgeschwister/story/26224134.

Peltier, Elian. "France Repatriates Several Orphan Children Who Were Stranded in Syria." The New York Times. The New York Times, March 15, 2019. https://www.nytimes.com/2019/03/15/world/europe/france-isis-repatriates-children.html.

Perry, Marvin, and Howard E. Negrin. *The Theory and Practice of Islamic Terrorism: An Anthology*. Basingstoke: Palgrave Macmillan, 2008.

Perry, Marvin, Howard E. Negrin, and Mary R. Habeck. "Knowing the Enemy, Jihadist Ideology and the War on Terror." Essay. In *The Theory and Practice of Islamic Terrorism: An Anthology*. New York, NY: Palgrave Macmillan, 2008.

Piazza, James A. "Poverty, Minority Economic Discrimination, and Domestic Terrorism." *Journal of Peace Research* 48, no. 3 (2011): 339–53. https://doi.org/10.1177/0022343310397404.

Piscatori, James, and Amin Saikal. *Islam Beyond Borders: The Umma in World Politics*. Cambridge: Cambridge University press, 2019.

"Posture Statement of General Kenneth F. McKenzie Jr., Commander, United States Central Command, before the House Armed Services Committee on March 10." U.S. Central Command, March 10, 2020. https://www.centcom.mil/MEDIA/Transcripts/Article/2111126/transcript-gen-mckenzie-sasc-testimony/.

Prashad, Vijay. *The Death of the Nation and the Future of the Arab Revolution*. Oakland, CA: University of California Press, 2016.

Radio Television Suisse (RTS). "Une Lausannoise, Ex-Djihadiste En Syrie, Souhaite Revenir En Suisse." rts.ch. Radio Télévision Suisse, February 9, 2019. https://www.rts.ch/info/suisse/10205792-une-lausannoise-exdjihadiste-en-syrie-souhaite-revenir-en-suisse.html.

Radio Télévision Suisse. "Faut-Il Créer Un Tribunal International Pour Juger Les Djihadistes?" Radio Télévision Suisse, June 4, 2019. https://www.rts.ch/info/monde/10482439-fautil-creer-un-tribunal-international-pour-juger-les-djihadistes.html.

Rashid, Ahmed. *Taliban: Islam, Oil and the New Great Game in Central Asia*. London: I.B. Tauris, 2009.

Rashid, Norul Mohamed. "Security Council Resolution 1373 (2001) on Threats to International Peace and Security Caused by Terrorist Acts," 2001. https://www.un.org/ruleoflaw/blog/document/security-council-resolution-1373-2001-on-threats-to-international-peace-and-security-caused-by-terrorist-acts/.

Razdykova, Gulnaz. "Presentation." *The Vienna Conference on Foreign Fighters by the OSCE*. Speech presented at the the Vienna conference on foreign fighters by the OSCE, February 11, 2020.

Renard, Thomas, and Rik Coolsaet. "From the Kingdom to the Caliphate and Back: Returnees in Belgium, in Returnees: Who Are They, Why Are They (Not) Coming Back and How Should We Deal with Them?" *Egmont Paper* 1010 (2018): 37.

Robinson, Glenn E. "The Four Waves of Global Jihad, 1979–2017." *Middle East Policy* 24, no. 3 (2017): 70–88. https://doi.org/10.1111/mepo.12287.

Ruf, Maximilian, and Annelies Jansen. "Study Visit: Returned Women and Children—Studying an Ongoing Experience on the Ground, 10–11 December 2019." Migration and Home Affairs. Radicalisation Awareness Network (RAN) Centre of Excellence, December 2019. https://ec.europa.eu/home-affairs/pages/page/study-visit-returned-women-and-children-studying-ongoing-experience-ground-10-11_en.

Rumsfeld, Donald. "Pentagon Briefing on Military Response to Terrorist Attacks." The Washington Post. WP Company, September 18, 2001. https://www.washingtonpost.com/wp-srv/nation/specials/attacked/transcripts/rumsfeld_091801.html.

Sahinkaya, Ezel, Rikar Hussein, and Edlira Bllaca. "Why Is Kosovo Taking Home Islamic State Members?" VOA. Why is Kosovo Taking Home Islamic State Members?, January 16, 2020. https://www.voanews.com/a/extremism-watch_why-kosovo-taking-home-islamic-state-members/6182667.html.

Sainazarov, Keneshbek, and Cholpon Orozobekova. Interview. Personal, May 6, 2020.

Savage, Charlie. "American-Born Woman Who Joined ISIS Is Not a Citizen, Judge Rules." The New York Times. The New York Times, November 14, 2019. https://www.nytimes.com/2019/11/14/us/hoda-muthana-isis-citizenship.html.

Save the Children's Resource Centre. "The Paris Commitments to Protect Children from Unlawful Recruitment or Use by Armed Forces or Armed Groups: Consolidated Version." Save the Children's Resource Centre. Save the Children's Resource Centre, 2007. https://resourcecentre.savethechildren.net/library/paris-commitments-protect-children-unlawful-recruitment-or-use-armed-forces-or-armed-groups.

Scheinin, Martin. "Back to Post-9/11 Panic? Security Council Resolution on Foreign Terrorist Fighters." Verfassungsblog, September 25, 2014. https://verfassungsblog.de/back-post-911-panic-security-council-resolution-foreign-terrorist-fighters/.

Schneider, Oscar. "Iraq Wants 2 Million Euros for Each Foreign Fighter Tried . . . " Brussels Times, October 1, 2019. https://www.brusselstimes.com/news/belgium-all-news/71090/iraq-wants-2-million-euros-for-each-foreign-fighter-tried-on-its-territory/.

Schulz, Jacob. "France Makes a Play to Try Foreign Fighters in Iraq." Lawfare, June 7, 2020. https://www.lawfareblog.com/france-makes-play-try-foreign-fighters-iraq.

Shakimova, Lola, and Cholpon Orozobekova. Personal, April 5, 2020.

Sjoberg, Laura, and Caron E. Gentry. "Reduced to Bad Sex: Narratives of Violent Women from the Bible to the War on Terror." *Kvinder, Køn & Forskning*, no. 2 (2013). https://doi.org/10.7146/kkf.v0i2.28175.

Sjoberg, Laura, and Caron E. Gentry. *Women, Gender, and Terrorism*. Athens: University of Georgia Press, 2011.

Sjoberg, Laura. "Jihadi Brides and Female Volunteers: Reading the Islamic State's War to See Gender and Agency in Conflict Dynamics." *Conflict Management and Peace Science* 35, no. 3 (2017): 296–311. https://doi.org/10.1177/0738894217695050.

Sonn, Tamara. *Is Islam an Enemy of the West?* Cambridge, UK: Polity Press, 2016.

Spadaro, Alessandra. "Repatriation of Family Members of Foreign Fighters: Individual Right or State Prerogative?: International & Comparative Law Quarterly."

Cambridge Core. Cambridge University Press, November 26, 2020. https://www.cambridge.org/core/journals/international-and-comparative-law-quarterly/article/abs/repatriation-of-family-members-of-foreign-fighters-individual-right-or-state-prerogative/C140146AC9F78E453B3AAFF1A2225008.

Speckhard, Anne. "Admin." ICSVE. International Center for the Study of Violent Extremism, August 26, 2017. https://www.icsve.org/inside-the-isis-machine-turning-children-to-monsters/.

Staffell, Simon, and Akil N. Awan. *Jihadism Transformed: Al-Qaeda and Islamic State's Global Battle of Ideas*. Kettering, US: Oxford University Press, 2016.

Stewart, Frances. "Crisis Prevention: Tackling Horizontal Inequalities." *Oxford Development Studies* 28, no. 3 (2000): 245–62. https://doi.org/10.1080/713688319.

Stigall, Dan E. "Repatriating Foreign Fighters from Syria (Part 1)." Just Security, March 18, 2020. https://www.justsecurity.org/69244/repatriating-foreign-fighters-from-syria-international-law-and-political-will-part-1/.

Sulce, Marija. "The Syrian Armed Conflict Nearing the End," January 2019. https://www.geneva-academy.ch/joomlatools-files/docman-files/The%20Syrian%20Armed%20Conflict%20Nearing%20The%20End.pdf.

Swiss Confederation. "Chiffres Des Voyageurs Du Djihad—Février 2019." Département fédéral de la défense, de la protection de la population et des sports. Swiss Confederation, 2019. https://www.vbs.admin.ch/fr/securite/recherche-renseignements/voyageurs-djihad.html.

Tanya Mehra. "European Countries Are Being Challenged in Court to Repatriate Their Foreign Fighters and Families." ICCT, November 11, 2019. https://icct.nl/publication/european-countries-are-being-challenged-in-court-to-repatriate-their-foreign-fighters-and-families/.

Taub, Amanda. "A New COVID-19 Crisis: Domestic Abuse Rises Worldwide." The New York Times. The New York Times, April 6, 2020. https://www.nytimes.com/2020/04/06/world/coronavirus-domestic-violence.html.

Tiersky, Ronald. "'Isis's Deadliest Weapon Is the Idea of Heaven.'" HuffPost. HuffPost, September 22, 2017. https://www.huffpost.com/entry/isiss-deadliest-weapon-is_b_12087084.

Toguslu, Erkan. "Caliphate, Hijrah and Martyrdom as Performative Narrative in Isis Dabiq Magazine." *Politics, Religion & Ideology* 20, no. 1 (2018): 94–120. https://doi.org/10.1080/21567689.2018.1554480.

Tokaeva, Asem. "Появилось Еще Одно Видео 'Казахских Джихадистов в Сирии' One More Video of Kazakh Jihadists in Syria Has Been Published." Появилось еще одно видео "казахских джихадистов в Сирии." Радио Азаттык, Radio Azattyk, July 29, 2014. https://rus.azattyq.org/a/video-jihadistov-iz-kazakhstana-v-sirii-i-irake/25463575.html.

Tumelty, Paul. "The Rise and Fall of Foreign Fighters in Chechnya." *Jamestown Foundation: Terrorism Monito* 4, no. 2 (2006): 8–10.

UK Home Office News. "Factsheet: Syrian Travellers." Home Office in the media. UK Home Office, February 15, 2019. https://homeofficemedia.blog.gov.uk/2019/02/15/fact-sheet-returnees-from-the-conflict-zone-in-syria/.

UK Parliament. "Counter-Terrorism and Border Security Act 2019." Legislation.gov.uk. Queen's Printer of Acts of Parliament. Accessed October 23, 2020. https://www.legislation.gov.uk/ukpga/2019/3/contents/enacted/data.htm.

UK Parliament. "Counter-Terrorism and Security Act 2015." Legislation.gov.uk. Queen's Printer of Acts of Parliament. Accessed October 23, 2020. https://www.legislation.gov.uk/ukpga/2015/6/contents/enacted.

UK Parliament. "Immigration Act 2014." Legislation.gov.uk. Queen's Printer of Acts of Parliament. Accessed October 22, 2020. https://www.legislation.gov.uk/ukpga/2014/22/contents/enacted.

UN Human Rights Council. "Arbitrary Deprivation of Nationality": United Nations. United Nations, January 26, 2009. https://digitallibrary.un.org/record/647823.

UN Security Council Counter-Terrorism Committee Executive Directorate. "Gender Dimensions of the Response to Returning Foreign Terrorist Fighters: Research Perspectives." RESOLVE, February 1, 2019. https://www.resolvenet.org/research/publications/gender-dimensions-response-returning-foreign-terrorist-fighters-research.

UNITAD. "Our Mandate | Investigative Team to Promote Accountability for Crimes Committed by Da'esh/ISIL (UNITAD)." United Nations. United Nations. Accessed June 8, 2020. https://www.unitad.un.org/content/our-mandate.

UNITAD. "The European Union and Unitad Sign Agreement to Support Digitization of Evidence of ISIL Crimes in Iraq | Investigative Team to Promote Accountability for Crimes Committed by Da'esh/ISIL (UNITAD)." United Nations. United Nations. Accessed June 6, 2020. https://www.unitad.un.org/news/european-union-and-unitad-sign-agreement-support-digitization-evidence-isil-crimes-iraq.

United Nations Security Council. "S/RES/2178 (2014) Security Council." United Nations. United Nations, 2014. https://www.un.org/securitycouncil/s/res/2178-%282014%29.

United Nations Security Council. "Tenth Report of the Secretary-General on the Threat Posed by ISIL (Da'Esh) to International Peace and Security and the Range of United Nations Efforts in Support of Member States in Countering the Threat (S/2020/95)." United Nations Security Council, February 4, 2020. https://www.un.org/sc/ctc/news/document/title-s-2020-95-tenth-report-secretary-general-threat-posed-isil-daesh-international-peace-security-range-united-nations-efforts-support/.

United Nations. "Guidance to States on Human Rights-Compliant Responses to the Threat Posed by Foreign Fighters." United Nations, 2018. https://www.un.org/sc/ctc/wp-content/uploads/2018/08/Human-Rights-Responses-to-Foreign-Fighters-web-final.pdf.

United Nations. "Key Principles for the Protection, Repatriation, Prosecution, Rehabilitation and Reintegration of Women and Children with Links to United Nations Listed Terrorist Groups." UNCCT Annual Report. United Nations, 2020. https://resolvenet.org/research/key-principles-protection-repatriation-prosecution-rehabilitation-and-reintegration-women.

United Nations. "Key Principles for the Protection, Repatriation, Prosecution, Rehabilitation and Reintegration of Women and Children with Links to United

Nations Listed Terrorist Groups." United Nations, April 2019. https://www.un.org/counterterrorism/sites/www.un.org.counterterrorism/files/key_principles-april_2019.pdf.

US Central Command. "Posture Statement of General Kenneth F. McKenzie, Jr . . . " US Central Command, 2020. https://docs.house.gov/meetings/AS/AS00/20210420/112498/HHRG-117-AS00-Wstate-McKenzieK-20210420.pdf.

Vidino, Lorenzo, and Seamus Hughes. "ISIS in America, From Retweets to Raqqa." Program on extremism. The George Washington University, 2015. https://extremism.gwu.edu/isis-america.

Vinet, Fabienne. "Joint Statement on Human Rights and Humanitarian Concerns . . . " United Nations Office of the Special Representative of the Secretary-General for Children and Armed Conflict, November 11, 2019. https://www.un.org/sexualviolenceinconflict/press-release/joint-statement-on-human-rights-and-humanitarian-concerns-related-to-conflict-affected-women-and-children-in-syria-and-iraq/.

Zakon.kz. "Three Kazakhstani Women Executed in Syria for the Murder of Their Compatriots and a Child." Редакция. zakon.kz, October 26, 2018. https://www.zakon.kz/4943322-tri-kazahstanki-kazneny-v-sirii-za.html. translated by the author from Russian

Zhurikhina, Elena. "Foreign Fighters from Central Asia: Between Renunciation and Repatriation." Prague Institute of International Relations, October 3, 2019. https://www.ispionline.it/en/pubblicazione/foreign-fighters-central-asia-between-renunciation-and-repatriation-24072.

МАЙКОЗОВА, Акмарал. "'Мама, Считайте Меня Мёртвой' Mom, Consider Me Dead." Время, November 7, 2018. https://time.kz/articles/risk/2018/11/07/mama-schitajte-menja-mertvoj. Translated by the author.

МЮ РК. "Ministry of Justice of Republic of Kazakhstan: Those Who Are in the Territory of the Country Won't Be Revoked Citizenship for Terrorism." МЮ РК, May 24, 2017. http://today.kz/news/kazahstan/2017-05-24/742936-zhivuschih-v-strane-kazahstantsev-mogut-ne-lishat-grazhdanstva-za-terrorizm---myu-rk/.

Index

About the Author

Cholpon Orozobekova is a conflict analyst and terrorism expert based in Geneva, Switzerland. She has been researching religious extremism, jihadism, and state policies toward ISIS fighters since 2016. She lectures at the Geneva Centre for Security Policy and is a Member of European Expert Network on Terrorism. Currently, Cholpon is a director of the Bulan Institute for Peace Innovations, the research institute based in Geneva. She holds three MA degrees from Geneva-based public universities. Cholpon worked in different international organizations and media for more then twenty years.